EUROPEAN UNIFICATION INTO THE TWENTY FIRST CENTURY

FADING, FAILING, FRAGILE?

Frans A.M. Alting von Geusau

FOOTPRINTS OF THE TWENTIETH CENTURY VOLUME IV

"Tous les pays de l'Europe sont impregnés de civilization chrétienne. Elle est l'âme de l'Europe, âme qu'il faut lui rendre"

Robert Schuman

"A revolution, that is, an event in the spiritual sphere, is authentic to the degree it is bloodless. The spirit rules through persuasion and not through fear. This is why a truly great revolution is, at the same time, a holiday of the liberation of a human being from the fear of other human beings."

Józef Tischner, The Spirit of Solidarity

In gratitude
to my beloved wife

To our children and grandchildren,
who deserve to live in a united Europe,
conscious of her Christian heritage
and her mission to serve justice and peace.

EUROPEAN UNIFICATION INTO THE TWENTY FIRST CENTURY
FADING, FAILING, FRAGILE?

Frans A.M. Alting von Geusau

ISBN: 978-90-5850-779-2
Second Revised Edition of European Unification in the Twentieth Century

Website: www.fransamaltingvongeusau.com

This book is the fourth volume in Footprints of the Twentieth Century:
1. Cultural Diplomacy: Waging War With Other Means? 2009
2. The Illusions of Détente, 2009
3. Western Cooperation. Origins and History, (second edition) 2009
4. European Unification, 2012

For more information take a look at our website:
http://www.wolfpublishers.com

Published by:
Wolf Legal Publishers
Tel: +31 13 582 13 66
Fax: +31 84 837 67 00
E-Mail: info@wolfpublishers.nl
www.wolfpublishers.com

PREFACE TO THE SECOND EDITION

The first edition of this book was published in December 1998. It was based on University Courses I had given over four years on the Theory and History of European Unification. In December 1998 I offered it to the universities concerned as a valedictory present, hoping that the history of European Unification would not be neglected in the European law and relations curricula. It was followed in 2002 by a similar two volume work on "*Western Cooperation, origins and history.*" A second and revised edition of this latter work was published in 2009 in a new one volume format; the documents discussed and referred to are accessible separately on my website: **www.fransamaltingvongeusau.com**

This second edition of European Unification follows the same format as the second edition of Western Cooperation. The documents referred to can also be found on this now enlarged website. Documents referred to in this second edition can be found under the heading:

EUROPEAN UNION

The website documents are organized in the following way:

Historic documents in Part I: EH. 1 - EH. 17

General documents in Part II: EU/EUD: Basic Treaty Texts/Draft texts

EC: the full list of Conclusions from Summits and European Council sessions.

Documents for each Chapter in Part II: E. number chapter. Number doc.

This second edition is an entirely new book, in fact. It is no longer a treasury of readings with brief comments. It has become a critical analysis on the history of European Unification into the twenty-first century in two parts.

The history proper of the European unification efforts is presented in Part II, THE PEACEFUL ORGANISATION OF COMMON ACTION.

Its first chapter is a general survey of Euro-pean Unification from the 1948 Congress of the Hague to the entry into force of the Reform Treaties of Lisbon in 2009. The second chapter reviews the central feature of European Unification, the enlargements of the Communities and the European Union from France and Germany to twenty seven member states at present. Chapter 3 deals with the European Economic and Monetary Union, a briefer chapter, as I am not an economist and the future of EMU is uncertain at best at the time of completing my manuscript. In Chapter 4, attention is focused on the evolution of the intended European constitution, including the evolution with respect to a European Charter for human rights. Chapter 5 deals with external relations and the efforts to unify member states' foreign policies.

Part I in this second edition is completely different from Part I in the first edition. The broader history of efforts towards Western and European cooperation in the twentieth century is already given in Part I of the second revised edition of my *Western cooperation Origins and history*, published as the third volume in my series footprints of the 20th century. Western cooperation and European Unification belonged together and to a large extent still do in the second decade of the 21st century. There is no need to be repetitious. The newly written first part in this volume gives some European background history in four chapters; meant to help the reader in better understanding the reality of Europe and the uniqueness of the unification project since 1950. Part I is not a full history but more a reflection on history.

I am most grateful to Willem-Jan van der Wolf, Monika Stojova and Simone Fennell-van Esch for editing and publishing this volume.

October 2011 Frans A.M. Alting von Geusau

Table of Contents

CHAPTER 2

TWO —> MANY? THE ENLARGEMENTS OF THE EUROPEAN COMMUNITY/UNION

LIST OF ABBREVIATIONS

CAP:	Common Agricultural Policy
CEEC:	Central and East European Countries
CFSP:	Common Foreign and Security Policy
COMECON:	Council for Mutual Economic Assistance (Communist countries)
CSCE:	Conference for Security and Cooperation in Europe
EC:	European Communities
ECB:	European Central Bank
ECHR:	European Convention for Human Rights
ECSC:	European Coal and Steel Community
ECU:	European Currency Unit
EEA:	European Economic Area
EEAS:	European External Action Service
EDC:	European Defense Community
EEC:	European Economic Community
EFTA:	European Free Trade Area
EMS:	European Monetary System
EMU:	Economic and Monetary Union
EPC:	European Political Cooperation
EU:	European Union
ICTY:	International Criminal Tribunal for Yugoslavia
IGC:	Intergovernmental Conference
NATO:	North Atlantic Treaty Organization
OECD:	Organization for Economic Cooperation and Development
OEEC:	Organization for European Economic Cooperation
PHARE:	Poland-Hungary Assistance for the Reconstruction of the Economy
SEA:	Single European Act
TEU:	Treaty on European Union

TFEU:	Treaty on the Functioning of the European Union
UN:	United Nations Organization
US:	United States of America
VAT:	Value Added Tax
WEU:	Western European Union
WTO:	World Trade Organization

INTRODUCTION

Europe is old, the idea of Europe is quite recent and the project of European unity is still in its infancy. Sixty-two years at the end of three millennia from Hellas to the present, represent just 2% of Europe's years in history covered by Norman Davies in his masterful book *Europe. A history*; that must be read before this volume. Sixty-two years are not enough to draw meaningful conclusions about the future of European Unification. They are more than enough to need a history for those born after 1990, who never heard about Robert Schuman, Konrad Adenauer or Jean Monnet. What happened to the plan Schuman of 1950 will be discussed extensively in Part II of this volume.

Before that second part of this book, we must reflect on what brought Europe to the moment in its history when such a radical new departure was called for. Emperors, kings and philosophers in the past did have plans for extending their dominion over the peoples of Europe. From Charlemagne to Napoleon, Hitler and Stalin, none of them really worked. The shock of two disastrous World Wars in the 20th century aroused the conscience of some of Europe's post war leaders, as we shall see in our first chapter. As a civilization, Europe is characterized by a fundamental ethical dualism between Christian virtues and pagan traditions.

In our second chapter we highlight two distinct examples - where Christian virtues prevailed, the humanization of law by the canonists in the 12th and 13th century and the victory of *Solidarnosc* over communist repression in the 20th century. The values of Europe, our current political leaders proclaim as age old ones, are quite new in fact and the source of much confusion (chapter 3). They have much to do with the philosophies of the 19th century. The ideologies they produced in the 20th century are not from another country and may not be forgotten. Chapter 4 should remind us that the worship of collective human power and its abuse are not aberrations of the past. They are still with us in the guise of the attachment to full national sovereignty and the ideologies of nationalism.

The history-proper of European Unification began in Western Europe in 1948, when the European Congress convened at the Hague in the presence of most post-war political leaders from Western Europe. The governments of Western Europe had responded to the American Marshall plan of 1947 by the creation of the Organisation for European Economic Cooperation (OEEC) as the framework for developing a joint program of economic recovery and liberalisation of trade and payments. The Soviet Union had rejected Marshall-aid as a capitalist plot and had forced its satellites to do likewise. Soviet domination over Eastern Europe had been completed by the coup d'état in Prague in February 1948. Negotiations on a peace treaty with Germany had broken down. France, Britain and the Benelux states had signed the Western Union Treaty, as a framework for self-defence, co-operation and mutual assistance.

The spectacle of ruins left by the Second World War, the onset of the Cold War, together with visionary American leadership convinced West European leaders of the urgent necessity to organise Europe on the basis of reconciliation between France and Germany. A joint European commitment to respect fundamental human rights and the rule of law was required to prevent individual states from again violating these rights on the scale practised by the totalitarian regimes of Nazi-Germany, the Soviet Union and fascist Italy. Economic recovery was needed to rebuild West European states from widespread devastation and chaos, and to regain sufficient strength to resist further Soviet expansion.

So it began, after the OEEC, with the Council of Europe, the Schuman Plan and the European Convention on Human Rights, as discussed in chapters 1 and 4 in the second part called "The Peaceful Organisation of Common Action." Chapter 1 follows the process from the Schuman Plan through the European Communities, the crises of the sixties, the stagnation of the seventies, the Single European Act of 1986 and the long drawn out efforts to transform the communities to a European Union. Two efforts - in 1953 and 2003 - to agree on a Constitution for Europe both failed, the first one due to a negative vote on an EDC in the French National Assembly, the second due to the negative outcome of referenda in France and the Netherlands. The six original members of the European Communities had to wait for the resignation of French President Charles de Gaulle before embarking on the first enlargement of the European Communities with Great Britain, Ireland and Denmark in 1973 as will be discussed in chapter 2. Together with the agreement on political co-operation, discussed further in chapter 5, the five also accepted a French proposal to work towards Economic and Monetary Union before the end of the decade of the seventies, as shall be dealt with in chapter 3. It did not happen, but supported by the plans of the European Commission in 1985 for completing the internal market before 1992, the issue remained on top of the agenda. During the same decade Greece, Spain and Portugal entered the Communities following their return to democracy in the seventies.

The end of the Cold War in 1989-1991 offered Europeans another spectacle of ruins left by Soviet domination and the Cold War. The peaceful revolutions in East and Central Europe were events of world historic importance (touched upon in part I, chapters 2 and 3). They caught the European Community Members by surprise and it took them long years before they finally agreed to the enlargement of the European Union to the East, as will be discussed in chapter 2, the leading chapter on Enlargement. After the enlargement to the West in 1973, to the South in the 1980s, with the neutral European countries in 1995, and to the East in 2004 and 2007, Malta and half of Cyprus were also added. There is no lack of further candidates for membership, but there certainly is lack of enthusiasm on the part of the present membership.

The end of the Order of Yalta also brought the re-unification of Germany and the inclusion of the former German Democratic Republic (GDR) into Member State Germany, an enlargement not much applauded by the French, the British and some others. It made the French insist on accelerating the Monetary Union, a decision taken by the European Council of Maastricht in December 1991. Germany re-united is clearly in the centre of Europe again. Despite the enlargement to the East and due to Britain's role as the odd man in with lots of treaty opt-outs, political leadership still lies between Berlin and Paris. Their leadership is less than forceful and imaginative.

Chapter 5, finally, tells the sad story how the European Community according to Schuman went astray to be transformed into a European Union. When the original purpose of federal unity was replaced by the illusion of world prominence, the six, later the nine, the twelve, fifteen and twenty seven, joined the Echternach procession from political cooperation to external action. The chapter reflects an unending history of pretence and impotence, of confusion and failure, wrapped in the kind of Eurospeak one finds in article 21 of the Lisbon Treaty. The heritage of Gaullism lives on in the steady rise of the number of European Council meetings as can be read throughout all five chapters in part II of this European Unification into the twenty-first century.

PART I

EUROPE IN HISTORY

"For this reason it seems to me that Europe may be destined to find an unsensational, but profoundly vital mission in the critical assessment of power."

Romano Guardini

CHAPTER 1

EUROPE:
A PRINCESS, A PLACE, A PAINTING OR A PROJECT?

EUROPE, in Greek mythology, was a beautiful Phoenician princess abducted by the god Zeus. To us she is a subcontinent, a construction of the human mind based on a poorly defined geography. She is also a civilisation and she is an idea.

Geography

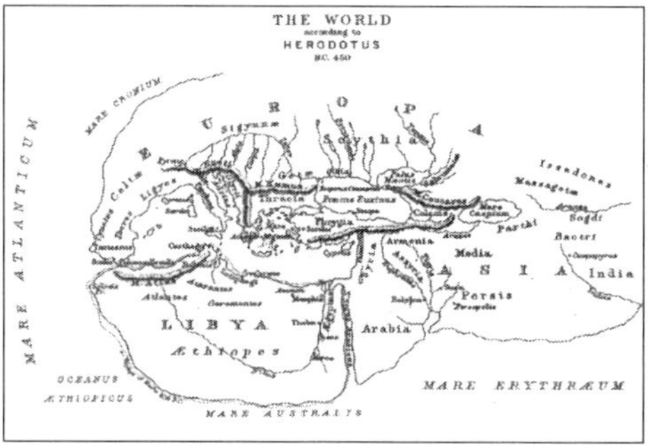

Herodotus mentioned Europe as one of the three continents around Greece. Sebastian Münster (1570) saw Europe as a Queen in the centre of the world. In today's atlas of the world (made in Europe), Europe still occupies the centre and extends to the Urals, including the Baltic republics, part of Russia and the former Soviet republics of Beylorussia, Ukraine, Moldavia, Armenia and Georgia. In the North, West and South she is surrounded by the Barents Sea, the Norwegian Sea, the Atlantic Ocean and the Mediterranean Sea.

"We are accustomed to regard Europe as a continent and to place it therefore in the same category as such mighty formations as America, Asia and Africa. Are we right to do this?"[1]

---

1 Romano Guardini, Europe - Reality or Mission. Our leading document EH. 1. As indicated in the preface all of the documents can be found at: www.fransamaltingvongeusau.com

Most consider the Bosporus as the sea border and the Urals as the land border between Europe and Asia. The Turks and Russians disagree. Istanbul is on this side; the Ottomans were in Europe for centuries. Modern Turkey belongs to most Western international organisations and wants to become a member of the European Union. The Russians never made up their mind whether they belong to Europe or not. In any case, the Urals are no border; they run right through the middle of Russian territory. Siberia used to be populated by many exiled citizens from European countries. Historically, modern Turkey is the successor to an Empire from another civilisation. Russia is different. Unlike Samuel Huntington, I see Russia - with Pope John-Paul II - as the other lung of European civilisation deeply formed by the faith in Christ.[2]

Although once a part of the Roman Empire, North Africa is not seen as part of Europe, nor are the Eastern Mediterranean countries. They share a long history of the spread of the Christian faith. For many centuries the Christian faith flourished in North Africa, the Middle-East and the Persian Empire rather than in Europe. Overrun by the Muslim armies since the seventh

---

2 Samuel Huntington, *The Clash of Civilizations and the Remaking of World Order*, Simon & Schuster 1996.

century, Christian churches have almost disappeared.[3] The regions are considered to belong to another civilisation.

Few would doubt the fact that the British Isles are part of Europe, except for a considerable number of Britons, who say they travel *to Europe*, when they board the Eurostar to Paris or Brussels. "In a way, Britain still sees itself as the sceptered isle, cut from the continent by divine will. If God had wanted to tie it to the rest of Europe, He would evidently not have dug the Channel."[4] Not so the Irish, they consider themselves true Europeans.

In Politics and Culture

In politics and culture Europe's borders are uncertain and changed often, especially to the South and to the East.

The break-up of the Roman Empire in the fifth century resulted in two ruptures of political organisation and culture: between the East and West Roman Empires leading to the Great Schism of 1054; and between North and South, when Africa and the Middle-East were lost to the Islam in the seventh and eight centuries.

The East and West Roman Empires both followed the tradition of Theodosius Roman Empire. The Christian faith was the official religion of the state.[5] Both were at the origin of a millennial empire. The East Roman Empire became Byzantium and lived

---

3 Cf. Philip Jenkins, *The Lost History of Christianity: The Thousand-Year Golden Age of the Church in the Middle East, Africa, and Asia - and How It Died,* Harper one 2008.

4 From Luigi Barzini, *The Impossible Europeans,* Weidenfeld & Nicolson 1983, p. 59.

5 See Document EH. 2.

until the conquest of Constantinople in 1453 by Mehmed II, Sultan of the Muslim Ottoman Empire. Its tradition of symbiosis between the temporal power and the spiritual power in the persons of the Emperor and the Patriarch survived thereafter in the countries which had accepted to belong to the Greek Orthodox Patriarchate of Constantinople; it survived however within each country separately, most clearly so in Russia with the creation of the Moscow patriarchate in the late sixteenth century.

The West Roman Empire collapsed under the weight of migrations and the invasions of Italy and Rome; until Charles the Great built up his European empire through a series of hard fought wars. On Christmas day in the year 800 he was crowned Emperor of the Holy Roman Empire by Pope Leo III. The Holy Roman Empire - of the German nation since 1250 - survived until Napoleon broke it up and arranged its liquidation between 1803 and August 1806.[6] Its history, at least until the Thirty Years War, was dominated by the complex struggle for supremacy between Pope and Emperor. The conflict between ecclesiastical or spiritual power and political or temporal power continued in the "West" until our time.

As A Concept of Civilisation

As a concept of civilisation, Europe henceforward was limited to Charlemagne's Empire that was a Western Empire. Although it was short-lived, its dream lived on. In real history it was no empire at all. As Christopher Dawson wrote: "It claimed to be the Roman Empire, but it was in fact the Frankish monarchy, and so it embodied two contradictory principles, the universalism of the Roman and Christian traditions on the one

6 Friedrich Heer, *The Holy Roman Empire,* Weidenfeld & Nicolson 1968, Translated from the German.

hand, and the tribal particularism of barbaric Europe on the other." The Emperor, however, was no longer the hereditary chieftain and war leader, but became an almost sacerdotal figure "anointed by the grace of God to rule over the Christian people and to guide and protect the Church. This involves, as we have seen, a strictly theocratic conception of kingship, so that the Carolingian Emperor was regarded, no less than the Byzantine Basileus, as the vicar of God and the head of the Church as well as of the State." The Carolingian theocracy, according to Dawson, however: "differed from the Byzantine in that it was a theocracy inspired and controlled by the Church. There was no lay bureaucracy as existed in the Eastern Empire; its place was taken by the episcopate, from whose ranks the majority of the Emperor's advisers and ministers were drawn.

Consequently, as soon as the strong hand of Charles the Great was removed, the theocratic ideal led to the exaltation of the spiritual power and the clericalisation of the Empire rather than to the subordination of the Church to the secular power"[7]- as has been the case in the Eastern Churches and would be the case in Europe after 1648.[8]

"It is impossible - writes Dawson - to understand early mediaeval culture on the analogy of modern conditions, which are based on the conception of the single all-inclusive society of the sovereign state. There were in fact two societies and two cultures in early mediaeval Europe. On the one hand there was the peace society of the Church, which was centred in the monasteries and Episcopal cities and inherited the tradition of later Roman culture. And, on the other hand, there was the

---

7 Christopher Dawson, *The Making of Europe; An Introduction to the History of European Unity*, The Catholic University of America Press 2003, pp. 227, 228, 231.

8 The Peace of Westphalia. Cf. Document EH. 7.

war-society of the feudal nobility and their following, whose life was spent in incessant wars and private feuds." Dawson concludes his chapter on the rise of the Mediaeval Unity as follows: "the close of the tenth century saw the birth of a new series of Christian states extending from Scandinavia to the Danube. The eleventh century saw the passing of Northern paganism and the incorporation of the whole of Western Europe into the unity of Christendom."[9]

Among the general conclusions Christopher Dawson draws in his book, two must be emphasised in this chapter. As a concept of civilisation, "the culture that we regard as characteristically Western and European was confined in the main within the limits of the former Carolingian Empire, and found its centre in the old Frankish territories of Northern France and Western Germany." It was not a closed culture: "(This) contact with the higher civilisation of the Islamic and Byzantine world had a decisive influence on Western Europe and was one of the most important elements in the development of mediaeval culture."

His second conclusion is most relevant to the question whether Europe is a Christian civilisation. "(Indeed), throughout the Dark Ages, Western Society had been characterised by an ethical dualism that corresponds to the dualism of culture. There was one ideal for the warrior and another for the Christian, and the former still belonged in spirit to the barbaric world of Northern paganism. It was not until the eleventh century that the military society was incorporated into the spiritual polity of Western Christendom by the influence of the crusading ideal. The institution of knighthood is the symbol of the fusion of Nordic

---

9 *Op. cit* pp. 239, 249.

and Christian traditions in the mediaeval unity."[10] The fusion did not create a Christian Europe, but a Europe characterised by an ethical dualism between Christian virtues and pagan traditions.[11]

In a way the Papacy belonged to both: As the Holy See it belonged to the Church and as Ruler of the Ecclesiastical State, the Papacy became part of the war-society; a duality that survived the Middle Ages and only came to its end in 1870.

Europe's rulers continued to dream of the imperial crown, whether they were from the house of the Hohenstaufen, the Habsburgs or the French and English kingdoms. When Napoleon had liquidated the Holy Roman Empire, he let himself be crowned Emperor in Paris, although the Austrian imperial monarchy would become the successor to the Holy Roman Empire. Napoleon III proclaimed himself emperor of France in 1851; in September 1870, the Empire collapsed in the defeat in war against Prussia. The Prussian King William I was proclaimed German emperor (much against his will) on 18 January 1871 in the Hall of Mirrors at Versailles. The dreams were more about imperial status than about European unity. For Charles the Great and his imitators, Europe was no more than the conventional name for the continent on which they happened to live and wage wars.

Europe is 'a construction of the human mind based on a poorly defined geography', we saw already. Emperors were conquerors and rulers, considering the lands they conquered

---

10 *Op.cit* pp. 252,254, 253. Cf. *The Song of Roland*. Copy of a modern translation in Document EH. 3. Also: Sir Thomas Malory, *Le MORTE DARTHUR*, Edited by R. M. Lumiansky, Macmillan 1982.

11 See also Denis de Rougemont, *L'Amour et l'Occident*, Librairie Plon 1972.

and the people they ruled their private property. Through wars and weddings (or occupation and succession) borders changed continuously. The concept of a fixed, demarcated, linear border is of very recent origin, just as passports are. Before the First World War, one could travel through Europe without a passport and without always knowing when one crossed a border. During the long history of conflict between the Austrians and the Ottomans battle lines kept changing and Serb militias fought for both sides. Territorial sovereignty as a concept needed a long time to emerge from private property. Empires dominated European history until their demise in the Twentieth Century. The Habsburg Empire, the German Empire, the Ottoman Empire and the Czarist Empire perished in the First World War. The British claim to empire was restricted to India and disappeared with the independence of the Indian subcontinent in 1947. The successor to the Czarist Empire - the Soviet Union - disappeared in 1991. Their disappearances left Europe with conflicting, national territorial claims and fixed but unclear borders - despite U.S. President Wilson's idea in 1919 to rearrange the map of Europe on the basis of the principle of national self-determination.

The Europe of sovereign states

The Peace of Westphalia marked the ultimate transformation to the Europe of sovereign states. During the Thirty Years War, "religious issues, so prominent in the early years, declined, and power politics never absent, finally predominated." It was the last European war in which religious motivation played a role and in which religion might have acted as a force of constraint upon the use of physical violence. Richelieu "furthered the notion that the interest of the state formed the basis for political and military actions. This attitude was strengthened when Catholics as well as Protestants ignored the Pope's solemn protest against the clauses of the peace treaties which were injurious to the Catholic church. The claim of a supranational religious authority to interfere in affairs of state was rejected." The Thirty Years War "brought into being a new awareness of the danger involved in the domination by any one power, a danger which could be met only by concerted diplomatic action, or if necessary by war."[12]

Reduced to power politics, i.e. to politics to try for domination or to resist such efforts, the development of the public law of Europe indeed restricted itself largely to reflecting the shifting power relations. These relations, indeed, shifted continuously.

The Thirty Years War codified the impotence of the German Emperor probably prevented the establishment of Habsburg hegemony, but prepared the way for Louis XIV's attempts towards domination. His failure was followed by the emergence of Prussia as a new great power. Russia entered the scene as a leading power in European affairs and Sweden lost its previous position as a leading power. In this highly volatile situation the bid for European hegemony by revolutionary France under Napoleon underlined the extreme weakness of a 'balance of power' system for 'lasting accord' between shifting dynastic interests. It proved once more that real danger of domination could be met only by war. Concerted 'diplomatic action' would be effective only in situations of minor danger.

When Napoleon finally lost, the European great powers and Russia turned out to be as intoxicated by their victory as had been the case with the sovereigns at the end of the Thirty Years War. They rejected the lofty principles of the French revolution - the solidarity, brotherhood and equality of men - and returned to the balance of power as the foundation for

---

12 Quotations from *Cambridge Medieval History, Vol. V.,* Chapter IX., p. 325.

the post war system. The Congress of Vienna[13], in essence, did in 1815 what the Peace of Westphalia had done in1648.

It rearranged the map of Europe in such a way that the newly arranged balance of conflicting powers could be maintained. The effort towards restoration and balance, however, could not contain the nineteenth century ideologies of revolution and nationalism. The new century was a period of continuous conflict and change. Europe may have been the powerhouse of the world, but primarily in the sense of revolution, ideology, war and colonial domination. The Concert of European great powers, conceived as an instrument for regular consultation, ceased to function as early as 1822; it finally broke down completely as a result of the Crimean war in the early 1850's. Major changes in the relations between the great powers prepared the way for the Austrian-Prussian war in 1866, the French-German war in 1870 and, finally, the First World War in 1914.[14]

The American and French Revolutions inaugurated the modern nation-state, marked by increased popular participation in the conflicts between sovereign states, despite the efforts at the Congress of Vienna in 1815 to return to a monarchical Europe. Europe continued to be conceived as a provisional framework for the secular and sovereign nation-state of the nineteenth century, especially in Europe*'s great powers*. They saw themselves as the centres of an expanding world of colonial domination.

---

13 Text and maps in Document EH. 9.

14 This section based on my: *European Perspectives on World Order,* Publications of the John F. Kennedy Institute, Center for International Studies, Nr. 10, Chapter 1, pp. 30-31.

The fate of superior spiritual power

The Latin Church kept Rome as the See of the Pope - except for the 50 years of the Avignon papacy in the fourteenth century - but its evolution was marked by the ongoing conflict for supremacy between the Pope in Rome and the Emperor of the Holy Empire, who did not have a permanent capital city. When the Holy Roman Empire was progressively weakened, political power moved to the new sovereign monarchies of Spain, France and England in particular. Reformation split the Latin Church into the Roman Catholic Church and the Churches of the Reformation. *Cuius regio eius religio* became the ruling principle for church-state relations and not only in the protestant countries. It was first agreed upon in the German Empire by the religious peace of Augsburg in 1555.[15] It surely is one of the ironies of European history that the fierce struggle for predominance between the spiritual and temporal powers in (Charlemagne's) Europe resulted in a return to the old model of unity between the two powers, now within the Empire and in each of the new sovereign states. The Head of State ruled by divine right and would also be head of the official church.

Enlightenment and the French revolution further split the relationship between the Catholic Church and secular states. Faith-based loyalty disappeared in favor of loyalty to the nation. The principle of freedom of religion - introduced by the Americans - marked and further promoted the idea of religion as a private affair rather than a collective commitment. In the early twenty-first century, "*everyone his or her own faith*", appears to have become the leading principle. The state must translate that principle into "neutral" positive laws.

---

15 Document EH.6 and 6A. Document EH.6 offers an English translation of the most relevant paragraphs. Document 6A gives the full text of the original document in German.

As neutrality in religion is an illusion, it is again the temporal power of the state on which the affairs of religion depend!

As many concepts of Europe as there are nations, leaders and thinkers

As a construction of the human mind, there are as many Europe's as there were nations, political leaders and intellectuals, most of them self-serving. Duroselle distinguished four concepts of Europe throughout its history:

(1) Europe as an embodiment of a basic principle - the idea of a Christian empire or republic;

(2) Europe as a continent of diversity - governed by the balance of power;

(3) Europe as an area to be united by force - the policies of Napoléon and Hitler;

(4) Europe to be constructed by mutual agreement.[16]

Duroselle's distinction reflects preferences and (in his case) a look at history through the prism of the proud French nation. His preference is for the fourth concept as devised by Schuman and Monnet and for the second one, a system of the balance of power, practised at the time of French predominance in the 18th century. Two omissions are interesting. The first one is the nineteenth century, the era of nationalism in Europe. The second one is the omission of the policies of Lenin and Stalin. Julien Benda and Dénis de Rougemont deal with both of them. Nationalism offers a distorted ideology on Europe as a

---

[16] From: J.B. Duroselle, *L'Idée d'Europe dans l'histoire,* Préface de Jean Monnet, DENOËL 1965.

continent of diversity; it is the concept of Europe as one's own nation writ large and being superior to the other nations. Hitler, Lenin and Stalin are the policy makers of the anti-European concept according to Benda and de Rougemont.[17]

Napoleon preferred to see himself as the successor to Charlemagne rather than Louis XIV. He wanted to rule over Europe, including Russia, liquidating whatever came in the path to his imperial dreams. With the exception of the fourth concept so far, the European area has always been formed or deformed by force of arms.

The *first concept*, while still dreamt of by some, lost its relevance in the seventeenth century, according to Duroselle. In reality that concept lost its relevance long before the peace of Westphalia - already when the Roman Empire of Theodosius fell apart in the fifth century. Even within the confines of Charlemagne's Europe, Popes, Emperors and Kings (especially those of Spain, France and England) waged many wars to prevail and did not hesitate to call in the Saracenes or Ottomans for support to that end. Nevertheless, the idea lived on, also beyond 1648 in philosophy, literature, the arts and music; some of them profoundly inspired by the faith in Christ and many of those works of art commissioned or sponsored by the same warring leaders. The works of art continue to be relevant for understanding 'Europe' in the sense of Dostoyevsky's famous dictum that beauty will save the world. Beauty surely saved Europe and much of it was saved despite wanton destruction in the many large scale, devastating wars.

The *second concept* perished in the trenches of the First World War. As a political concept it never reflected the reality of

---

17 In *L'Esprit Européen*, Neuchâtel 1947, Textes des rencontres internationales de Genève, September 1946.

power politics in Europe after the Peace of Westphalia. So called balances of power are inherently unstable and cannot do else but end in wars. The Holy Alliance, concluded at the time of the Congress of Vienna, was a short-lived illusion. With the rise of Northern Germany through the *Zollverein* and the policy of Bismarck in the centre of Europe, it crumbled and collapsed in the wars with Austria and France and finally perished in the First World War.

Anti-European Ideologies

Duroselle's third concept is no concept of Europe at all. The French Revolution is at the origin of the anti-European ideologies of the nineteenth and twentieth century. The French Revolution following its initial years of terror and the Jacobin totalitarian-democratic dictatorship[18], produced Napoleon Bonaparte. Napoleon set out to redraw the map of Europe and impose such "democratic" regimes by force of arms, thus planting the seeds of the ideology of nationalism, especially in Germany. German resistance against the universally applicable ideas of the Enlightenment was articulated by Herder, who had great contempt for "the illusions of the philosophers of Paris, who claim to civilize 'toute l'Europe' and 'tout l'univers'."

It was not without significance that he brought in the tale of the Tower of Babel (from the Bible) to emphasise his theory of national diversity, when he wrote: "Distinct nations were formed, each with its own language, not only as a result of migrations, but also because of discord in the course of great common concerns. They are, so to speak, the debris of the confusion of peoples". What makes a Volk (a nation) according to him, is

---

[18] Cf. J.L. Talmon's trilogy: 1. *The Origins of Totalitarian Democracy; 2. Political Messianism; 3. The Myth of the Nation and the Vision of Revolution,* Secker & Warburg/University of California Press 1980.

not only the possession of a common culture, but also conflict with other nations. Herder rejected the dynastic 'machine-state' and the "wild mixing of various races and nationalities under one sceptre". He saw little in Montesquieu's "ideal form of constitution", but favoured an 'organic' *Volks-Staat* (nation-state) in which political government gave expression to the shared national culture.[19] Like Johann Gottlieb Fichte, Herder evolved from an admirer of the Enlightenment philosophers to a romantic German nationalist.[20] Writers and scholars, as Denis de Rougemont wryly remarked, express loyalty to the most threatening party so as to avoid the worst trouble. Such intellectual cowardice will be multiplied towards the totalitarian regimes in the twentieth century; another reason why studying the philosophers of the past is not very helpful to understand the idea of Europe after the Second World War.

The Revolution also is at the origin of the revolutionary messianism, inspiring nineteenth century thought and twentieth century ideologies, among them Lenin. The Bolshevik *coup d'etat* under Lenin's leadership set out to promote "world revolution". His successor Stalin extended Soviet totalitarian rule to the Elba in the heart of Germany. It was the outcome of Stalin's conspiracy with Hitler in 1939 and the Grand Alliance against Hitler in 1941.[21] Hitler came to power in 1933 and set out to conquer Europe and exterminate its Jewish and Slavic populations until he met total defeat in the Second World War. The three totalitarian regimes of twenty century Europe - Mussolini's fascism in addition to Lenin/Stalin's communism and Hitler's National Socialism - were the poisoned products

---

[19] Johann-Gotfried Herder, *On Social and Political Culture,* Translated, edited and with an introduction by F.M. Barnard, Cambridge University Press 1969, Quotations from pp. 202, 169, 324.

[20] Cf. Fichte's Addresses to the German Nation.

[21] Cf. my *Western Cooperation, Op. cit.* Chapter I.4 and I. 5.

of the ideologies of the nineteenth century and the First World War. They were the harbingers of the anti-Christian and anti-European policies of totalitarian repression. The depth of destruction and disorientation required a radically new approach. Even those who fought totalitarian repression had been infected by the totalitarians' anti-Christian and anti-Semitic fury, by their nationalism, and by the madness of the police state, their lawlessness and their rule of the lie and the informer.

After the Second World War

After the Second World War, only the *fourth concept* would still make sense. The post-war Idea of Europe to be constructed by common agreement, did not come to *Robert Schuman* and *Jean Monnet* by the study of philosophers from the past, but by the spectacle of ruins left by two World Wars. Their project to unify Europe after the Second World War was a creative response to the reality of war, repression and destruction, rather than a reception of earlier ideas.

Their conscience and recent experience told them, that (Western) Europe could survive only if it was prepared to reconcile and unite. The spectacle of bombed-out cities, total chaos, death, displacement and immense suffering, made them and others realize what Romano Guardini said in 1962 and available as the opening document to this volume:

> "(Europe) has had time to shed many an illusion. The real Europe harbours no unqualified optimism, no fundamental belief in universal and inevitable progress. The values of the past are still so real to it that Europe knows what is at stake. It has already lost so much that is irrecoverable, its long destructive wars have laid upon it so heavy a load of guilt that it can feel not only the

creative possibilities but also the dangers, even the tragedy, of human existence. It is mindful no doubt of the mythical figure of Prometheus, who brought fire from Olympus, but also of Icarus, who fell from the sky because he flew too close to the sun. Europe is familiar with the achievements of learning and of conquest, but it has no belief in the certainty of progress or in Utopian dreams of universal happiness. It knows too much for that. For this reason it seems to me that Europe may be destined to find an unsensational, but profoundly vital mission in the critical assessment of power. Its criticism will not be negative, nor will it be timid or reactionary. I believe, however, that the care of man is entrusted to Europe, because Europe has experience of power, not as the guarantee of assured triumphs, but as part of its destiny, uncertain though it be whither it may lead."
(..)
But, Guardini continues: "Europe (also) gave birth to the concept of freedom, both for man and for man's work; its primary duty, its concern for man's humanity, will be to protect freedom even in opposition to man's own work."[22]

The contrast between power and freedom, between repression and resistance, between revenge and reconciliation in revolution and between national sovereignty and European unity, can be recognized throughout European history. It manifests both the tragedy of Europe and the freedom of Europeans to follow their conscience and revolt in name of the dignity of the human person. Most histories of unification efforts may have overlooked that Europe's long history is marked by these contrasts. The dominating feature of Europe's political

---

22 Romano Guardini, *Europe - Reality or Mission,* See and study Document EH. 1.

history is ongoing division not growing unity. The hopeful contrast is the freedom of conscience of the Europeans to revolt and make a new beginning.... time and time again.

While using different words, Guardini, Benda, Dawson and Jaspers appear to agree on the fundamental dualism in Europe as a civilization:"the ethical dualism between Christian virtues and pagan traditions" as Dawson called it. Karl Jaspers referred to it as the polarities typical for European civilisation; the antithesis between antiquity and Christianity, between Church and State or between faith and science. Julian Benda emphasised the contrast between the reality of a European civilisation and the virtual absence of the awareness of Europe as a political and spiritual unity.[23]

The awareness of European unity came in response to the wild triumphs of the anti-European and anti-Christian ideologies and to the spectacle of the ruins after two World Wars. The fathers of European Unification after the Second World War represented and practiced the Christian virtues necessary to that end. They could not be assured of success, nor can we be at present. The European Union no longer is what Schuman wanted it to become. The current leaders do not resemble their fathers of Europe.

---

[23] In *L'Esprit, Op. cit.* Julia Benda, *Discours à la nation européenne,* Folio essais, Gallimard 1979.

CHAPTER 2

EUROPE:
CHARACTER AND CULTURE

"No culture has appeared or developed except together with a religion".[1]

Culture, writes Christopher Dawson, means "a common social way of life - a way of life with a tradition behind it, which has embodied itself in institutions and which involves moral standards and principles." In a later chapter, Dawson writes that all civilizations have always been both social and religious: "two worlds of reality bound together by a visible fabric of institutions and laws, and by objective conceptions of justice and authority which gave them validity".[2] Law developed from such moral standards and principles, which themselves found their origin in religion and sacred customs.

Throughout history, culture, religion and law have thus always been closely linked to each other and with the concept of people or a nation. It would be difficult to visualize a universal common social way of life with a tradition behind it and originating from a universal religion or kept at peace by a common acceptance of a universal rule of law. The world of men has always been a world of cultural, religious, legal and national diversity.

Europe no doubt has developed together with the Christian

---

1 T.S. Eliot, *Christianity and Culture*, A Harvest Book 1976.

2 Christopher Dawson, *The Historic Reality of Christian Culture*, Harper N.Y. 1960, pp. 13 and 86.

faith. Within Christianity, we observe great diversity. Already within the European Union, there are Greek Orthodox, Greek Catholic, Roman Catholic, Lutheran, Anglican and Reformation Christians.

Such diversities may be enriching, but have also been sources of tensions and conflicts. Religious believers and churches may be imbued with respect for divergence, they also claim exclusiveness or superiority. In the domain of culture, some might claim that man's spiritual and creative activity is universal by definition, while others would claim that every thought and every habit is determined by the spirit of the people to which a person belongs. The former tend to reject cultural diversity, the latter reject the existence of any standards or values common to various nations. Both claims have a grain of truth and an amount of falsehood within them.

European civilisation has been formed profoundly and decisively by the Good News, the Gospel of Jesus-Christ. As our Saviour, Christ is unique: not the last of the prophets but the first of the risen from the death. As divine reality His coming into this world is a historic reality. He is not only memory but living presence. From a Christian point of view, human history and the history of salvation are intertwined. History has a sense and a direction, advancing towards the end of times. As Karl Jaspers wrote: freedom, history, science are three typically European characteristics.[3] Therefore "tradition" implies more than just interpretation of the Word of God recorded in the Bible. It implies progress towards some end. Europe's conception of man and woman and their fundamental dignity is fundamentally shaped by Jesus-Christ. He Himself was fully aware of His mission to complete the Law (the *Torah*) and to bring the faith of Israel to all the nations. He was also aware of

---

[3] In *L.' Esprit Européen. Op. cit.* above in Chapter I.

being "A Sign of Contradiction" in the world. In that sense He was a revolutionary and teaches those who want to follow Him to be and to do the same. Important changes or turning points in European history are the outcome of major revolts against the existing order. Some of them bring change for the better, others for the worse, again others with mixed results. We shall discuss two examples relevant to the theme of this book.

It must be well understood: what makes the difference are Christ and the Bible and not so much we Christians. Europe's history is full of tragedy, conflict, injustice and violence. Like others, Europeans do good and commit evil, practice virtue and care for others and are blinded by power, egoism or subject to hatred. Formed by Christ does not mean that we Europeans are superior to others, only that abundant grace has been given to us. Our shortcomings are worse than those of others. Europe as a civilisation is full of gripping stories of courage and compassion, resistance and revolt and faith and fortitude; but also of cowardice and complicity, revenge and repression and fault and failure.

THE PAPAL REVOLUTION

The humanization of law over the centuries is the first theme giving evidence of such decisive importance. Ancient and traditional customs are known to be harsh and cruel. Some of them are described in the Book of Genesis, like the treatment of Joseph by his half-brothers (Jacob had several wives) or the response of the brothers to the dishonouring of their sister Dinah.

From the Ten Commandments in the Book of Exodus to the Sermon on the Mount in St. Mathew's Gospel, the Bible narrates of God's effort to humanise men's cruel laws - an effort continuing through Tradition. The first commandment behind this effort is to "love the Lord your God with all your heart, with all your soul, with all your mind and with all your strength. The second is this: You must love your neighbour as yourself. There is no commandment greater than these." (Mk.12,30-31). There can be no true justice without such charity.[4] In the legal history of the West, the process of humanisation can be followed through the formation of Roman law, Canon Law and the codification of law in continental European countries. For the formation of the European and Western legal tradition, the Papal Revolution in the eleventh century has been a decisive turning point.[5] It was a turning point in the relations between spiritual and temporal power, as a result from the reform policies of Pope Gregory VII following the Great Schism between East and West in 1054. The Papal claim to superior spiritual power broke the tradition of symbiosis between the two powers in the Roman Empire, resulting after ages of conflict in the separation between church and state.

Separation between church and state

The separation between spiritual and temporal power, between faith and politics, between church and state is not an invention of the era of Enlightenment, as most of us have been taught. The concept has its origin in the Gospel itself, where Jesus in reply to a question by some Pharisees and Herodians, says: "Pay Caesar what belongs to Caesar - and God what belongs to God."[6] History provides ample evidence of the wisdom of this concept. One of man's greatest temptations is the abuse of power over men. The best remedy is the separation of powers. The separation between spiritual

---

4 Armand Abécassis, Droit et religion dans la société hébraique, *Archives de Philosophie du Droit,* Tome 38,1993.

5 Harold J. Berman, *Law and Revolution; The Formation of the Western Legal Tradition,* Harvard University Press 1983.

6 This story appears in Mathew, Mark and Luke.

and temporal or political power opened the road to a system of checks and balances we call democracy, to freedom of conscience and religion and to human rights.

In Robert Schuman's view, democracy owes its existence to Christendom. It was born the day man was called to realise in daily life the dignity of the human person; and to do so in individual liberty, in respect for the rights of everyone; and to practise fraternal charity to all. Never before Christ have such ideas been formulated.[7]

Spiritual and secular power in Western history

We should not forget that the symbiosis between spiritual and political power has been the custom in human history. Such was the case in the Roman Empire of the 4th century and in Byzantium thereafter. It was the case in the countries of the Reformation, according to the principle *cuius regio eius religio.* It was the case in the countries with an Orthodox majority and seems to be returning to Russia. It was the case in the Islamic world and today in Iran in particular. The symbiosis easily leads to repression and seldom or never to democracy.

The major exception to the custom of symbiosis is the Roman Catholic Church - at the time of the persecutions in the Roman Empire before Emperor Theodosius in 380 and after the Papal revolution in the eleventh century. The history of Europe and the West has been deeply marked by the turbulent relationship between Popes and Emperors of the Holy Roman Empire, from 800 (rule of Charles the Great) to the Peace of Westphalia in 1648. For centuries it was an adversary relationship, not always

---

[7] René Lejeune, *Robert Schuman, Père de L'Europe 1886-1963, La Politique, Chemin de sainteté,* Fayard 2000, p. 220. See also Berman, *Op. cit.* Chapter 2.

edifying but surely fascinating. In this history three periods must be remembered in particular.

The first one is the era following the Great Schism of 1054 between East and West. The Papal Revolution (Gregory VII) against the political power of the Emperor dominated Europe for over two centuries. It began as an effort to free the Pope from imperial oversight.[8] It was the era of the great crusades against the Turks and Byzantium. More positive was the creation of Europe's first modern universities. Bologna devoted itself to law, Paris to theology. The former was instrumental in the creation of the first Western system of law, the canon law. The latter, through such great saints and teachers as Albertus Magnus and Thomas Aquinas, helped revive philosophy, *fides et ratio*. The era came to an end with the failed effort (Boniface VIII) to assert papal supremacy over the king of France.[9]

The second one is the era of Reformation and religious wars, from Luther to the Peace of Westphalia in 1648[10] - also the era of the great discoveries. While the Americas were discovered and colonised, Europe (the West at the time) fell apart. The Peace of Westphalia sanctioned a new system of sovereign states, whose princes accepted no higher authority than their own and no other law than that promulgated under their own authority.

The third one is the era of Enlightenment and the revolutions in America and France. French Enlightenment and Revolution were distinctly irreligious and anti-catholic Church. The Pilgrim Fathers, who fled religious persecution in England and sailed (after 11 years in Holland at Leiden University) to North

---

8 See Document EH. 4. The ten dictates of the pope.
9 See documents EH. 5. Unam Sanctam, Pope Boniface VIII.
10 Cf. Document EH. 7. Peace of Westphalia.

America, were most religious. They sought full freedom for practising their own version of Protestantism. The American Colonies in 1776, revolted against the King of Great Britain because of his usurpation of power. Inspired by the writings of John Locke, their new Republic was built on Christian foundations. Freedom of religion was one of its fundamental principles. After the Second World War, the West and Europe embarked on their new course of Atlantic cooperation and European Unification. The American model of a state founded on freedom of religion, rather than the French one founded on the *laicité* of the republic prevailed - also in the Declaration *Dignitatis Humanae* of the Second Vatican Council![11]

A Variety of solutions to the relations between Church and State

The United States of America is the only Western country in which freedom of conscience and religion was a founding principle from the beginning. The European states moved gradually from the situation of a dominant Church to accepting freedom of conscience and religion - in some of them not until after the Second World War.

A strict regime of separation between Churches and State prevails in the United States and France. This proved problematic in France, as we saw already, but it is working well in the United States. It enabled full freedom for the churches. The relationship is the subject of continuous and lively discussion. Many cases have come before the Supreme Court for judgment. Strict separation also prevailed in the former

---

11 The chief intellectual architect of the Declaration was the U.S. Jesuit theologian John Courtney Murray. George Weigel, *Freedom and Its Discontents, Catholicism Con-fronts Modernity,* Ethics and Public Policy Center 1991, At p.37.

Soviet Union, but in a devious variant. The Soviet and other communist constitutions separated the state from the church and the church from education. That is to say: the State abused education to impose atheism and the church was kept out of the educational system. Russia, after 1991, officially wrote the separation of Church and State in its Constitution, but in reality the Russian Orthodox Church is considered as the national church.

At the other end of the spectrum are England, the Nordic states, Greece and several Swiss cantons with the regime of an established church. Under the influence of post-war developments towards freedom of religion and equality of treatment, the regime of a state church is little more than a formality.

In between one finds religiously pluralist countries like Germany and the Netherlands in which a mixed system of cooperation and separation prevails. In Germany churches have a special status. They receive their income through the system of *Kirchensteuer*. In the Netherlands religious and state schools and universities are equally financed.

In between one may also find countries like Belgium, Ireland, Italy, Poland, Portugal and Spain - all in majority Catholic. A system of separation based on freedom of religion and equality of treatment is in force. In fact the Catholic Church still is the more equal one, by its size, by its organisation and in a number of these countries by the fact that its rights are enshrined in a Concordat with the Holy See.

Especially since the Second World War, the regimes for the separation between Churches and States tend to converge. This is partly due to the attractive model presented by the United States but also to the European Human Rights Convention, giving prime of place in its article 9 to freedom of conscience and religion. This development in itself underlines the importance of the separation between religious and political power for the humanisation of law and the state. Two things, however, must be kept in mind. The European Human Rights Convention - like the Schuman Plan - was a response to the massive violation of human rights in war and by the totalitarian regimes. The variety of solutions reflected a variety of Christian denominations. It may be that these solutions are no longer adequate for our current problems. Among them are the dechristianization of our societies and the growing presence of Muslim minorities, who do not recognise the separation of church and state.

THE HUMANIZATION OF LAW

The Papal Revolution of the eleventh century was also a turning point in the formation of the European and Western legal tradition as such. In the chapter on The Origin of Western Legal Science in the European Universities, Harold Berman explains that the twelfth century was the century in which the Western legal tradition was formed, in the new method of teaching and in the method of analysis and synthesis of legal texts.

From the theory developed by the canonists, four should be emphasised as particularly important. The *first* one is the principle, as a matter of natural law, that: "princes are bound by and shall live according to their laws."

The *second* is the theory: "that customs must yield to natural law", rightly underlined as "one of the greatest achievements of the canonists." Berman than continues: "Elaborate criteria were developed to determine the validity of a custom: its duration, its universality, its uniformity of application, its reasonableness - tests still used in the twentieth century. This meant that custom lost its sanctity; a custom might be binding or not."[12]

The *third* one is that the canonists and Romanists of the twelfth century "combined the Greek capacity for philosophy with the Roman capacity for law. In addition, they deepened the earlier concepts of reason and equity by adding to them the Judaic and Christian concept of conscience, which they related to mercy and love."

The *Fourth*, "the European jurists of the twelfth and thirteenth centuries converted the Roman law rule (*vim vi repellere licet*) into a general principle, which they juxtaposed with the so-called pacifist utterances of Jesus ('turn the other cheek'), and from the opposing maxims they developed a general concept of justification for the limited use of force applicable to a whole series of interrelated categories systematically set forth: force necessary to execute the law, to defend oneself, to defend another, to protect one's property, to protect another's property."[13]

Some examples may clarify the extent of this influence. When asked about the right of a husband to divorce his wife (Mt. 19,1-9), Jesus makes clear that no man should separate what God has joined. What he means is marriage as a union between one man and one woman. We also learn that Moses still accepted divorce, because of the people's stubbornness. Monogamy became the cornerstone of Western family law. The marriage vow is given special protection, although recent changes in secular law have made divorce easier. Such protection is bound to be undermined by recent developments

---

12 *Op. cit.* p. 145.

13 Berman, *Op. cit.* pp. 146-148, "Force may be used to repel force"is the translation of the Roman Law Rule.

giving unions between two persons of the same sex the same rights and status. Done in the name of the principle of equal treatment, it shows the extent of philosophical and moral confusion now pervading modern secular society.

Another example concerns the power of a father over his wife and children. Traditional custom gave him power over their life and death. Western law has gradually abolished that power. A death sentence can be pronounced only by a competent and independent court under strict rules of criminal law and procedure. Revenge killing or honour killing have been outlawed. Under the European Human Rights Convention, the death penalty itself has been abolished (Protocol Nr. 6).

So how do we deal with the case of a young Turkish woman in a European City, who was killed by her 12 year old brother?[14] The case was widely discussed in the local Turkish community and the boy found substantial support for what was considered an act to protect the honour of her family, permitted under *Shari'a* or Islamic Law. Under existing criminal law in Europe (but also in modern Turkey) honour killing is forbidden by law. The practice according to reports from the UN, however, is still widespread in Islamic countries and growing in Europe and not always prosecuted. Legal authorities can and do react variably. The Public Prosecutor can decide not to do anything as the killing has not been reported to him, he can indict the boy only, or the father as accomplice, or both son and father for deliberate murder. The Judge, similarly, has a variety of options at his disposal: from a lenient sentence for the boy and acquittal of the father to life sentence for both for murder. Seen in perspective, the answer appears to be quite clear.

---

[14] There were at least six such cases in 2005 in one major city. To protect the persons concerned, this case combines elements of some of them.

What is claimed to be *shari'a* is in reality accepted ancient custom. No such "religious" claim can be accepted against current criminal law as the outcome of a long process of its humanisation. Father and son ought to be condemned for premeditated murder.

Another example with a long history is the abolition of slavery. Already in the *Corpus Iuris Civilis* we can read that slavery is contrary to natural law. It took the West until the nineteenth century until slavery was abolished by law. Still, the theory that customs must yield to natural law is one of the greatest achievements of the humanisation of law and of the canonists in particular.

A final example concerns the issue of war under international law. Essentially, we are faced with a very sad history and an unsolved issue. Still from times of St. Augustine and Thomas Aquinas onwards, efforts have been made to restrain warfare, the latest step being the prohibition to use force in the UN Charter. Just war theory is not meant to justify the use of force but to limit war between states.

The humanisation of law is closely related to the separation between church and state and has often been the outcome of the revolt of the human spirit against cruelty and abuse of power - to which we shall now turn.

THE REVOLT OF THE HUMAN SPIRIT

Jesus Christ was neither a warrior nor a political revolutionary. His kingdom was not of this world, in the world He was a sign of contradiction. His message is addressed to the conscience of every human being, to our inner sanctuary where we must decide between the good to do and the evil to avoid. In conscience we may decide to disobey a law and the ruler.

"The principle of civil disobedience was in fact inherent in the experience of the early church, since Christian worship was itself illegal."[15] The principle found its way into the laws of Europe and the West. The right or even the duty to disobey the law is not limited to tyrannical laws. As we can read in the Encyclical *Evangelium Vitae* of Pope John-Paul II: "Abortion and euthanasia are thus crimes which no human law can claim to legitimize. There is no obligation in conscience to obey such laws; *instead there is a grave and clear obligation to oppose them by conscientious objection"*[16]

Throughout our history, courageous men and women revolted in the name of their conscience and thereby changed the course of history. We owe the principle of freedom of conscience and religion to those who, most concretely, objected to the death penalty for heresy in the name of tolerance.[17] Tolerance, ever since, is a duty for state authorities.

In our time, we owe Europe's peaceful unification to those who opted for reconciliation with Germany instead of revenge. In Washington D.C. George Marshall and Dean Acheson decided to offer Marshall Aid also to Germany (1947). From Paris Robert Schuman launched his proposal for reconciliation and European unity with Germany (1950). The plan was drafted by Jean Monnet and strongly supported by Alcide de Gasperi in Rome and Konrad Adenauer in Bonn. These men changed the course of European and Western history, acting from the depth of their faith as Christians. Robert Schuman was fully aware of being an instrument of Providence, Who used

---

15 Harold J. Berman, *Op.cit.* p. 167.

16 Encyclical of John-Paul II. Par. 73.

17 Stefan Zweig, *Castellio gegen Calvin oder Ein Gewissen gegen die Gewalt,* Fischer Taschenbuch 2003; Voltaire, *Traité sur la Tolérance,* Flammarion Paris 1989.

him to achieve what goes beyond our human capacity.[18].

The Spirit of 1989: Living Within the Truth

The early autumn of 1989 showed two fascinating scenes. On 5 September a new government with Tadeusz Mazowiecki as Catholic Prime Minister of a non-communist government took office in Warsaw and was greeted, not by Soviet intervention, but by Gorbachev's approval. Already in May, the Hungarians had begun cutting the barbed wire in their section of the Iron Curtain, enabling East Germans to escape across it. In early September the Hungarian authorities decided to let them leave officially, and the trickle turned into a massive exodus of East Germans through Hungary and Austria to the West German Federal Republic. Thereafter the Order of Yalta collapsed with breath-taking speed. The Berlin Wall was opened on 9 November 1989. The velvet revolution in Prague followed the same month, on 17 November. It caught people and politicians in Western Europe and North America unprepared and fully surprised.

Within a year after the crumbling of the Berlin Wall, Germany was peacefully re-united. By virtue of the Treaty on the Final Settlement with respect to Germany of 12 September 1990 Britain, France, the Soviet Union and the United States terminated their rights and responsibilities relating to Berlin and Germany.

In November 1990 the Heads of State or Government of the states participating in the Conference for Security and Cooperation in Europe (CSCE), created by the Helsinki Final Act, gathered in Paris to adopt the Charter of Paris for a new

---

18 René Lejeune, *Robert Schuman, Père de l'Europe 1886-1963.* Fayard 2000, p. 15.

Europe. According to the Charter they proclaimed a new era of democracy, peace and unity.

The Charter of Paris was presented as a follow-up to the Final Act of Helsinki of 1975, but in fact contradicted the latter on most major points. The Charter renounced the status quo of a divided Germany by declaring that: the establishment of the national unity of Germany is an important contribution to a just and lasting order of peace for a united, democratic Europe.

German re-unification - for long conceived as the possible outcome of a long process of détente - now became the starting point for the new Europe. The Treaty of 12 September 1990 was and still remains the first and principal legally binding agreement with respect to the new Europe. It confirms the right of the united Germany to be an enlarged (West-German) Federal Republic and to continue its membership of NATO and the European Community. It confirms the definite nature of its existing borders as an essential element of the peaceful order in Europe. It commits Germany to peace, the renunciation of nuclear, biological and chemical weapons, and a reduction in its armed forces. It committed the Soviet Union to a complete withdrawal of its armed forces from the territory of the (former) GDR. As a Western democracy, the united Germany is to be the cornerstone of Europe's new architecture.

The euphoria of the Charter of Paris was short-lived and the transition to a new Europe would prove to be difficult and painful. Neither the West, nor the new leaders in the former East were prepared for the difficulties of the transition process. From under the rubble (the phrase comes from Solzhenitsyn) of the collapsed communist system, the ghost of nationalism emerged in its new shape as the ethnic-nationalist warrior, bent on carving up the territories of the failed states into ethnically cleansed new states. Its principal victim was Yugoslavia. In the West, Yugoslav national communism had for a long time been conceived as the model for the liberation of Eastern Europe from Soviet domination. Few people cared about the slow disintegration of the republic following Tito's death. The Serbian memorandum of 1986[19] went virtually unnoticed until 1991, when it was too late to save the country from disaster.

The year 1991 was the year in which the 12 Member States of the European Communities agreed on a new Treaty on European Union. The year 1991 also was the year in which the Soviet Union disintegrated into 15 independent republics.

The collapse of the Soviet Union and Yugoslavia contained a mixed message for Europe's unification efforts. Common action clearly has its limits when dealing with serious political crises. At the same time it operates as a barrier against the escalation of conflicts. Major powers are more reluctant to intervene unilaterally in local conflicts. States seeking membership of European organizations have an additional interest in earning admission by peaceful behavior.

In the 1980s we have experienced how the revolt of civil society in Poland, Czechoslovakia and Hungary peacefully brought down communist repression and the Soviet system. The "Spirit of 1989"[20] overcame the post-war division of Europe and created the conditions for the peaceful enlargement of the European Union. The Spirit of 1989 found its source in the Christian faith. When Pope John-Paul II visited Poland in 1979, he asked his fellow-Poles: "What are you in favour of? Of conformist

---

19 Text in Document EH. 14. Chronology of the collapse of Yugoslavia in document E. 2. 26.

20 Frans A.M. Alting von Geusau, *Cultural Diplomacy: waging war by other means?*, Wolf Legal Publishers 2009, Chapter 8, 'The Spirit of 1989: Europe on the Threshold of a new Era?'.

consent to totalitarian coercion or of the inviolable right in God's and man's order of things for human beings to live in freedom and dignity?"[21] The answer came on the spot and within a year with solidarity strikes at the Gdansk Shipyard and the creation of *Solidarnosc*, the first free trade union behind the Iron Curtain. The peaceful collapse of the communist system did not come by chance, it was so intended. The "Spirit of Solidarity" sought revolution as an event in the spiritual sphere and not a violent revolution based on the principle of revenge. "Solidarity means to carry the burden of another person and so fulfil God's law, it is a virtue born of itself from the heart. The key to our cause is faith in the Son of Man."[22] This faith was the key to the Spirit of 1989 and to the peaceful re-unification of Europe.

The Founding Fathers of the 1950's had caused European Unification to become a reality. The leaders of Civil Resistance in East and Central Europe from 1968-1989 caused Europe's re-unification to become a reality. Its Founding Fathers are Pope John-Paul II and the leaders of *Solidarnosc* in Poland and *Charta 77* in Czechoslovakia. They initiated and organised the peaceful revolution of the spirit against totalitarian repression. Totalitarian communism has been peacefully overcome by *Solidarnosc* in Poland and by *Charta 77* in Czechoslovakia, in both cases in the name of human dignity. It brought the end of Europe's division and the enlargement of the European Union from 12 to 27 Member States.

The success of civil resistance against the most intrusive totalitarian system known in human history indeed is a message of hope. However deeply the system managed to intrude the inner sanctuary of man, it ultimately failed to paralyse

---

21 A selection of documents from the civil resistance in East and Central Europe in EH. 11.

22 Józef Tischner, *The Spirit of Solidarity*, Harper and Row 1982.

his conscience. As Pope John-Paul II wrote in the Encyclical *Veritatis Splendor*:

> "54. The relationship between man's freedom and God's law is most deeply lived out in the "heart" of the person, in his moral conscience. As the Second Vatican Council observed: "In the depths of his conscience man detects a law which he does not impose on himself, but which holds him to obedience. Always summoning him to love good and avoid evil, the voice of conscience can when necessary speak to his heart more specifically: 'do this, shun that'. For man has in his heart a law written by God. To obey it is the very dignity of man; according to it he will be judged (Cf. *Rom* 2:14-16)".

Such obedience to the law written in their heart gave birth to *Charta 77* and to *Solidarnosc* in 1980. Their obedience changed the history of their country and of Europe.[23]

The creation of *Solidarnosc* acted like a forceful earthquake in the communist system. No building any longer stood solid or reliable. No martial law, no masterminded assassination attempt on the Pope and no internment of the trade union's leadership could any longer break civil resistance. The most intrusive and, in a way, the most powerful totalitarian system collapsed without major violence. No armies were moved, no battles fought no frontiers crossed.

It was not Michael Gorbachev, who changed history with his *Glasnost and Perestroika*; he wanted to reform the system from above (and obviously failed), his principal contribution was to refrain from the use of force when Poland formed its first non-

---

[23] Text of Charta 77 and the Gdansk agreement of 1980 in documents EH.12. and EH. 13.

communist government in September 1989. That moment all other communist leaders knew that their days were numbered. Nor was it the West that "won the Cold War". Western leaders and intellectuals were all taken by surprise. Not a few of them had acted on the belief that the communist system was there to stay and could at best be assisted in reforms from above by *détente* and negotiation.

It was the spirit of solidarity by which non-violent civil resistance was organised and prevailed over repression. As Józef Tischner told his fellow-members of Solidarnosc: the key to our cause is faith and it is our task to "carry one another's burden and in this way fulfil God's law."[24] It was a call for the solidarity of consciences. This virtue does not need to be imposed from the outside by force, it is born from the heart. It does not need an enemy to grow, but unites us in pursuing truth and justice. What happened in the years prior to 1989, can be summarised in the following way:

Against the "Secrets" Of the System:		*Civil Society replied with*
Official atheism	←	Live in Faith
Propaganda, mass mobilisation	←	Turn away, organise ourselves
The organised lie	←	Live within the truth
Organised forgetting	←	Active remembering
Betrayal and distrust	←	Solidarity of consciences
Persecution and humiliation	←	Organise assistance
Apathetic subjection	←	Restore sense of responsibility
Violence against citizens	←	Non-violent revolution of the spirit
Usurpation	←	Live as if you are already free

24 Jozef Tischner, *The Spirit of Solidarity*, Harper & Row 1984 (translated from Polish).

As Vaclav Havel wrote: "There are no terms whatsoever in which living within the lie can coexist with living within the truth, and therefore everyone who steps out of line denies the system in principle and threatens it in its entirety."[25] The same can be said of living the faith and practicing our Christian virtues: they threatened the system in its entirety. As a consequence, 1989 became the *year of truth* for communism and Europe.

When John-Paul II visited his country as the Pope for the first time in 1979, none of the standard communist banners had been removed, but some had been edited privately. Under the banner "The Party is for the People", somebody had added: "But the People are for God." Making fun of the omnipotent Party was another weapon of civil resistance against communist repression.[26]

I have no doubt that Pope John-Paul II and the leaders of civil resistance in East and Central Europe should be counted among the founding fathers of Europe, in particular of her re-unification and the peaceful enlargement of the European Union. The reply of civil society against the "secrets" of the totalitarian communist system (see figure above), are an excellent point of departure for a discussion on "European values", together with the reply of the post-war founding fathers to the ruins of war.

---

25 Vaclav Havel, *The Power of the Powerless; Vaclav Havel or Living in Truth,* Edited by Jan Vladislav, Meulenhof with Faber and Faber 1986.

26 Milan Kundera, *The Book of Laughter and Forgetting.*

Fading Spirit

More than twenty years after the breakdown of communism, Europe has not become what many of us hoped for in 1989. The spirit of solidarity seems to have faded with the communist system, despite the enlargement of NATO and the European Union. The effort to live within the truth is still threatened. The family - as foundation of our society - is still under attack, no longer by totalitarian regimes but by private initiative and parliamentary majorities. Instead of official atheism, we are now faced with an aggressive secularism. Apparently (according to a majority in the European Parliament) it is politically more correct to be dishonest than to be a convinced catholic. Interestingly, it also seems to be politically correct no longer to want to learn from history: communism was bad, yes, but is now past history and should be forgotten. Could it be that aggressive secularists have something to suppress in their memory as far as their attitude to communism before 1989? Could it be that they have something to deny loudly as it does not fit in their schemes for a secular European Union, namely that the communist ideology was defeated by the Gospel?

CHAPTER 3

EUROPE: IDEAS HAVE CONSEQUENCES AND THE PAST IS NOT ANOTHER COUNTRY

Article 2 Treaty on European Union (TEU) Lisbon.

> *The Union is founded on the values of respect for human dignity, freedom, democracy, equality, the rule of law and respect for human rights, including the rights of persons belonging to minorities. These values are common to the Member States in a society in which pluralism, non-discrimination, tolerance, justice, solidarity and equality between women and men prevail.*

This article of the TEU Lisbon clearly suffers from over-kill formulation. The first sentence is similar to the original EU Treaty. Only "principles" have been replaced by "values." The meaning of the second sentence is unclear. It reads as a kind of afterthought without legal or even political significance. At best it is pretentious.

THE SEARCH FOR VALUES

A brief excursion to Europe's modern history teaches us that the search for "values" invariably indicates a desire to distinguish oneself, or stand apart from and contrast with somebody or something else. After the Second World War, Western Civilization with its common heritage and common values contrasted with the East (the Soviet Empire). The Atlantic Alliance was to become the dynamic counter-attraction to Communism. Teaching the history of great ideas from Plato to NATO[1], should raise the awareness of a Western identity. Within the West dominated by the United States of America, France since President Charles de Gaulle looked for arguments to distinguish the emerging European Community, it wanted to dominate, from America. Its search for a "European identity" (since the 1970s) tried to discover typical European values distinct from American ones. There was a time when the European Left in fact supported this attempt. In the era of East-West *détente* and the nuclear balance of terror, many on the left and among the liberals felt closer to Moscow's bureaucratic socialism than to America's outright capitalism. Among them was the " counter-culture" being established in our universities after the student revolts of 1968 in Paris. By the time of the end of the so called Cold War in 1990, this counter-culture had been transformed into "widely accepted conventional wisdom, a new form of conformity, values that are taken for granted."[2]

Of course both (France and the European left) got a little lost when communism collapsed, Germany re-united and America remained as the only "super power". During the decade of the nineties, America clearly took the lead in shaping a new order directed towards the advance of democracy and the market economy. Europe reluctantly imitated and followed by its own approach towards deepening and widening European

---

1 *From PLATO to NATO*, is the title of a book by David Gress, The Free Press 1998.

2 Paul Hollander, *Decline and Discontent, Communism and the West Today*, Transaction Publishers 1992.

Unification. While the first stagnated, enlargement irresistibly continued.

"9/11", the terrorist attack on America, would be another turning point. In the new "war against terror" declared by U.S. President Bush jr., Europe wanted her identity to be more clearly distinguishable. The search for common European values was to serve the effort to give an enlarging European Union a firmer foundation in a European Constitutional document. At the same time it should set Europe apart from American and Islamic culture: more peaceful and secular than the former, more democratic and more tolerant than the latter.

The values-debates referred to so far, have one thing in common. They all reflect an effort to prove the superiority of one's own culture over others. The study of history and the reading of classical texts should prove it. The common values enumerated in the Constitution for Europe and repeated above, are of this kind. They are taken for granted and dutifully recited whenever asked.

To the best of my knowledge, no ideas of any consequence have been advanced so far. It is not by lack of effort. Two prestigious European institutes devoted substantial efforts and time to the debate on values. The Vienna Institute for Human Sciences (IWM) set up a high level Reflection Group on the Spiritual and Cultural Dimension of Europe, on the invitation of Romano Prodi (former) President of the European Commission. The Tilburg Nexus Institute organised a series of high level conferences on *"Europe A Beautiful Idea"*, during the Dutch Presidency of the European Union in 2004. At the end of a confused and often contradictory report, the Reflection Group of IWM concluded that: "There is no essence of Europe, no fixed list of European values. There is no "finality" to the process of European integration."[3]

Such a conclusion is saddening rather than surprising. Europe's debate on values is hardly a century old and began with Nietzsche's "God is dead" philosophy. The underlying philosophical crisis has not been overcome as yet...on the contrary; it has deepened by the counter-culture that became a new form of conformity.

Beyond Good and Evil?

Until Nietzsche, value meant a measure: a mathematical rather than a moral category. One spoke of the value of a property (to be expressed in monetary terms), of the estimated price for a good, value added tax, the exchange value of a currency, as the precise meaning of a word, or in art as the relative lightness or darkness of a colour. It was Nietzsche who initiated a new way of speaking about values, primarily in an effort to move mankind beyond categories of good and evil as taught through the Christian faith. He did most clearly so after "Thus spoke Zarathustra" in "The AntiChrist":

> "What is good? Everything that heightens the feeling of power in man, the will to power, power itself.
> What is bad? Everything that is born of weakness.

[3] *The Spiritual and Cultural Dimension of Europe*, IWM, Vienna/ Brussels, October 2004. A more interesting, but largely ignored effort to define the values of Europe can be found in Document EH. 15, The Charter of European Identity 1995, initiated by Vaclav Havel.

> What is happiness? The feeling that power is growing, that resistance is overcome. ."[4]

I quoted from Nietzsche's aphoristic book, to underline the astonishing and insufficiently noticed phenomenon, rightly exposed by Allan Bloom: "there is now an entirely new language of good and evil, in an attempt to get "beyond good and evil" and preventing us from talking with any conviction about good and evil anymore. Even those who deplore our current moral condition do so in the very language that exemplifies that condition. The new language is that of *value* relativism, and it constitutes a change in our views of things moral and political as great as the one that took place when Christianity replaced Greek and Roman paganism." It is much easier to reduce the tension between values than the tension between good and evil. "The term "value" meaning the radical subjectivity of all belief about good and evil, serves the easygoing quest for comfortable self-preservation" Use of the value language, however, leads us in two opposite directions - "to follow the line of least resistance, and to adopt strong poses and fanatic resolutions."[5] Freud and Weber - both profoundly influenced by Nietzsche - "are the immediate source of most of the language with which we are so familiar"[6] according to Bloom.

---

4 Quotations are from The Antichrist as translated by W. Kaufmann and R.J. Hollingdale. See also document EH.10 for a longer excerpt. In: *The Portable Nietzsche,* The Viking Press 1954. The term "moraline" means hypocritical moral opinions.

5 Allan Bloom, *The Closing of the American Mind, How Higher Education has failed democracy and impoverished the souls of today's students,* New York 1987 at pp. 141,142,143.

6 On p. 148. Also: Alasdair MacIntyre, *After Virtue,* University of Notre Dame Press 1984.

Values have thus taken the place of good and evil. They are purely subjective and relative. Their possible number is unlimited. They are preferences to pursue rather than norms or standards of behaviour to observe, but they can be imposed by force. All it needs is the will and the power to do so.

Allan Bloom wrote his book before the collapse of communism about the intellectual state of the American Union. Despite the "Spirit of Solidarity"[7] that brought down communism, the new language of value relativism spread like wildfire across America and Europe (East and West) after 1989. Its use, indeed, leads in two opposite directions. On the one hand, we often take the line of least resistance when accepting different Chinese, Asian or Islamic values in discussions on human rights. On the other hand, *laïcistes* and secularists tend to adopt strong poses and fanatic resolutions against Christian moral principles. Some examples in the European Union are well-known: the fanatic pursuit of the right to abortion for women in developing countries under the heading of "Reproductive Health Care and Rights"; resolutions in the European Parliament condemning homophobia or rejecting the appointment of Buttiglione as European Commissioner; the elimination of any reference to the Christian heritage in the Preamble and the modernisation of the language in Part II (Charter of Fundamental Human Rights) of the Constitution for Europe [8]- in contrast with appeasement towards the perpetrators of violence against harmless Danish caricatures on Mohammed.

---

[7] Jozef Tischner, *The Spirit of Solidarity*, Harper & Row 1984. Translated from the Polish, it demonstrates the profound faith that fuelled the movement of civil resistance against communist rule.

[8] See Document EUD.4.

Ideas do have consequences, indeed. In his last book, *Memory and Identity,* [9] Pope John-Paul II wrote that the ideologies of evil in the twentieth century were deeply rooted in the history of European philosophical thought. The same applies to our new language of value relativism. Nietzsche's impact has been so great, because of his central place in the context of that history from Descartes, through the Enlightenment, the nineteenth century's philosophies of progress-as-power, to existentialism and neo-Marxism.

Any effort on our part to contribute to a debate on common values must take this context into account. Christian Europeans are caught between aggressive secularists and fanatic Islamists - Europe's two culture wars as George Weigel called it[10] - while most of us in between are indifferent, are afraid to stand up or take the line of least resistance. That is very dangerous, writes Weigel in his concluding paragraph: "Nihilism rooted in scepticism, issuing in the bad faith of moral relativism and Western self-loathing, comforting itself with a vacuous humanitarianism: not only is this not marvellous, it has contributed to killing Europe demographically, and to paralyzing Europe in the face of an aggressive ideology aimed at the eradication of Western humanism in the name of a lethally distorted understanding of God's will."

Ideas have consequences, indeed. Still, honesty forces us to admit that the ideas of philosophers, too often, have been sources of confusion rather than living sources for action. Where such ideas were the sources for political ideologies of evil, the consequences have been disastrous, as we all know from the history of the twentieth century.

---

9 Published by the Vatican Press in April 2005.

10 George Weigel, 'Europe's Two Culture Wars' *Commentary May 2006.* p. 29-36.

Monnet's ideas about European integration did not come from a study of the philosophers. They came from the spectacle of the ruins left by the Second World War. The same can be said of Robert Schuman's ideas as expressed in his Declaration of 9 May 1950. His proposal to make German-French reconciliation the cornerstone for future peace had the same origin. From experience and observation he knew that another Treaty of Versailles[11] would not bring peace. He equally knew that such reconciliation would not result from solemn declarations. It required true and effective solidarity to be carefully developed under the authority of common institutions and common rules (and within the Western alliance).

The political context at the time was important. Europe was emerging from the dreadful experience of the war and faced at the same time a new totalitarian threat from Stalin's Soviet Union. Most governments had returned from exile with little more in mind than national recovery. The depth of the moral and material crisis was such, that only a fundamental change of policies could save Western Europe. George Marshall with Dean Acheson in Washington, Jean Monnet and Robert Schuman in cooperation with Konrad Adenauer and Alcide de Gasperi, had the courage to launch such changes. The Marshall plan and the Organization for European Economic Cooperation (OEEC), the North Atlantic Alliance and the European Coal and Steel Community (ECSC) indeed changed the policies of the states concerned.

---

[11] The Peace Treaty of 1919, stating Germany's responsibility for the outbreak of the First World War and imposing heavy reparation payments. Compare my *Western Cooperation: Origins and History*, Wolf Legal Publishers, Second Revised Edition Wolf Legal Publishers 2009, Part I, Chapter 1.

I cannot escape the conclusion that the European values debate that flared up around the abortive effort to write a constitution for Europe, is dominated by the secularist apprentices of Nietzsche. They like to talk about the European Union as a community of values, but not of Christian values. They went as far as disowning their own past by refusing any reference to our Christian heritage in the Preamble to the Constitution. As Nietzsche wanted it, everyone with a strong enough will is entitled to his own common values.

CLARITY AND CONTRADICTION

As the very concept of 'common values' is a dubious one from the outset, it is bound to present us with a number of pitfalls. The first one is: a beautiful list of values - we want our neighbour to live by. Another one is an unlimited list of subjective preferences - personal, collective or national ones. Still another one is a claim to superiority - Western European against Eastern European values or European against American values. Last but not least is the concept of values as an instrument to delegitimize the Christian heritage of Europe. There is a need for clarity and contradiction through discernment and distinction.

Let Principles Be Principles!

Clarity comes first. When we deal with a legal text like a basic EU Treaty,[12] we need principles to be observed, either as general principles of law or as principles to be transposed into binding legal rules.

There were no good reasons to replace "principles" by "values" in the Constitution for Europe and in the TEU of

---

12 At present: the Lisbon Reform Treaties entered into force on 1 December 2009.

Lisbon. In fact it meant a downgrading from observable and eventually enforceable principles to subjective and unenforceable preferences. The new formulation is confusing and open-ended. According to article 2, the Treaty is no longer founded on principles to be observed but on the values to respect. The list is enriched by the value of respect for human dignity, whatever that may mean. The "values of respect for" are declared to be common in societies "in which pluralism, non-discrimination, tolerance, justice, solidarity and equality between women and men prevail." This mish-mash is highly confusing and dangerous. Human dignity is an inspiring Christian and philosophical concept. Pluralism and non-discrimination have become code-words for value relativism. Tolerance is a principle by which public authority has the obligation to respect freedom of religion. Justice and solidarity are primarily virtues to be practiced and secondarily principles to be transposed into legal rules. Equality between women and men is already a prescription of European law. The mish-mash appears to be highly stimulating for proclaiming and promoting a great variety of personal preferences. It opens the way for declaring abortion a fundamental human right, for accepting the equality of same-sex marriage as required by the value of non-discrimination, or for allowing *sharia* for the sake of tolerance and equality.

At the same time, we should be conscious of the frailty of those very principles, now turned into values. Liberty, democracy, respect for human rights and the rule of law are no age-old European values but bitterly fought principles in the short period after the Second World War for the original member states. They are still to be realised in the member States which joined in the twenty-first century. Assuring respect for these principles and for their transposition into binding legal rules is bound to be a perennial effort.

Exposing the hidden persuaders

In the affluent societies of the European Union, there is a strong tendency to reduce the values we cherish to mere economic values: what serves shareholders value, competition and the free market, what promotes the culture of consumption and what contributes to economic growth. In the era of globalisation and in an EU giving priority to economic and monetary matters, moral considerations are being marginalised in decision-making. Governments and their (bloated) bureaucracies are turned into managers - like universities, hospitals, utilities, public transport etc. - acting in conformity with market principles. Public service for the purpose of the common good is being replaced by privatisation schemes for the sake of efficiency and better profit. Values are the façade, competition is the rule behind.

As Jonathan Sachs writes: "It is difficult to talk about the common good when we loose the ability to speak about duty, obligation and restraint, and find ourselves only with desires clamouring for satisfaction."

Later in the same book, when discussing why competition came to occupy centre stage in modern thought, he challenged the theory behind it. It is a fallacy to think that "private vice would become public virtue, when society was so organized as to turn passions into interests".[13] Contracts are not the only and certainly not the most fundamental forms of association. Markets, according to him, depend on virtues learned in more

---

[13] Jonathan Sack, *The Dignity of Difference, How to avoid the clash of civilizations,* Continuum 2002, pp. 23,144. See also Part II, Chapter 3 below.

fundamental associations like marriage and family, he calls Covenantal[14] relationships sustained by trust.

The hidden persuader here, to be exposed in a debate on common values, is what I would like to call *the dictatorship of economic values.* Under this dictatorship we are supposed to be concerned only about economics and such economic values as competition, efficiency, profit and growth.

As we are well aware, behind the façade of the UN Millennium goals is the reality of a growing gap between rich and poor - inside our own countries and between countries - and growing violent conflict e.g. in Africa and the Middle-East. The reasons are obvious. Nowhere occupies the search for the common good a more reduced place than in international relations. In our world of sovereign states, there is little or no room for the pursuance of the universal common good. Globalisation can run rampant as there is nothing - except the parochial interests of the major powers - to restrain the dictatorship of economic values. Neither the United States nor the European Union sees it to be in their interest to promote such restraint.

That dictatorship must also be exposed inside the European Union. Without the vision and the sense of responsibility of the founding fathers, the principal interest appears to be to keep the process of economic and monetary integration going. Insufficient transparency enables the national and European bureaucracies to promote certain liberal or secularist agenda's in e.g. human rights and social policy with the argument that the functioning of the common market so requires. There is hardly any room for evaluating measures on other than economic values.

---

14 Covenantal after the biblical Covenant between Yahweh and the Jewish people.

Finally, it is important to expose and reverse the trend to introduce economic values like competition into the more fundamental covenantal associations. The protection of marriage and the family is not just a traditional reflex but an urgent responsibility. Without the virtues learned in these associations, we can not build justice and peace.

THE PAST IS NOT ANOTHER COUNTRY

On 8 November 1989 West-German Chancellor Helmuth Kohl - on his first official visit to post-communist Poland - went to Częstochowa, Poland's famous place of pilgrimage to the Black Madonna. As he knelt down in front of the shrine, the priest invited him to pray for an intention particularly dear to him, adding that Mary always answers such prayers. Kohl prayed for German re-unification… and the same night he had to rush back home where the hated Berlin Wall had collapsed.

I remember most vividly when it happened and where I was the ninth of November in 1989.

Mr. Kohl and almost all politicians in Europe - East and West - were taken by surprise. Long after the communist dream had turned into a nightmare, did Europe wake up to the evil of totalitarian repression. For the collapse of communist rule, nobody really was prepared.

Why did it take so long to achieve the breakdown of communism? Lenin took power in 1917 and Gorbachev only resigned in 1990 - neither Yeltsin nor Putin brought Russia much closer to democratic rule. By all accounts, communism in its Leninist variety was evil and absurd if not outright criminal[15] How could such a system be expanded from Petrograd to the

---

[15] Cf. Stéphane Courtois, *Le Livre Noir du Communisme*, Paris 1997.

Elba, to China and survive for so long? It is a pressing question.

In fact, we deal with two histories - the internal one of man in his dignity and the external one of the political system. As a consequence, my question is twofold:

- Which were the "secrets" of totalitarian communism by which it could intrude into the hearts and minds of men and women, their "inner sanctuary", so that their conscience could be paralysed or even locked up?

- What was wrong with the dignity of man that he prostrated himself for the false utopia and the lies of the totalitarian regimes and failed to have sufficient an impact on the course of political history in the twentieth century?

We should ask these questions, because *Solidarnosc* and *Charta 77* taught us that men and women who act in the name of human dignity can change history. We also must ask these questions today, because the very Christian spirit from which civil resistance acted and through which it prevailed, seems to be under attack and vanishing again today.

Lenin's Soviet Republic was a descendant from the First World War and its moral and intellectual confusion - like Mussolini's fascism and Hitler's Nazism. The latter two perished in the Second World War. Soviet totalitarianism allied itself in 1941 with the West and survived. Terror was its method from the outset. But, as Aleksander Solzhenitsyn wrote in *One Word of Truth* (his Nobel Peace Prize address):

> "Violence does not exist alone and can not survive in isolation. It is inevitably bound up with the lie. Between them there is the most intimate, most natural, fundamental link: violence can only be concealed by

> the lie, and the lie can be maintained only by violence. Anyone who has once proclaimed that violence is his method is inevitably forced to choose the lie as his guiding principle."

One can understand how people, subject to this system of terror, tried to survive in various ways. Much more troublesome, to me, is the extent to which the West accommodated, acquiesced, looked the other way, condoned terror and legitimised one-party rule as "really existing socialism." The Grand Alliance between Roosevelt, Churchill and Stalin in 1941 may have been a necessity, but was no less shocking an alliance than the Molotov - von Ribbentrop Pact of 1939.[16] Even more shocking was the acceptance of ethnic cleansing in East and Central Europe after the war as "orderly transfer of populations." The American policy of containment (1947) was based indeed on a proper assessment of the Soviet threat and achieved its primary purpose, but at the price of a nuclear arms race. This latter race resulted in a nuclear balance of terror and a dubious policy of *détente*, through which communist rule attained moral equivalence with democratic government in the minds of many politicians and intellectuals in the free West. It could thus happen that many intellectuals fell under the spell of a new (neo)Marxist dream at the very time - Prague 1968 - East Europeans began to wake up from the nightmare of Marxism-Leninism and to resist.

As Vaclav Havel said: "We had all become used to the totalitarian system. We accepted the system as unchangeable, thus helping to perpetuate it." Indeed, one way or the other, we bear responsibility for the longevity of the communist system. Teaching its history is a moral obligation. Dealing with

---

16 Cf. my: *Western Cooperation, Origins and History,* Wolf Legal Publishers 2009, Second Revised Edition, Part I., Chapter 4.

communism as a relic of the past to be forgotten, is a neglect of duty. One may have understanding for those (many) politicians and intellectuals, who try to silence their bad conscience of complicity by forgetting the past, but we should never accept it, if only to prevent history from repeating itself.

"Secrets" of totalitarian communism

> "In our system - Vaclav Havel wrote - the violence is spiritual rather than physical. Designed to achieve the gradual destruction of the human spirit, of basic human dignity... people live their lives in a state of permanent humiliation."
> (...)
> "Totalitarianism is a system which absorbs the whole society. It enters every vein and artery of the social organism, usurping and controlling all aspects of human life."[17]

Organised violence was the principal instrument for the pulverisation of civil society and the atomisation and isolation of the individual. The spheres of autonomy in which man finds his identity and his dignity - family, friends and church - were the primary targets of persecution and destruction. Autonomous associations were to be replaced by undifferentiated mass organisations as instruments to manipulate the masses and destroy the fabric of interpersonal relations. The Churches were singled out as special targets, because total control over people could be achieved only, if man would be deprived of faith as the ultimate source of his spiritual freedom and resistance against political power.

---

17 *The Power of the Powerless*, In: *Vaclav Havel, or Living in Thruth*, Edited by Jan Vladislav, Faber 1986; Second quote from: East European Reporter, Vol 2., Nr. 2

Totalitarian communism perverted human relations as betrayal of one's parents, children, friends or neighbours was taught a citizen's duty. Fear and distrust took the place of friendship and trust. The virtues of compassion and care were treated as crimes against the state; they disappeared from the vocabulary and ceased to be practised. Thinking came to be treated as a mental aberration; whoever questioned the "official truth" was sent to a lunatic asylum for psychiatric treatment. "Newspeak" (so well described in Orwell's *1984)* was primarily meant to eliminate other forms of thought and to deprive people of their memory.

Behind the façade of a Constitution a state structure and official laws, the communist system was fundamentally a system of lawlessness. Political power did not reside in the institutions of the state but in the conspiratorial body called the Party, controlling everything and every institution from within. As one of my Czechoslovak friends told me years ago, the difference between legality and socialist legality is the same as the difference between a chair and the electric chair.

Life under totalitarian communism thus was permeated with hypocrisy and lies. One party rule was called a people's democracy, humiliation was called liberation and military intervention, fraternal assistance. The regime falsified the past, the present and the future, thus depriving man of any certainty, identity or memory.... thus trying to intrude his "inner sanctuary" and destroy his human dignity.[18]

Worse and more lasting than centrally planned economic mismanagement, is the morally debased environment left

---

18 Cf. my: *Beyond Containment and Division, Western Cooperation from a Post-Totalitarian Perspective,* Chapter 2, Martinus Nyhoff Publishers 1992.

behind by communist rule and its acceptance as a legitimate form of government. Against the totalitarian assault on human dignity, far too many perished in the *Gulag* or suffered humiliation. Far too many also passively accepted, complied or were accomplices in helping to perpetuate the system.

Remember Europe's recent past … properly

The enlargement of the European Union this century should be seen as a major event in the spiritual realm rather than just an inevitability in the economic realm. As Norman Davies rightly emphasised in his latest book[19] there is a long history of misunderstanding, neglect, sense of superiority and ignorance of Western Europe towards East and Central Europe. As a result of the Cold War, "the East" was something like a black hole to most in the West. Worse than the hostile image of Eastern Europe was the well-established convention of ignoring Eastern Europe completely writes Norman Davies. Few of us in the Western part of Europe understood the profound significance of the spirit of 1989; because few of us really understand how different the Eastern experience with totalitarianism has been from our Western experience. The majority of the new member states were squeezed between the two ideologies of evil for most of their national life in the twentieth century. In all these countries, people have great difficulty to deal with the moral heritage of these ideologies and the superficial and materialist view on economic progress brought in from the West. In a "debased moral environment" (Vaclav Havel) it is difficult to resist the Western dictatorship of economic values. The inability to come to grips with the communist past and the new dictatorship is proving to be a poisonous mixture. Judging by political developments in the new member states and the

---

19 Norman Davies, *Europe East & West*, Jonathan Cape 2006.

arrogant comments on them in the West, there still is a long way to go.

The original EU member states have their own past to come to grip with; from the Nazi-Soviet partnership and the Grand Alliance (1939, 1941) [20] to their détente policies of the 1980's; and from their fellow-travellers in the 1930s to their neo-Marxists and appeasers of the détente era. The longevity of totalitarianism in the East had a lot to do with Western acquiescence, indifference and ignorance. The new member states need support and understanding in the long and difficult process of transitional justice and reconciliation.

If the European Union continues to give priority to the process of economic integration, it is heading nowhere according to Norman Davies. It is a nice irony, he writes, that the peoples of the new member states may well have a more rounded vision of the Europe to which they wished to return than the often arrogant West Europeans who reluctantly let them in.[21]

Europe's re-unification today like the initiation of its post-war unification needs the living sources tapped by the founding fathers in the 1950's in the West and in the 1980s in East and Central Europe.

Christian heritage

As Christians we live under the Covenant, as we read in Genesis chapter 9:

> "And this', God said,' is the sign of the covenant

---

20 Compare my: *Western Cooperation: Origins and History,* Second Revised Edition, Wolf Legal Publishers 2009, Part I, Chapter 4.

21 *Op. cit.* p.42

which I now make between myself and you
and every living creature with you for all ages to come
I now set my bow in the clouds and it will be the sign
Of the covenant between me and the earth."

It is an eternal Covenant, extended to all nations and deepened in the salvation through Christ. Ever since, we are part of human history and part of the history of salvation. We live under the contract and the Covenant. When we dare speak about a Christian Europe, we speak of the Grace we received and not the results we achieved. The good news of the Bible, Jesus Christ and not European Christianity made the difference. The Covenant teaches us love, loyalty, responsibility, obedience, equity, compassion, reconciliation; the building blocks of what St. Ambrosias called a civilisation of love. The Covenant is our living source of inspiration, enlightening our search for justice and constantly reminding us of our weaknesses. It is where Europe's founding fathers found their source of inspiration for doing what they did to change the history of Europe. They organised true and effective solidarity under the authority of common institutions and common rules - the supranational European Communities. Much the same way, as we saw above, did the leaders of civil resistance in Central Europe truly and effectively respond to day-to-day repression.

When I follow the debates on common European values today, I cannot help remembering the following fable:

Once upon a time, a spider was sitting on the branch of a lovely tree rising high unto a starlit sky. A perfect place, he thought to weave his web. On his own thread, firmly fixed to the branch, he gently descended downwards and , going around, wove a most intricate cobweb in beautiful octagonal figures. At sunrise, when he saw the threads reflected in the sunlight, he looked at his web and was very proud of his work.

With himself in the centre of the web, he thought it would be even more beautiful, when cutting his first thread from the branch of the tree. And so he did. The web collapsed and he found himself amidst a confusing heap of threads far down below on the ground. The more he tried to move around, the more he became entangled in the threads he had himself produced with so much pride.

This is where disowning Europe's Christian heritage leads us, a confused and disorderly debate on values without any apparent structure or hierarchy. To return to the path laid out by the Schuman Declaration of 1950, four things appear to be necessary.

First, we must challenge the concept of value relativism, the idea that everyone is entitled to his or her subjective values. We must not fall into the trap that the principles we profess are accepted as our preferences in the private sphere now that "religion has made a comeback". When we join the search for common European values, we must make clear from the outset that we are interested in principles. Values as preferences you can have; principles must be observed. Our search for these principles finds its living sources in the Covenant.

Second, in debates on values we must introduce clear distinctions between virtues, principles, rights and obligations. Virtues must be taught in the family and at school; they must be practised in daily life. They form our inner sanctuary, enabling us to distinguish between the good to do and the evil to avoid. Principles are to be found and formulated. They can be found in Holy Scripture and in natural law. We must propose a selection of principles of fundamental importance to the European project. Rights and obligations are the "translation" of principles into positive law. Virtues can be distinguished from principles but are to be seen as inseparable. There can be no true justice or solidarity without them being practiced as a virtue. Rights and obligations must be properly balanced in positive law. Protection of rights requires the obligation to respect them.

Third, once we accept to focus on principles rather than talk about values and have been in a position to select principles relevant to the European project, we must consider the hierarchy between them. Are they of equal standing? Which one is to prevail in case of conflict?

Fourth, principles must be observed and human nature is such that society must dispose of the means to enforce them, if necessary. Democracy and the rule of law enshrined in a Constitution are the necessary condition for their observance. Principles that cannot be enforced are unsuitable as living sources for the European project.

Europe's living sources, indeed, are in Christ's grace given to us Europeans. It would be a shame to lock the EU up in a secularist, neo-liberalist ghetto. As Romano Guardini wrote shortly after the Second World War: Europe will be Christian or it will not be.[22]

---

22 In his text on *Der Heilbringer in Mythos, Offenbarung und Politik,* First published in 1946, republished in 1979 as Topos Taschenbuch.

CHAPTER 4

EUROPE:
STATE, NATIONAL SOVEREIGNTY AND NATIONALISM

'Europe' is something political, economic and technical; above all it is an attitude of mind, and formidable obstacles confront the creation of that attitude. The primitive mentality - and its influence is still felt everywhere - regarded anything strange as wrong, dangerous, hostile in fact, and this psychological formula finds a place also in political theory. The State is presented as a structure which may have enemies - or friends; but especially enemies. These formulas remind us how strong is the resistance to such processes as the creation of a truly European attitude of mind and of how much must happen before it comes about.

To mention only one task that shows the magnitude of what there remains to be done: if Europe is to become a reality, it is first essential that every European nation shall re-think its history and see its past in the light of this great construction of tomorrow. How much self-conquest and self-analysis does that not call for! History is there to warn us how little it can be taken for granted and how great is the danger of failure.[1]

Romano Guardini spoke these words in 1962. What he then said, is still relevant today. The European Union of the Treaties of Lisbon is something political and technical, it is very much and primarily something economic. It offers a large zone of peace, open borders and cheap travel. 'Europe', nevertheless, has hardly become an attitude of mind or a shared vision on the

---

1 Full text in document EH. 1.

future. Most of us take 'Europe' for granted in material terms, resent it when it comes to politics and ignore it as an attitude of mind. 'Europe' has become something economic, expensive or intrusive and no more. Little or no progress has been made in creating a truly European attitude of mind. With the exception of Germany, few European nations are re-thinking their history in the light of the construction of the enlarged European Union. European Unification is and always was meant to be a political process, a project to change and re-organize relations between European States, as we shall see in the second Part of this book. In the view of the fathers of Europe after the Second World War, it meant a new concept of power to be exercised over man, the transfer of national powers to new, supranational institutions and the victory of a new attitude of mind over the ideologies of nationalism, socialism, Nazism and fascism. It is important to be aware of the radical novelty of the new concept - not only against the ideologies of the twentieth and nineteenth centuries, but against the whole tradition of politics in Europe since modernity.

FORCE, VIOLENCE AND STATE SOVEREIGNTY

> *"La raison et lumière naturelle nous conduit à cela, de croire que la force et violence a donné source et origine aux Républiques"* wrote Jean Bodin in 1576.[2]

Bodin wrote his treatise in the middle of the religious wars, ravaging Europe from the beginning of the Reformation in 1525 to the Peace of Westphalia in 1648. The wars were fought all over Europe from England through France (1559-1598), the Netherlands (1566-1648), to the Holy Roman Empire (1618-1648).

---

2 Jean Bodin, *Les Six Livres de la République,* Edition et presentation de Gérard Mairet, Livre de Poche, Librairie Générale Française 1993, Livre Premier, Chapitre VI, p. 92.

They were complex and interrelated, cruel and destructive. They involved the Papacy, the Emperor, the Kings of Spain, England, France and Sweden, the feudal lords, princes and bishops and the church communities. They caused immense suffering especially throughout the territories of the Empire.

The lasting importance of his treatise resides in his radical departure from the conceptions of power at the time. He extensively quotes from Mosaic Law and the authors from classic Greece and Rome, but makes no reference to the St. Paul, Church Fathers like St. Augustine or other authors in the Christian tradition. Bodin is best known and most quoted for the modern concept of state sovereignty he developed in his books. Sovereignty, he defines in the First Book, Chapter VIII is "the absolute and perpetual power of a republic." It is to be vested in the "Prince", the sovereign exclusively as such power cannot be shared with others or divided between institutions. As the sovereign he can make and break the law; it depends purely on his will. He himself is not subject to the law - contrary to the precepts of canon law as it had developed, but in conformity with ancient Roman law.

Background to his concept of sovereignty is the attempt to offer a theory for restoring public order in France damaged by the religious wars; to legitimate the emancipation of the French King from Pope and Emperor and to support the subjection of the feudal lords to his rule. His Republic is essentially a secular state centralizing and exercising "temporal power" only. In doing so the sovereign is not subject to any "spiritual power" or divine law. The Christian concept of revelation is completely absent in his theory. In the exercise of his sovereign powers, the Prince is not restrained by any rule of divine or natural law, although he is himself "the image of God on earth."[3] *"Puisqu'il*

---

3 As he writes in Chapter X of his first book.

n'y a rien plus grand en terre, après Dieu, que les Princes souverains, et qu'ils sont établis de lui comme ses lieutenants, pour commander aux autres "homes", il est besoin de prendre garde à leur qualité, afin de respecter et révérer leur majesté en toute obeisance, sentir et parler d'eux en tout honneur, car qui méprise son Prince souverain, il méprise Dieu, duquel il est l'image en terre." As the image of God on earth, the Prince, obviously, is expected to practice virtue, to obey God and to pursue the common good, but there is nobody to call him to task. As Alain Benoist writes in the paragraph titled: *Divine Absolutism Becomes Royal Absolutism:*

"It is not difficult to detect the religious foundations of Bodin's doctrine. Bodin's understanding of political power is merely a profane transposition of the absolute way God and the Pope exercise power over Christians, even though he denounces the medieval concept of power as merely a delegation of God's authority. For Bodin, the prince no longer is satisfied to hold power by "divine right." By granting himself the power to decree and annul laws, he acts like God. He forms a distinct entity, ruling the social body in the same way that God governs the cosmos. Thus, the sovereign's absolute rectitude is nothing more than the transposition into the political sphere of the Cartesian God, who can do everything except desire evil. Surreptitiously, sovereignty became infallible. In other words, Bodin makes sovereignty profane by taking it away from God, and then makes it again sacred in a profane form: he takes leave of God's monopolistic and absolute sovereignty and ends up with the monopolistic and absolute sovereignty of the state. All of modernity resides in this ambiguity: on the one hand, political power is secularized; on the other, the sovereign, now identified with the state, becomes a person granted quasi-divine political power."[4]

---

4 Alain Benoist, *What is Sovereignty?*, Reprinted in document EH. 16 as one of two short leading texts with this Chapter, p. 102.

For the purpose of this chapter, it must be emphasized that Bodin's concept of sovereignty produced royal absolutism in France. The French Revolution abolished the *Ancien Régime*, but preserved the concept of sovereignty as, again, Benoist observes:

"The French Revolution preserved the very content of the concept of sovereignty embodied in the absolute monarchy, and took credit for giving it back to the nation. Hence the difficulty for the republican tradition to reconcile the first two articles of the Declaration of Rights, which affirmed the pre-eminence of universal individual rights, with the third article, which decreed that the nation is the supreme authority: "The principle of sovereignty resides essentially in the nation; no body, no individual can exercise authority not emanating from it." The idea of absolute sovereignty not only remained constant from the *ancien régime* to the Revolution, but the revolutionary idea of the pre-eminence of national sovereignty was also stressed from the beginning of the movement, i.e., prior to 1792 or 1793, and, thus, before the Jacobinist party came to power."[5]

In fact, the French Revolution turned the concept of sovereignty into the ideology of the absolute sovereignty of the nation state of the nineteenth century. As Jacques Maritain writes:

"At the time of the French Revolution that very concept of the State considered as a whole unto itself was preserved, but it shifted from the King to the Nation, mistakenly identified with the body politic; hence Nation, Body Politic and State were identified. And the very concept of sovereignty - as a *natural* or *innate* and *inalienable* right to

---

5 *Loc.cit,* p. 105. See also, Tocqueville, *L, Ancien régime et la Révolution,* Editions Gallimard 1967. The text of the Declaration of Rights (*La Déclaration des droits*) can be found in Document EH. 8.

supreme *transcendent* power - was preserved, but shifted from the King to the Nation. At the same time, by virtue of a voluntarist theory of law and political society, which had its acme in eighteenth century philosophy, the State was made into a person (a so-called moral person) and a subject of right, in such a way that the attribute of absolute sovereignty, ascribed to the Nation, was inevitably, as a matter of fact, to be claimed and exercised by the State."[6]

Later in the same chapter, Maritain writes:

"That concept of the State, enforced in human history, has forced democracies into intolerable self-contradictions, in their domestic life and above all in international life. For this concept is no part of the authentic tenets of democracy, it does not belong to the real democratic inspiration and philosophy, it belongs to a spurious ideological heritage which has preyed upon democracy like a parasite. During the reign of individualist or "liberal" democracy the State, made into an absolute, displayed a tendency to substitute itself for the people, and so to leave the people estranged from political life to a certain extent; it also was able to launch the wars between nations which disturbed the XIXth Century. Nevertheless, after the Napoleonic era the worst implications of this process of State absolutization were restrained by the democratic philosophy and political practices which then prevailed. It is with the advent of the totalitarian regimes and philosophies that those worst implications were released. The State made into an absolute revealed its true face. Our epoch has had the privilege of contemplating the State totalitarianism

---

6 Jacques Maritain, *Man and the State,* University of Chicago Press 1951, Quotation is from Chapter 1 an excerpt of which can be found as Document EH. 17.

of Race with German Nazism, of Nation with Italian Fascism, of Economic Community with Russian Communism."[7]

It is better not to nurture any illusions. The fact that state totalitarianism has been overcome, does not mean that the ideology has disappeared with it. As Denis de Rougemont said in the *Rencontres Internationales*[8], we are all infected by the ideologies we lived with and we overcame. The idea of the nation state as the source of our values and the focus of our loyalties, is still alive in the European Union of the twenty-first century. As such it is closely allied with the Nineteenth Century ideology of nationalism, another consequence of the ideology of the French Revolution and the German response to it.

ON NATIONALISM AND EUROPEAN UNIFICATION

"The ideal of a single, scientifically organized world system governed by reason was the heart of the program of the Enlightenment", wrote Isaiah Berlin in his essay on Nationalism. "Among the assumptions of rational thinkers of the liberal type in the nineteenth and for some decades in the twentieth century were these: that liberal democracy was the most satisfactory or at least, the least unsatisfactory form of human organization; that the nation-state was, or at least had historically come to be, the normal unit of independent, self-governing human society; and finally, that once the multinational empires had been dissolved in their constituent parts, the yearning for union of men with common language, habits, memories, outlooks, would at last be satisfied, and a society of liberated, self determined nation states would come into existence, and, inspired by a patriotism not tainted by aggressive nationalism

7 *Loc.cit.* Document EH. 17

8 *'L'Esprit Européen 1947, Op. cit.*

would live at peace and in harmony with each other, no longer impeded by the irrational survivals of a servile past".[9]

It were these assumptions President Wilson brought with him to Versailles in 1919 and by which he unfolded his plans to make the European world safe for democracy. Through the exercise of the right of national self-determination, the "constituent parts" of the multinational empires would fall into place as "liberated, self-determining nation-states." International guarantees for the inviolability of the new borders between them, would assure that these nation-states "would live in peace and harmony with each other." The borders drawn at the 1919 Peace Conferences, could eventually be changed peacefully by popular referendum.

At this point attention must be drawn to a crucial divergence in cultural development and political thought between the United States on the one side and Europe, Germany in particular on the other. The Constitution of the United States was itself a product of Enlightenment and a broad Lockean consensus on the best form of government. The Constitution and the development of the American form of government confirmed according to American political thought the assumptions of rational thinkers of the liberal type. In American political thinking, the expansion of democracy continues to be looked at in terms of the universal validity of liberal democracy as the most satisfactory form of government.

Nationalism, as it emerged in Germany and Europe during the nineteenth century, stressed the national differences in cultural development and political organisation. Unlike American political thought, European nationalist thinking challenged

---

[9] Isaiah Berlin, *Nationalism: Past Neglect and Present Power,* In: *Against the Current,* London 1979, pp. 353, 351.

rather than supported the assumptions of rational thinkers of the liberal type. Until this very day, the differences manifest themselves in the cultural diplomacy of the United States and the principal European states. American "public diplomacy" is geared towards the advancement of liberal democracy. The cultural diplomacy of France, Britain and Germany is geared towards the promotion of the national language, *la mission civilisatrice*, the British way of life or *Deutschtum*, and the export of Voltaire, Shakespeare or Goethe. The cultural diplomacy of the smaller European states is geared towards the protection of their national, cultural identity.[10]

Historical Background

In Western Europe, the nation-state has, indeed, come to be the normal unit of independent, self-governing human society. Such at least is the case for France, England and the Netherlands and maybe for Denmark, Sweden, Portugal and Spain. In these countries, nation-building followed the emergence of independent monarchies and the formation of defined territorial units. Germany and Italy were late-comers in the process and built their nations through war. By the end of the nineteenth century the nation-state had come to be the normal unit; although many Germans, in particular, lived outside the borders of Bismarck's North German Reich - spread mainly over a large area to the East and into Russia (Volga Germans) and the Balkans.

In Central Europe, Poles - for historic reasons - kept a strong sense of identity, despite Poland's partition between three empires. Hungarians had a strong sense of identity through their distinct language and as one of the ruling "nations" in

---

10 See further my: *Cultural Diplomacy: waging war by other means?*, Wolf Legal Publishers 2009, Chapters 3, 4, 5.

the Habsburg Empire. The Greeks, who gained independence from Ottoman rule in the early nineteenth century, formed a distinct nation though with uncertain borders. Otherwise, the areas belonging to the Russian, Habsburg and Ottoman Empires, were inhabited by a rich variety of ethnic groups and warring tribes living pell-mell without distinct boundaries between them. Serbs, Bulgarians and Romanians formed groups large enough to develop a memory of their history and a sense of identity. They could claim a heartland, where they formed a majority of the population, but mostly - as in the case of the many smaller ethnic groups - they could not be distinguished by the territories on which they lived. They were distinguishable by the place they occupied in the hierarchical structure of the empires, their religion or their language. The mosaic of peoples reflected the continuously changing borders between empires and the old fault-lines between Orthodox Christians, Latin Christians and Muslims. The Serbs fought for or against their Habsburg and Ottoman masters; they were predominantly orthodox with a strong affinity to the orthodox and Slavic Russians. The catholic Slovenes were benignly ruled from Vienna. Slovaks and Croats were subject to Budapest's policies of "magyarisation"; Hungarians lived in areas now forming part of Slovakia, Croatia, Voivodina and Romania. Romanians, Bulgarians and Serbs are predominantly orthodox; Slovaks and Croatians are catholic; Hungarians are evangelical and catholic. Albanians - living in Albania and Kosovo, the heartland of historic Serbia - are predominantly Muslim. Before the war erupted in 1992 in Bosnia-Herzegovina, its population consisted of a plurality of Muslims, a sizable minority of Serbs and a smaller minority of Croats.

When the empires disintegrated - the Ottoman Empire over a long period ending in the First World War, the Habsburg Empire in 1918, and the Russian/Soviet Empire in 1991 - these "multinational" empires could not just be dissolved in their constituent parts. No such parts with definable territories were in existence or could be called into existence, without creating serious minority problems.[11]

The Time Zones of Europe

At this point, it may be useful to introduce the distinction, Ernest Gellner made between the four "Time Zones of Europe".[12] The manner in which nationalism manifested itself in Europe, he wrote, varies from region to region, and one might distinguish four time zones.

1. The first Western most time zone is that of the Atlantic coast of Europe. From the late Middle Ages it was occupied by strong dynastic states, which roughly correlated with cultural areas. When nationalism came, and political units had to adjust themselves to cultural boundaries, no very great changes were required. Some turbulence there was and still is to this day as in Northern Ireland, the Basque region or Corsica, but the map of this part of Europe does not look very different from what it was in the past. "Induced forgetfulness rather than invented memory was the national bond, as Ernest Renan insisted".

2. The next time zone to the East was an area of quite exceptional political fragmentation. The effective political units were much smaller than the geographical extension of the two locally dominant, German and Italian, high cultures. The existing high cultures had to be endowed with a political roof, and this task was accomplished by military and diplomatic means in the later part of the nineteenth century: the unification of Italy and Bismarck's Germany.

---

11 See further my: *The Illusions of Détente,* Wolf Legal Publishers 2009, Chapter 8.

12 Ernest Gellner, *Conditions of Liberty. Civil Society and its Rivals.* Penguin Books 1994, Chapters 15-17.

3. The third time zone to the East presented the greatest problems from the viewpoint of the implementation of the nationalist principle of one culture, one state. The area presented an appallingly complex patchwork of diverse cultures without any coherence in political, cultural and religious boundaries. The effort to implement the nationalist political principle went through five stages. In the first stage, the old dynastic-religious system is still in place, but nationalism entered the scene under bureaucratic centralisation and standardization imposed by the enlightened despots. In the second stage, nationalist irredentism was successful in culture but not in politics, with the exception of the creation of a number of more or less national buffer states in the Balkans. In the third stage from 1918-1939, nationalism was triumphant and self-defeating. The system of supposedly national states, set up in the name of national self-determination, collapsed like a house of cards with the outbreak of the Second World War. War-time and post-war "ethnic cleansing" on a massive scale left the region a seething mass of oppressed ethnic resentments - the fourth stage. In the present fifth stage, ethnic resentment has erupted into civil war in former Yugoslavia but appears not to spread further. The wish to join "Europe" and the West restrains desires to seek implementation of the nationalist principle or a change of existing boundaries imposed after the Second World War.

4. The fourth time zone corresponds more or less to the territories of the erstwhile Czarist empire. In this area, the search for the implementation of the nationalist principle was frozen by seventy or forty years of Bolshevik ideocracy. The Soviet Union broke up from the center down and not from any nationalist irredentism. Implementation of the nationalist principle had nowhere been a program. The new states emerging from the collapsed Union found themselves suddenly in a political and cultural vacuum and without the means to build an

independent political, economic or cultural entity out of the chaos left behind.

The Peace of "Versailles" and the "Order of Yalta"

Even under the best possible circumstances, President Wilson's plans for the formation of nation-states in Central and Eastern Europe, were thus bound to fail; and the circumstances were less than good. Czechoslovakia and Yugoslavia were new and artificial creations. The borders of Hungary were dictated by revenge. The Baltic States acquired independence as a consequence of the Brest-Litovsk Peace Settlement (abrogated by Lenin shortly thereafter). Civil war in Russia enabled Poland to move its borders Eastwards. None of the newly created states - with the exception of Czechoslovakia - became democracies in which there was a chance to properly deal with ethnic conflict or minority rights.

The Second World War and the "Order of Yalta" in its aftermath, just added new chapters of cruelty, conflict, revenge and repression, by which the formation of self-determined nation-states was made virtually impossible. As a consequence of the Molotov-von Ribbentrop Pact of August 1939, the Baltic States were annexed by the Soviet Union and Poland was partitioned. Czechoslovakia - already dismembered by Hitler in 1938 - and Yugoslavia disappeared. Slovakia and Croatia became "independent" German satellites, like Hungary, Romania and Bulgaria.

After the War, "Yalta" enabled Stalin to impose his solution to the problem of nationalities on Eastern Europe. The Baltic States, 48% of pre-war Polish territory, Transcarpathian Slovakia and Romanian Bessarabia were annexed by the Soviet Union. Poland was compensated with pre-war German Silesia and Pomerania. Populations were massively "transferred" (expelled) in a huge operation of "ethnic cleansing". National, ethnic or minority identities were suppressed in the name of socialist internationalism.

The desintegration of the Soviet Empire revived "nationalism" in a new and destructive way. In its first phase, the liberation of Poland (within its "Yalta" borders), Hungary, Czechoslovakia and East Germany went peacefully, as did - more slowly - the liberation of Bulgaria. In Romania, Ceausescu was violently replaced by a new regime of questionable bearings; in the meantime democracy has sufficiently taken hold to be a member state of the EU since 2007. The Soviet Union has chaotically come apart in hastily proclaimed new states - none of them looking like a viable, liberated, properly governed and self-determined nation-state. Yugoslavia violently came apart in a cruel civil war. Slovenia, Croatia and Macedonia have proven viable. Bosnia-Herzegovina's problems seem insoluble. The future of Serbia, Montenegro and Kosovo remains uncertain.

Convictions of the nationalist creed

It is against this historical background that we must now look at the four characteristic convictions of the nationalist creed, discussed by Isaiah Berlin.[13]

First is the conviction, "that men belong to a particular human group, and that the way of life of the group differs from that of others; that the characters of the individuals who compose the group are shaped by, and cannot be understood apart from, those of the group, defined in terms of common territory, customs, laws, memories, beliefs, language, artistic and religious expression, social institutions, way of life...; and that it is these factors which shape human beings, their purposes

13 *Loc. Cit.* at p. 341 ff.

and their values". In the name of that conviction, nationalism challenges the validity of any law for the sake of the free expression of the creative (national) will."

Second is the conviction, "that the pattern of life of a society is similar to that of a biological organism". What the organism needs for its development "constitutes its common goals"; and "these goals are supreme"... "Whence it follows that the essential human unit in which man's nature is fully realised is not the individual, or a voluntary association which can be dissolved or altered or abandoned at will, but the nation". The fusion of nationalism with *etatisme* and industrialization resulted in the doctrine of the supremacy in all spheres of the nation-state, "working together to build up Great Powers, each of which claimed to be a universe in itself".[14]

Thirdly, "this outlook entails the notion that one of the most compelling reasons, perhaps the most compelling, for holding a particular belief, pursuing a particular policy, serving a particular end, living a particular life, is that these ends, beliefs, policies, lives, are ours. Rules or doctrines or principles should not be followed because they lead to virtue, or happiness, or justice, or liberty, but because "these values are those of my group and my nation."

Finally, "full-blown nationalism has arrived at the position that, if the satisfaction of the needs of the organism to which I belong turns out to be incompatible with the fulfillment of the goals of other groups, I, or the society to which I indissolubly belong, have no choice but to force them to yield, if need be by force...There is no overarching criterion or standard, in terms of which the various values of the lives, attributes, aspirations, of

---

14 Cf. Arnold Toynbee, *A Study of History,* Oxford University Press 1972, at p. 34, New and Revised Abridged Edition.

different national groups can be ordered, for such a standard would be super national, not itself immanent in, part and parcel of, a given social organism, but deriving its validity from some source outside the life of a particular society".

What gives these convictions such a destructive character, are the historical circumstances in which they could develop into aggressive, nationalist ideologies. The way of life of the own group or nation not only differs from that of others. It is considered to be superior, while the other is inferior. If the pattern of life of a society is similar to that of a biological organism, the "health" of the organism thus requires that inferior minorities are expelled or exterminated like infectious diseases.

Hitler embarked upon a "scientific" program to exterminate Jews, Gypsies and Poles to purify the Aryan race and the German nation. Serbs and Croats in the Yugoslav civil were engaged in ethnic cleansing of each other and the Bosnian Muslims in territories they claim as theirs.

Full-blown nationalism in areas where ethnic or national borders cannot be meaningfully drawn, thus is bound to fuel continuous war, conflict and revenge. Combined with ideologies of national superiority, it produces a chain-reaction of war and revenge, destruction and cruelty. The targets of nationalist warfare are not the armies of the enemy, but innocent citizens, cities, cultural monuments and the society of the nations or ethnic groups, deemed to be inferior.

The convictions of the nationalist creed, as they made their appearance in Europe, are - like the ideologies of racism and totalitarian communism - diametrically opposed to every single idea of Europe.

The Nationalist Challenge to the Idea of Europe

The assumptions with respect to the formation of nation-states (formulated by American President Wilson) have proven to be fallacious. The success of the EU policy to overcome nationalism by membership of the European Union, without addressing the issue of imposed borders, is still to be proven. The forming of a "European attitude of mind" turned out to be difficult already in the nation states of the first and second zones. It may be even more so in the third time zone for the majority of the states members since 2004. For them it seems to be even more necessary to belong to a Europe organized in the spirit of Schuman and *Solidarnosc,* that is to say a supranational or Community Europe with common institutions and common rules.

More in particular, the European Union of 27 needs:

(1) Common principles, rules and mechanisms for European supervision with respect to the observance of fundamental human rights, including the rights of persons belonging to minority groups;

(2) Agreement on the gradual removal of economic and cultural barriers and on diminishing the importance of political frontiers between states;

(3) Promotion of the development and growth of an open and transnational civil society with autonomous and voluntary associations;

(4) Acceptance of significant transfers of state-sovereignty to common institutions, including judicial institutions.

As Guardini said in 1962[15], power can be exercised over man in two ways, the way of dominion or the way of service. This second way is not "under the compulsion of weakness, but in virtue of the ascendency of strength made legitimate, too, by divine ordinance in a way which is not an expression of arrogated superiority or 'majesty', but to restore honorable status to a discredited word, of 'humility'. It is the humility of a strength which desires that right shall reign on earth. There is no splendor, no majesty in power, displayed, in this form, it is purely practical. All the same, it may be the real meaning behind the present worldwide revolutionary ferment, for men all desire a valid order backed by power, but it must be an order which renders service. Perception of this truth and its realization in fact might also be a task for Europe, that same Europe that has practiced so much violence and oppression in the name of a superiority that has lost its substance."

The required European attitude of mind must be based on virtue and realism; the virtue of humility for the purpose of exercising power in the way of service and realism about our human defects; to understand why Europe needs common, supranational and democratic institutions and common enforceable rules.

FIDELIO

As Ludwig von Beethoven gave Europe the tune and the text for the European Anthem - Ode to Joy from his 9th symphony - we may just as well rely on his Opera Fidelio to conclude the first part of this volume.

Fidelio stands for the three European virtues of Courage, Fidelity and Love, by which Leonora saved the life of her husband

---

15 Cf. Document EH. 1 Europe Reality or Mission.

Florestan, about to be killed in revenge by Don Pizarro, governor of a state prison. Disguised as a boy, Leonora managed to be employed as an assistant to jailer Rocco. With him she descended into the deepest and darkest pit of the subterranean prison, where her husband was chained dying from hunger, thirst and cold. She went to help Rocco, who was ordered by Pizarro to dig a grave for Florestan, he wanted to kill and be buried there in secret. When Don Pizarro came down and drew his dagger to kill Florestan, Leonora threw herself between them, ordering Pizarro to stand back: "First you will have to pierce my breast! Death will surely punish your cruel lust for blood." Pizarro hurls her out of the way, but she comes back to shield her husband again, singing "First kill his wife!" In the ensuing confusion, Pizarro after a while recovers: "Am I to be frightened by a woman?" On which Leonora produces a small pistol and pointing it to Pizarro, sings: "Another sound and you are dead."

At that moment a trumpet call is heard from the tower, announcing the arrival of the Minister Don Fernando. "Ah, you are safe now, almighty God, almighty God, sings Leonora embracing Florestan who joins in.

"Love combined with courage, your freedom will achieve."

Don Fernando, the townspeople and the other prisoners join in with an ode of joy:

> "Hail, hail,hail, happy day
> Hail, happy moment
> Desired so long, yet unforeseen
> Justice, with graciousness united
> Stands before the doors of death,
> Let the wicked be punished,
> Who oppressed the innocent,
> Justice holds the sword of judgement

Ready poised for sentence!
Let the wicked one be punished.

Let all who have won fair wives
Join in our celebration
Never can we praise too much
The wife who saved her husband's life!
Praise, praise with joyous fervor
Leonora's noble courage!"

Without such virtue, the required European attitude of mind will not be formed and Europe's conscience will remain too fragile to sustain European unity as envisaged.

PART II

PEACEFUL ORGANISATION OF COMMON ACTION

"The European Union, if it continues to give priority to economic and monetary matters, is heading nowhere"

Norman Davies

CHAPTER 1

FROM THE SCHUMAN PLAN TO THE TREATY OF LISBON: A SYSTEM IN PERMANENT CRISIS

"European unity is the most important event in the West since the war, not because it is a new great power, but because the new institutional method it introduces is permanently modifying relations between states and men. Human nature does not change, but when nations and men accept the same rules and the same institutions to make sure that they are applied, their behaviour towards each other changes. This is the process of civilization itself."[1]

With these words, Jean Monnet concluded his reflections, entitled 'A Ferment of Change' on the European Unification process launched on 9 May 1950 by French Foreign Minister Robert Schuman.

The constitutional foundation for 'Europe' was laid by the Schuman-plan and the resulting agreement on the Treaty Instituting the European Coal and Steel Community (ECSC).

As J.B. Duroselle wrote, Jean Monnet's idea of European integration was not the outcome of studying previous plans for European unity, it came to him by the spectacle of ruins left by the World Wars.[2] Faced with the ruins of European policies of domination, Monnet and Schuman - like George Marshall and Dean Acheson three years earlier (1947 Marshall-plan) - chose

---

1 From an article published in *Journal of Common Market Studies 1,1962.*

2 Cf. *L'Idee d'Europe dans l'histoire,* Paris 1965.

for reconciliation with Germany and the peaceful organization of common action and cooperation. Their choice was not obvious at all, as we know too well from the history of Europe. In 1919 the victorious powers had chosen for revenge against and domination over Germany. In the other half of Europe after 1945, Stalin chose for totalitarian domination over allied and defeated states. Their choice was not even obvious for the French Government in which Schuman was Foreign Minister: he needed to invent some ruses to have his plan accepted, before he rushed to the press-room to announce it publicly![3]

The Schuman-plan was a unique document, in the situation it addressed and in the ideas underlying its proposals. Five European governments accepted the invitation to open negotiations on the basis of the principles enunciated in the Schuman Declaration; in April 1951 the six states signed the ECSC Treaty. As is made clear by the Preamble to the Treaty, the six states were in fundamental agreement on the purposes to be achieved. They were:

"*Convinced* that the contribution which an organized and vital Europe can bring to civilization is indispensable to the maintenance of peaceful relations;

Conscious of the fact that Europe can be built only by concrete actions creating a real solidarity and by the establishment of common bases for economic development;

Resolved to substitute for historic rivalries a fusion of their essential interests; to establish, by creating an economic community, the foundation of a broad and independent community among peoples long divided by bloody conflicts;

---

3 Rene Lejeune, *Robert Schuman, Pere de l'Europe,* Paris 2000

and to lay the bases of institutions capable of giving direction to their future common destiny."[4]

There was fundamental agreement indeed:
- on *purpose*: peaceful relations and true solidarity;
- on *the road to follow*: concrete actions and the fusion of essential interests;
- and on *the method of common action*: creating institutions capable of giving direction to their future common destiny.

This agreement on the peaceful organization of common action has been solid enough to provide the constitutional foundation for more than sixty years of peace and cooperation and for the growth from a six-member ECSC to a twenty-seven member European Union - with a common currency. The unification of Europe into the twenty-first century is a remarkable process and offers a fascinating history. It did not come about without major problems. It often stumbled from crisis to crisis. There were moments in which even the most optimistic 'European" no longer believed in its success, or in which they declared a shaky compromise to be a historic decision. Neither today's European Union nor European law can be properly understood or interpreted without knowledge of its history. European Unification went through so many crises that we can properly call it a system in permanent crisis. Hardly ever did European Unification experience attainment of the aims formulated originally. Never did the process degenerate into breaking off relations or resorting to war. Somehow, the constitutional foundation weathered all storms and survived every serious challenge.

---

4 The text of the Schuman Plan and the ECSC Treaty can be found in documents E.1.2 and EU. 2.

Against those who argue that the method of common action devised for a limited (coal and steel) community of six states no longer fits for a comprehensive union enlarged to twenty-seven states, stands the reality of its evolution. Ever since its creation, a growing number of European states sought admission. The peaceful organization of common action could extend to more and more states and its scope could continue to broaden.

Let us briefly look in this first chapter at the history of sixty years unification.

CONGRESS OF EUROPE AND THE COUNCIL OF EUROPE (1948-1951)

The years 1947 and 1948 were gloomy and critical years for post-war Europe. 1947 began with a severe winter, no government could adequately cope with. The US offered (Marshall) Aid. The Soviet Union imposed its one party totalitarian system on one after the other countries in East and Central Europe, culminating in the Coup d'Etat of February 1948 in Prague. The Prague Coup changed Europe. Political leaders in Western Europe began to realize that federalist plans for unity were no romantic dreams but urgent needs for political survival and freedom. What started as an effort to unite federalist movements became a Congress attended by major political leaders.

The Congress of Europe in The Hague turned the ideas of the federalists into a political program for post-war Western Europe. Its political resolution[5] called for a Union or Federation of Europe and proposed to draft a Charter on Human Rights. Within a year agreement was reached on the Statute of the

---

5 Text in document E.1.1.

Council of Europe.[6] Strasbourg was chosen as the seat of the new organization to underline its mission of contributing to the reconciliation between France and Germany. Already during the first session of the Council's Consultative Assembly (now called Parliamentary Assembly) Winston Churchill proposed to associate a free and democratic (West) Germany to the Western democracies. In 1950 the German Federal Republic was admitted as an associate member; it became a full member a year later.

The Council of Europe was a compromise between the French - who had preferred a constitutive parliamentary assembly to prepare a constitution for closer union, and the British - who wanted no more than a ministerial committee and a consultative assembly. As the excerpts from the Statute, reprinted as our second document, show, the real innovation of the Statute was that acceptance of the principles of individual and political liberty and of the rule of law was defined as a condition of adhesion.

Already during its first session the Committee of Ministers of the Council invited the Assembly to consider any changes in the political structure of Europe considered necessary to achieve greater unity between member-states of the Council. The Assembly adopted a resolution on 6 September 1949 stating that it is the aim of the Council of Europe to create "a European political authority with limited functions but real powers." The issue dominated the debates in the Assembly until December 1951. It soon became clear that the Assembly was split in two groups. The "federalists" - coming mainly from France, Italy and the Benelux - preferred "a European organization with real powers, governed by a central authority." The "functionalists" - mainly from Britain, Ireland and the Scandinavian countries

6 Text in document EU.1.

- wanted to achieve closer "European unity by a greater measure of intergovernmental cooperation in various fields." Even the compromise they reached was unacceptable to the Committee of Ministers.

It is important to realize that those were critical years for post-war Europe. The American Marshall Plan was rejected by Stalin and his East European satellites. The OEEC gave body to the American condition of cooperation among receiving states and played a major role in the distribution of aid and the liberation of trade and payments. Shortly after the Congress of Europe, Stalin ordered the Berlin blockade in an effort to force the Western Allies out of West Berlin. The successful airlift brought the blockade to an end and led to the creation of the (West) German Federal Republic in May 1949. A secure place for the new republic had to be found; membership of the Council of Europe did not suffice, as a solution had to be found for the control over German heavy industry - than under the Coal and Steel Authority headed by Jean Monnet. Jean Monnet and Robert Schuman realized that Europe needed a more imaginative plan than the Council of Europe to move forward. The Schuman plan was launched on 9 May 1950.

THE NEW COMMUNITY AND ITS FIRST CRISIS (1950-1954)

The new method of common action he proposed was the core of the Declaration made by Robert Schuman on 9 May 1950.

The aims Schuman wanted to achieve were reconciliation between France and Germany and a European federation. Such a Europe must be built through practical achievements that first create a sense of common purpose. To this end he proposed to place the production of coal and steel under a joint High Authority. Coal and Steel had been the basic industries for war. Pooled in a common market and placed under a joint Authority, they would contribute to peace and unification. His Declaration was addressed to Germany, Great Britain, Italy and the Benelux states. Britain stayed out. The other five replied positively in a joint communiqué of 3 June 1950. The Dutch government expressed some reservation with respect to the political responsibility of the supranational High Authority; an issue no yet settled in the French proposal.

In the negotiations resulting in the signature of the Treaty Instituting the European Coal and Steel Community on 18 April 1951, the foundations were laid for the new community method and the structure of the new community. Henceforward the development of the new community method would be the responsibility of the four core-institutions of the community: an independent High Authority, a Special Council of Ministers, a Common (Parliamentary) Assembly and a Court of Justice.

The abortive European Defence Community

In response to American pressure - following the outbreak of the Korean War in June 1950 - to agree to West German re-armament, René Pleven proposed a similar community to ECSC for joint European defence. A Treaty Instituting the European Defence Community (EDC) was signed by the same six states on 27 May 1952.[7] In August 1954 it was defeated in the French National Assembly.

This first crisis in the European integration process was quickly overcome. Already in October 1954 agreement was reached on West-German rearmament and its admission to NATO by

---

7 Compare my *Western Cooperation Origins and history* (second edition) and Documents II.6.1 and II.6.2.

way of a revision of the Western Union (known since as the West European Union).

The crisis and the solutions found, however, exacted their price. Defence and security policies were left outside the domain of the new community method - a problem plaguing European Unification ever since. With respect to the powers given to the institutions of the two new communities, the Council of Ministers emerged clearly as the most powerful institution.

A Draft Treaty Instituting a European Political Community

On 10 December 1951, the Consultative Assembly of the Council of Europe (still much involved in the debates on European Unification) acknowledged the impossibility of reaching agreement on a political authority with real powers among all members of the Council of Europe. The Assembly therefore recommended the creation of such an authority, duly controlled by a parliamentary assembly, among a limited number of continental Member States. Following the signature of the EDC Treaty, the Assembly proposed to confer that task to an Assembly capable of exercising it without delay and to draft a statute envisaging a European Political Community. On 10 September 1952 the six governments of the ECSC Member States invited their Common Assembly to transform itself - through co-opting nine new members from among the representatives to the Consultative Assembly of the Council of Europe - into the Assembly-ad-hoc with the task of drafting a Statute for a European Community. On 9 March 1953, the draft treaty concerning the Statute of a European Community was presented to the Foreign Ministers of the six ECSC Member

States.[8] After the rejection of the EDC Treaty in the French National Assembly, the draft disappeared in the archives. As the first effort to write a Constitution for Europe, it merits some attention.

The principal purpose of the European Political Community, according to the draft, was to merge the ECSC and the EDC into one European Community "of a supranational character". Among its functions are those already exercised according to the ECSC and EDC Treaties. In addition the Community shall contribute to a gradual establishment of a common market; and provisions are made for a coordination of foreign policies of member states. Specialised authorities can be set up, third states can be associated to the Community and relations with the Council of Europe are provided for in a special protocol. The Community shall have legal personality. The European Convention for the protection of Human Rights (Provisions of part I) "are an integral part of the present statute."

The Community shall have the following institutions:

1. A Bicameral Parliament;
2. A European Executive Council (for conducting international relations);
3. A Council of National Ministers;
4. A Court of Justice;
5. An Economic and Social Council.

---

8 In the Assembly, French delegate Michel Debré, to be Prime Minister of the Fifth French Republic later, proposed a pact for a union of European states that was rejected. See Document EUD. 1 for the text of the draft.

The Community shall have limited legislative, budgetary, administrative, treaty-making, coordinative and judicial powers.

The draft was extensively discussed by the six Foreign Ministers until August 1954 (when the French National Assembly rejected the EDC Treaty). The ministers accepted the institution of a single Court of Justice and a popular House of Parliament to be elected by direct suffrage. No agreement could be reached on the composition and election of the Senate nor on the appointment and responsibilities of the Executive Council. The principles and procedures to govern the establishment of a common market (Beyen-plan) received much attention. No agreement could be reached on association and accession of other states nor on the conduct of international relations. The magic formula for reconciling supranational power with the maintenance of national independence and sovereignty was still wanting.

RELAUNCHING EUROPEAN INTEGRATION (1955-1961)

Within a year the unification process was relaunched on the initiative of the three Benelux members. In May 1955, the Benelux states proposed to enlarge the common market to a comprehensive economic community and to the development of atomic energy.[9]

The new method of common action introduced by the ECSC Treaty was applied to the difficult and complex process of negotiating the two new treaties. The Ministerial Conference of Messina created an intergovernmental committee presided by Belgian Foreign Minister Henri Spaak and consisting of

9 Text of the Benelux Memorandum in document.E.1.3.

six delegations composed of diplomats and experts. The Committee associated civil servants from the ECSC, OEEC, the Council of Europe and the European Conference of Ministers of Transport to its work. It submitted its report to the six ministers of Foreign Affairs on 21 April 1956.[10] Thereafter the Ministers instructed the Committee to draft the necessary treaties to put the proposals into effect and decided to meet regularly themselves to be briefed by the heads of delegations and to take the required political decisions. On 26 June 1956 the Intergovernmental Conference resumed its work under Spaak's presidency.

On 25 March 1957, the Treaties Instituting the European Community and the European Atomic Energy Community were signed, again by the six original members of ECSC. Two new economic communities came into being with the same structure and institutions as those of the ECSC. New was the triangular relationship between the Council of Ministers, the Commission and the parliamentary Assembly. Unlike the High Authority of the ECSC, the role of the Commission was to propose legislation, whereas the Council of Ministers was given the final power of decision after having consulted the Parliamentary Assembly. The decisive role of the Council re-introduced the need for close cooperation between European and national civil servants (through Committee of Permanent Representative (COREPER)). The Treaties envisaged the possibility of strengthening the powers of the Commission and the Assembly, by the gradual introduction of (qualified) majority voting in the Council and election by direct suffrage for the members of the Parliamentary Assembly.

---

10 Text of the Spaak Report in Document E.1.4. (in French and in English translation).

Johan Willem Beyen: Founding Father of the European Common Market[11]

Johan Willem Beyen became Dutch Foreign Minister at the time the ECSC Ministers debated plans for a European Political Community in order to give ECSC and EDC a constitutional foundation. Contrary to his predecessor and most other members of the Dutch government he saw no conflict between further economic integration and political unification. In the first ECSC Foreign Ministers Conference he attended after taking office, he proposed to link the two. Political unification without economic integration would be just as unworkable as economic integration without political unity. The political community needed a common market, and a common market needed a supranational political authority in his vision. Chapter V, articles 82-87 in the draft Statute for an EPC was devoted to the progressive realization of a common market.

Throughout the negotiations on the statute and with the French, Beyen remained convinced that European Unification required a solid supranational basis in military as well as economic matters. It was a question of principle on which he was not prepared to compromise.

Early in 1955, when France had another new government, time was considered ripe for an attempt to relaunch the European integration process. Jean Monnet favored the sector by sector approach, transport and energy to be added to coal and steel. Beyen revived his earlier plan for a European

---

[11] Apart from the Mémoires of Paul-Henri Spaak, there is not much on the primary role of Minister Beyen in the Relance Européenne. In the Dutch language: W.H.Weenink, *Johan Willem Beyen 1897-1976 Bankier van de Wereld Bouwer van Europa,* Prometheus/NRC Handelsblad 2005.

common market. Thanks to Belgian Foreign Minister Paul-Henri Spaak, both plans were presented in the Memorandum from the Benelux countries to the Member States of ECSC of 18 May 1955. The Memorandum - rather than a French-German document for much more limited cooperation - won the day in the last night of the Ministerial Conference in Messina in June 1955. Under the leadership of Spaak a special committee was charged to study the institutional modalities for the realization and functioning of a common market and the creation of a common organization for the development of atomic energy. In May 1956 in Venice, it was agreed to open negotiations on a treaty to institute a common market and a treaty to institute an organization for atomic energy. Prior to his departure as Foreign Minister in 1956, the plan Beyen had received prime of place in the *relance européenne*. Soon after the entry into force in 1958 of the two Treaties of Rome, Euratom ran into serious difficulties and the EEC emerged as the centerpiece of the unification process. Just in time before the collapse of the Fourth French Republic and the advent of the considerably more nationalistic Fifth Republic, a European Common Market under a common supranational authority could begin to function.

A solid supranational basis for European Unification was a matter of principle for Beyen. He did not change his mind at the time (1958-1963) he was ambassador in Paris. He had just arrived, when a coup d'état brought the Fourth French Republic to an end and General de Gaulle to power. He left shortly after General de Gaulle's 'No' to Britain. He showed understanding for the efforts to create a more stable France, but disagreed with the President's European policies.

As one of the Founding Fathers - with Schuman, de Gasperi and Adenauer - Beyen (like Spaak by the way) was convinced of our Christian heritage. Already in his first appearance as

Foreign Minister in the Dutch Parliament, he reaffirmed that the Western world can neither survive nor blossom when it would renounce the Christian principles that are the foundation of its civilization. On 29 October 1962 Beyen was baptized into the Roman Catholic Church with French philosopher and friend Jean Guitton as a witness. For the founding fathers Christian principles apparently were living sources for political action.

It is most important to underline that Europe had founding fathers rather than founding countries. All of them looked beyond the perceived interests of their countries and had great difficulty to convince their fellow ministers. Schuman had to find a ruse to have his plan adopted by the French Government. Adenauer had to overcome resistance against integration in the West before German re-unification. Beyen had great difficulty in overcoming resistance in the Dutch government against supranational authority and economic union without Britain. Each of them was guided by what they understood to be their personal and political responsibility to change the pattern of European politics in the direction mentioned above: true reconciliation and effective solidarity to be carefully developed under the authority of common institutions and common rules.

Their commitment to action was not necessarily guided by some common values held by the public in their countries. In fact there was quite some resistance to it. A referendum on the Schuman plan in 1950 and on the Beyen plan in 1955 might not have received a majority in either France or the Netherlands. Well over 50 successful years later a majority in both countries voted against adopting the Constitution for Europe. This latest Constitution, finally, has produced its own ironies. The Convention preparing it was no true convention. The members accepted by consensus what ought to have been voted on article by article. The Constitution is no true constitution but a lengthy and complex document full of contradictions, non-binding proclamations and empty formulae. It undermines rather than promotes supranational authority and postpones the very decisions which had been the reason for launching the exercise.

Jean Monnet's Action Committee for the United States of Europe[12]

Jean Monnet - or Mr. Europe as he was referred to by his friends in Washington - had been the first President of the High Authority of the ECSC since 10 August 1952. After the crisis of August 1954 he informed his colleagues in November not to seek a second term after 10 February 1955. Urged by the Assembly to modify his decision, he informed the six governments that he was willing to do so. The French Government, nevertheless, decided not to pose his candidature.

On 13 October 1955 he announced the creation of an Action Committee for the United States of Europe, composed of delegates from the major political parties and trade unions in the European Community Member States. Their mission will be to express their determination to their governments and to public opinion to see the decisions of the Foreign Ministers in Messina (on 2 June 1955) as a step towards the United States of Europe. To reach these objectives intergovernmental cooperation would be insufficient. True federal institutions are indispensable and close association of Great Britain must be assured.

In terms of substance the Committee focused all its attention on a European Community for Atomic Energy (EURATOM), considered to be the engine for further unification. From late

---

12 Cf. Pascal Fontaine, *Le Comité d'Action pour les États-Unis d'Europe de Jean Monnet*, Centre de Recherches Européennes de Lausanne, 1974.

1956 onwards (but in fact too early) it focused its effort on a speedy ratification of the Treaties of Rome of 25 March 1957. In this respect they were successful. Parliamentary approval was obtained as early as July in France and Germany, and in Italy and the Benelux before mid October. On 1 January 1958, the two new communities could start to function, provisionally in Brussels, where of course they are still located today.

Contrary to the expectations in 1957, EEC - not Euratom - would become the engine driving the new method of common action, largely because of its scope and the provisions for a transitional period of twelve years for establishing the common market.

A System in permanent crisis

The new method proposed by Monnet, Schuman, Beyen and Spaak for the European integration process, implies that community-Europe can be characterized as 'a system in permanent crisis'. The difficulty to reach agreement on integrating further often leads to a decision to take the next step before an agreed dead-line. The EEC Treaty, as a consequence, in article 8 provided for a transitional period of twelve years subdivided in three stages, each to be concluded with a number of decisions prescribed by the Treaty. It provided for predictable crises every four years, producing the phenomenon of Marathon sessions - Council members 'locked up' in their conference centre until agreement was reached. The first such session took place in December 1961 to take the necessary decisions for moving to the second stage of the transitional period. The Commission had proposed that the essential objectives to be reached before that date (1 January 1962) included decisions on the principles of a common agricultural policy, on the application of the rules of competition (articles 85 and 86) and the principle of equal remuneration for the same work as between male and female workers (art. 119) and a more specific elaboration of the provisions with respect to the free movement of persons, services and capital (articles 48-73). To which the French government (supported by the Dutch) added: regulations to put the common agricultural policy into effect. At the last moment (on 12 January 1962) the French government introduced a draft regulation concerning the financing of a common agricultural policy.

Indeed, the Council and the Commission were still in Marathon session on 12 January 1962. The official clock had been stopped on 31 December 1961 and EEC New Year could only start on 14 January 1962. That day or rather that night, the package deal was agreed upon. As a method of decision-making it established a lasting practice and created perennial problems. The lasting practice includes an emphasis on structured intergovernmental negotiations. The presence of several ministers from each of the governments enables package deal decisions, requiring common agreement. The Commission's role is one of initiation and mediation. The Parliamentary Assembly remains on the side lines. Package deals run the risk of obscure agreements and declarations of intention to agree before a new deadline. Fatigue of the ministers may cost them dearly. Good example is the acceptance of the French draft regulation. The financing of the common agricultural policy was at the origin of some of the crises of the 1960s and still gives the European Union lots of trouble today.

It should be kept in mind that the first stage in the transition to a common market coincided with the first four years of the French Fifth Republic, replacing the Fourth after the *coup d'etat* of May 1958. The new Gaullist regime gave France more stability. As was realized only later, de Gaulle did not want Great Britain to become a member; he wanted a Europe of States instead of a Community Europe; and his foreign policy had a clear anti-American bias. Jean Monnet definitely was not his friend and adviser. The latter's Action Committee lost much of its impact. De Gaulle's support for the common market, for the decision in 1961 to accelerate the entry into force of the common market (on 1 July 1968 instead of 1 January 1970) and the breaking off of negotiations on a Free Trade Area, were seen as a pro-European stance rather than what they turned out to be later.

A Community of Law

It was a blessing for Europe that the three communities were in place before the Gaullist challenges of the 1960s. It enabled the European Court of Justice (common to the three communities of ECSC, EEC and Euratom) to establish its reputation as a "constitutional" Court and as an authoritative institution to interpret and clarify European law, often made obscure by Council decisions. The Court amply used its jurisdiction to make a preliminary ruling on the interpretation of the treaties and the validity and interpretation of acts of the institutions, to establish two basic constitutional principles of the European legal order.

The first principle, originally laid down in the Van Gend & Loos Case, concerns the direct effect of community law in the legal order of Member States. Individuals may derive rights directly from Community law. The fundamental argument behind the ruling is, that the EEC constitutes a new legal order of international law for the benefit of which states have limited their sovereign rights. When sovereign rights can be limited, sovereignty is divisible and loses its character as a holy and sacrosanct principle.

The second principle, laid down in the Costa v. ENEL case, concerns the well-known constitutional principle - first formulated by the US Supreme Court (Marbury vs. Madison

1804) - of the primacy of European law over any rule of national law. The primacy for European law extends to treaties and secondary European law. "Any rule of national law" includes the Constitutional law of Member States.[13]

Built upon these two fundamental principles, unity in the interpretation and application of European law can be assured. At the same time it helps to maintain the primacy of law over politics as a major asset in the effort to settle serious political conflicts peacefully.

THE GAULLIST CHALLENGE (1958-1969)

The second serious crisis in European unification came in 1958 with the coming to power of Charles de Gaulle as president of the new Fifth French Republic and lasted until his abdication in 1969. In name of the *grandeur* of France, de Gaulle challenged both American leadership in the Atlantic Alliance, and the new (supranational or community) method of common action.[14]

Setting the stage

General de Gaulle did not waste time once he declared his willingness to assume power on 5 May 1958 at the time of a threatening coup. First priority was to replace the Constitution of the Fourth Republic by a new one establishing a presidential system and curtailing the powers of the National Assembly. The text of the Constitution for the Fifth French Republic was drafted in the summer and approved by popular referendum on 28 September 1958. It entered into force on 4 October 1958

---

13 Text of the two cases in Document. E.1.5. Compare Koen Lenaerts and Piet van Nuffel, *Constitutional Law of the European Union*, Thomson Sweet&Maxwell, 2005 (Second edition).

14 Cf. my: *Western Cooperation, Op.cit.* Chapters II.2 and II.6.

and General de Gaulle was elected President on 21 December 1958. In the meantime he had written a personal letter to US President Eisenhower, with copy to British Prime Minister Harold McMillan to create a directorate of the three powers with global responsibilities - France, Britain and the United States - within the Atlantic Alliance to take joint decisions on global problems.[15] Foreign policy was a presidential domain:

> "The President of the Republic shall ensure due respect for the Constitution. He shall ensure, by his arbitration, the proper functioning of the public authorities and the continuity of the State. He shall be the guarantor of national independence, territorial integrity and due respect for Treaties."

This text of article 5 of the new Constitution makes it quite clear. General de Gaulle wanted the President (himself) to occupy the place of supreme head of the executive, at the same time arbiter (between government and parliament) and chief of foreign policy and defense. The President, in his own words: "*doit inspirer toute l'action gouvernementale*". Article 6 in the original version of the Constitution provided for election of the President by an Electoral College, a system that had some resemblance with the Electoral College in the American Constitution and with the way the Emperor of the Holy Empire had been elected. Already in 1962, an organic law introduced direct election by universal suffrage.

With the monarchical presidency in place and the claim to great power status in the White House, President de Gaulle could turn his attention to 'Europe', addressing inspiration and guidance to Europe's six prime ministers by sovereign, presidential Press Conference.

---

[15] Compare my *Western Cooperation*, pp. 158,159

On Stage

The 11 year reign of General Charles de Gaulle was both theater and tragedy. His re-appearance on the French political stage signaled the tragic end of the Fourth Republic. His sudden departure from the political stage on 28 April 1969, one day after the lost referendum on regionalization and the reform of the Senate was a personal tragedy. In between he definitely destroyed the consensus on the United States of Europe as the ultimate aim of the process of European unification launched by Robert Schuman. Underlying these tragedies were his illusions about his role and France's place and destiny in the world after the Second World War.

During the 11 years Charles de Gaulle offered lively theater, most of it in carefully staged press conferences in the Elysée Palace. Most of his major decisions on Europe were announced on this stage in beautifully turned French phrases. Despite the clarity of his views, his audiences came and left puzzled, convinced as they were that he who stabilized France must also be in favor of the United States of Europe. From the outset, however, he made crystal clear that he wanted to replace Community Europe by the Europe of States - and to replace a Europe firmly anchored in the Atlantic Alliance by an independent European Europe under French presidential leadership.

Before turning to the abortive negotiations on political union, I must briefly refer to the context of the Gaullist era. As Tony Judt described so well,[16] the latter part of the 1950s and the full decade of the 1960s were an age of prosperity and its discontents, but also of East-West détente and the Vietnam

---

16 Tony Judt, *POSTWAR, A History of Europe since 1945*, Penguin Books 2006, Cf. Part Two.

war. It was an age of new-won affluence, migration (so-called guest workers) and steady growth of real wages, productivity, trade and urbanization. It was the age also of the lost illusions of empire - the completion of the process of decolonization. Discontents of the age exploded in the May 1968 revolts in Paris and France. Prime Minister Georges Pompidou could handle the revolt, but President de Gaulle appeared to be lost in it. The age of détente was ushered in by two unlikely events: the building of the Berlin Wall in August 1961 - to stop the flood of East-German refugees to the Federal Republic; and the Cuba Missile crisis of October 1962 - that brought the US and the Soviet Union to the brink of nuclear war and initiated serious arms-control talks. President de Gaulle's illusion that his France could promote détente by forging a special relationship with Moscow, was rudely destroyed by the Soviet-led invasion of Prague in August 1968. His lost illusions in foreign policy contributed to his sudden departure in April 1969.

Political Union

His proposal for a 'European Political Union' was meant primarily to replace the new method of common action by traditional forms of intergovernmental cooperation as he made clear as early as on 5 September 1960 and after the breakdown of political union negotiations on 15 April 1962, of course in a press conference:

> *«Encore une fois, il est tout naturel que les Etats de l'Europe aient à leur disposition des organismes spécialisés pour les problèmes qui leur sont communs, pour préparer et au besoin pour suivre leurs décisions, mais ces décisions leur appartiennent. Elles ne peuvent appartenir qu'à eux et ils ne peuvent les prendre que par coopération. Assurer la coopération régulière de l'Europe occidentale, c'est ce que la France considère*

comme étant souhaitable, comme étant possible et comme étant pratique, dans le domaine politique, dans le domaine économique, dans le domaine culturel et dans celui de la défense. Cela comporte un concert organisé régulier des Gouvernements responsables et puis, aussi, le travail d'organismes spécialisés dans chacun des domaines communs, organismes subordonnés aux Gouvernements; cela comporte la délibération périodique d'une assemblée qui soit formée par les délégués des parlements nationaux et, à mon sens, cela doit comporter, le plus tôt possible, un solennel référendum européen, de manière à donner à ce départ de l'Europe le caractère d'adhésion et de conviction populaires qui lui est indispensable»

«Qu'est-ce que la France propose à ses cinq partenaires? Je le répète une fois de plus. Pour nous organiser politiquement, commençons par le commencement. Organisons notre coopération. Réunissons périodiquement nos Chefs d'Etat ou de Gouvernement pour qu'ils examinent en commun les problèmes qui sont les nôtres et pour qu'ils prennent à leur égard des décisions qui seront celles de l'Europe. Formons une commission politique, une commission de défense et une commission culturelle, de même que nous avons déjà une commission économique à Bruxelles qui étudie les questions communes et qui prépare les décisions des six Gouvernements».

The proposal foundered in 1962, primarily due to Dutch resistance. In February 1961, the six set up a political commission to study de Gaulle's initiative. Only the French chairman of the Commission, Christian Fouchet, tabled a draft treaty in November 1961. A second version was circulated in January. The official second version, adapted by de Gaulle in person came on 18 January and was immediately rejected by France's five partners, who submitted an alternative draft rejected by de Gaulle[17].

The texts clearly manifest fundamental disagreement on two fundamental tenets of European unification. De Gaulle wanted to replace the Community method of common action by traditional cooperation between sovereign states. He rejected the attribution of sovereign powers to supranational institutions. In his political union, the existing community institutions had to be reduced to preparatory commissions and parliamentary advice. What de Gaulle wanted was a European Union instead of a European Community. De Gaulle also wanted a 'European Europe' no longer embedded in the system of Western cooperation but under independent French presidential leadership. In the French draft of January 1962, the subject matter of the three European Community Treaties was included in the spheres for intergovernmental cooperation:

> "It shall be the aim of the Union to reconcile, co-ordinate and unify the policy of Member States in spheres of common interest: foreign policy, economics, cultural affairs and defence."

The other five were prepared to embark on intergovernmental cooperation in foreign policy but not to abolish the existing communities, as they formulated in their alternative draft:

> "This Treaty shall not derogate from the competence of the European Communities."

The second fundamental disagreement was played out on the issue whether to make reference or not to NATO and on

---

17 The three documents can be found in Document E.5. 2-3.

the question of British participation in the political union talks. For the Netherlands and Belgium, British membership of the communities was a condition for creating a political union. For de Gaulle it was not.

In 1963 de Gaulle said 'No' to the entry of Britain as too close an ally to the United States.[18] In the same month of January 1963, he concluded a bilateral cooperation treaty with Germany. The Treaty was intended as a bilateral substitute for the abortive political union and as a model for a future presidential European union of *"le cavalier et le cheval"*. On the official photo of the signing ceremony, one sees President de Gaulle in the center, flanked on one side by the French Prime Minister and on the other side by the German Chancellor Adenauer! The treaty would significantly contribute to further French-German reconciliation and far-reaching cooperation between the two states within the European communities/ union, but not in matters of defense and foreign policy.[19]

The Empty Chair

In 1965 de Gaulle ordered his ministers no longer to participate in decision-making in the EEC Council of Ministers - in a direct challenge to the community method of common action. The agreement reached in January 1962 on the financing of a agricultural policy provided for a final decision before 1 July

18 See the next Chapter. The French-German Treaty of 1963 can be found on my website under Western Cooperation Nr. II.6.2.

19 Compare my: *Beyond Containment and Division, Western Cooperation From A Post-Totalitarian Perspective,* Martinus Nijhoff Publishers 1992/1994. Chapter 5, Containment within Containment: France and the (West) German Federal Republic 1945-1989. The German *Bundestag* added a preamble of its own to the treaty, emphasizing Germany's adherence to NATO and close cooperation between Europe and America, p. 93

1965 on the system of financing the CAP for the years 1965-1970. In March 1965 the Commission proposed to finance the CAP from 1 January 1967 onwards from direct Community resources instead of contributions from Member States. The resources would come from the levies[20] on imported agricultural products, reason why the Commission proposed to give the Parliamentary Assembly budgetary power over the CAP and thus also strengthen its own power in relation to the Council of Ministers. This move to strengthen the supranational institutions in carrying out a CAP strongly pushed by France, backfired. It enormously angered de Gaulle[21] and upon his order French Foreign Minister Maurice Couve de Murville decided at midnight of 30 June that no agreement could be reached on financing the CAP. The Minister and the French permanent representative withdrew and left Brussels. The French chair remained empty until 17 January 1966. In a two part extra-ordinary session (on 17-18 and 28-29 January) of the Council of Ministers, agreement was reached on the so called "Luxembourg Compromise" by which the French would come back.[22] In reality, the compromise was a Gentlemen's Disagreement. The first part of the session concluded with the publication of a French *aide-mémoire* aimed at curtailing the powers of the Commission.

The second part concluded with an agreed text on:
a) the relations between the Commission and the Council;
b) majority voting in the Council.

---

20 The price difference between world market prices and the prices for these products inside the common market.

21 For his press conference of September 1965, see Document E. 1. 6. Note the contempt with which he referred to the European Commission as some technocratic, stateless and irresponsible assembly (*aréopage).*

22 See Document.1.7. for the Luxembourg compromise.

On the relations under a) a reaction from the Commission was required, but never came. On majority voting in the Council divergence remained. Still, they all agreed that efforts to reach agreement should first be made. On the principal decisions to be made with respect to the CAP members agreed on the decisions to be taken by common consent. They also agreed on the date when the instruments of ratification be posited on the Merger Treaty signed just before this crisis. By virtue of the Treaty, the three communities would have one Commission and one Council of Ministers in addition to one Court of Justice and one Parliamentary Assembly (merged already by the Treaties of Rome).

Last Act

The last act in de Gaulle's challenge to Community Europe was played in 1967, a year after de Gaulle had decided to withdraw France from NATO's integrated structure and expel NATO from France. It would be the shortest act. On 10 May 1967, Britain again submitted a request for membership of the European Communities. This time the French even refused to discuss the application for membership. After that, even perennial optimist Jean Monnet was no longer optimistic about Europe: "Nowhere are things moving in the right direction" he declared to the American weekly Newsweek in April 1968. Still, the common market was achieved ahead of time on 1 July 1968 with the exception of a common commercial policy. In my book Beyond the European Community, written before de Gaulle's departure (but with a post-script dated June 29, 1969), I shared his pessimism for which I was severely criticized by true European federalists and advocates of the community method of decision-making.

Nevertheless, the year 1968 produced not one but two revolutions with an impact that became manifest only later.

The May 1968 student Revolt in Paris and the Prague Spring followed by the Soviet-led invasion would be the beginning of the end of the Gaullist era. *Le Cavalier* dismounted in April 1969 and *Le Cheval* in Bonn embarked on an entirely new policy towards the Soviet bloc, called the West-German *Ostpolitik* of the new Chancellor Willy Brandt. President de Gaulle's more realistic and approachable successor George Pompidou understood that British membership would be in the French interest in the new situation of German prominence in Europe.

The Gaullist challenge did leave its footprints in the process of European Unification into the twenty-first century. Since the entry into force of the Treaty of Lisbon in December 2009, we all belong to the European Union. The name became official in 1992 with the entry into force of the Maastricht Treaty, when the European Community was reduced to one of the three pillars of the European Union. Today the relevant provisions are to be found in the "Treaty on the Functioning of the European Union". De Gaulle's love for Summitry has gradually been institutionalized in the European Council, consisting of Heads of State and of Government. The European Council grew out of occasional summits. In 1974 it was decided to meet three times a year in the European Council. As can be seen in the conclusions of the European Council, its nature gradually changed from the summit for foreign policy to the highest authority in the Union. The nature of the European Council strengthens the emphasis on intergovernmental cooperation at the expense of community decision-making. Amidst lots of prime ministers, the French Presidents enjoy their eminent position and still insist on arriving after and leaving before everybody else. The style of a monarchical presidency has been kept alive by all of the successors of President de Gaulle. Foreign policy and defense cooperation are still kept separate. Even for the original Member States of the ECSC, federal unity no longer is the ultimate aim. The first post-Gaullist Summit of

December 1969 in The Hague set the tone for what now is the European Union.

Ironies of History

Every history has its ironies. Walter Hallstein who initially supported the French in their resistance against a common market, became the first President of the new Commission for the European Economic Community. He successfully resisted the efforts by President de Gaulle to reduce the Commission to an advisory body. Whereas French resistance during the negotiations in 1956, could be overcome only by accepting a long (12 years and more) transitional period, completion of the common market was accelerated with de Gaulle's agreement - most likely in his efforts to keep Britain out. The initial success of the common market convinced President Kennedy and Prime Minister Harold MacMillan that Britain should be in - a belated recognition of Beyen's abortive efforts to associate Britain to the *relance européenne*. De Gaulle's Veto against British membership lasted as long as his presidency. The Hague Summit of December 1969 opened the road to British entry and political cooperation. Various British governments would turn out to be at least as anti-supranational as the French presidents of the Fifth Republic. Political cooperation would be the prelude to accepting the very Gaullist idea of regular meetings between the Heads of State and Government, not just for discussing foreign policy but for high level "inspiration" to all matters pertaining to the Communities and the Union.

FROM THE HAGUE SUMMIT TO THE SINGLE EUROPEAN ACT (1969-1986)

The departure of President de Gaulle did not mean the end of Gaullism in French foreign policy. At best it meant a better sense of reality and a willingness to compromise. The first Summit met on the initiative of France and at the invitation of the Netherlands in The Hague on 1 and 2 December 1969.

The Heads of State or Government reaffirmed the will to pass from the transitional period to the final stage of the European Community. They did so not because of having taken all the required decisions to that end. They did so primarily to lay down a definite financial arrangement for the common agricultural policy before the end of 1969 as required by France (par. 5). On French insistence they also accepted "not to exclude its adaptation by unanimous vote" (par. 7). [23]

They also accepted that a plan in stages should be worked out during 1970 with a view to the creation of an economic and monetary union. The Hague Summit inaugurated the period of long term plans for further community integration. Among them were the Werner report on the creation of an Economic and Monetary Union (EMU); the Thompson report on a European Fund for Regional Development; and Commission Action plans with respect to a common industrial policy and the social dimension of the integration process.

The most important break-through was to be found in paragraphs 13 and 15 of the final communiqué of the Summit. To save the face of Gaullist France, "they reaffirmed their agreement on the principle of enlargement of the Community", but specifically instructed their foreign ministers

---

[23] See Document EC. The Hague 1969.

to make proposals in the matter of political unification before the end of July 1970. The so-called Davignon Report was submitted in July 1970 to the six member-governments and the four would-be member governments. It was adopted on 27 October 1970.[24]

The break-through to the enlargement of the Communities, discussed below in Chapter 2, came with the French-British Summit on 20 and 21 May 1971 of Georges Pompidou and Edward Heath. To understand the political deal between the two gentlemen it is important to keep a few considerations in mind. British Prime Minister Edward Heath was, exceptionally, a pro-European Conservative governing between two Labor Governments under Harold Wilson. George Pompidou opted for British membership to create a counterweight to West-Germany. The latter had shown its political clout by refusing to revalue the Mark in the monetary crisis of 1968 (forcing France to devalue the French Franc); and by embarking on its new *Ostpolitik* in December 1969. For President Pompidou, admitting Great Britain, political cooperation and economic and monetary union belonged together to assure continued French leadership - after the agreement on the definite financial arrangements for the Common Agricultural Policy (CAP).

Process and context

The political context of the 1970's, however, was not propitious to assuring French leadership in the European Community. West-German *Ostpolitik*, in fact, created its own dynamics towards transforming East-West détente from a bilateral US-Soviet affair into a multilateral process - culminating in the Helsinki Accords on CSCE in 1975. Germany instead of France became the prime actor in East-West relations, also in the

---

24 See Chapter 5 below. Text of the Hague Summit, document EC.H.

1980s when significant frictions developed between Bonn and Washington on East-West relations. As the odd man out in NATO, France played no role in the negotiations on the modernization of medium-range nuclear missiles or arms-control. In addition, the 1968 devaluation of the French franc followed by the 1969 revaluation of the German mark had ended monetary stability within the Community.

The decision of US President Nixon in August 1971 to decouple the Dollar from the Gold–price ended the so-called Bretton-Woods system and gave rise to significant and lasting world monetary instability. Completing the Economic and Monetary Union before the end of the decade ceased to be an achievable aim. Shortly after the entry of Britain, Ireland and Denmark on 1 January 1973, the enlarged Community was hit by the first energy-crisis in the wake of the October 1973 Middle-East War. The first ever foreign policy declaration of the nine in November 1973 was an act of shameful cowardice and has never been followed up by joint action. There was no solidarity between Member States in coping with recession and the economic consequences of the crisis.

The decade, in addition, was marked by significant internal developments in the countries of (Western) Europe. The restoration of democracy in Greece, Spain and Portugal opened a new chapter of enlargement of the Communities, requiring significant institutional adjustments. Attention of several major member countries was turned inwards by serious internal disturbances like the Rote Armee Fraktion (RAF) in Germany, the Red Brigades in Italy, the ETA in Spain and the problem of Northern Ireland for Britain.

The British Challenge

For the further development of European integration, the most serious challenge, however, came from London. As Luigi Barzini wrote in his delightful book on The Impossible Europeans:

> "When they (the British) finally joined the European Common Market, disastrously, too late, too expensively, at the wrong moment, they did so reluctantly and somewhat squeamishly, though politely concealing their feelings, like decayed aristocrats obliged by adverse circumstances to eat in a soup kitchen for the needy."[25]

The first challenge concerned the re-negotiation of entry-terms as required by the minority Labor government, succeeding Heath's government in 1974; the second, the British contribution to the budget problem raised by Prime Minister Margareth Thatcher from 1979 and solved only in 1984.

Re-negotiation

Labour took office as a minority government in February 1974 and already on 1 April 1974 presented a demand for renegotiation at the general affairs EEC Council meeting in Luxembourg.

The demands were stiff and the legal position was doubtful at best. In his statement, the British Secretary of State for Foreign Affairs declared (a.o.):

> 'This is why we are immediately seeking a fundamental renegotiation of the terms of entry, for which we have spelled out our objectives in the following terms'

---

[25] Luigi Barzini, *The Impossible Europeans* Weidenfeld and Nicollson 1983, pp. 60-61. See also J.- P. Puissochet, *The Enlargement of the European Communities*, Sijthoff 1975.

'The Labour Party opposes British membership of the European Communities on the terms negotiated by the Conservative Government.'

We have said that we are ready to renegotiate.

In preparing to renegotiate the entry terms, our main objectives are these -

Major changes in the Common Agricultural Policy, so that it ceases to be a threat to world trade in food products, and so that low-cost producers outside Europe can continue to have access to the British food market.

New and fairer methods of financing the Community Budget. Neither the taxes that form the so-called 'own resources' of the Communities, nor the purposes, mainly agricultural support, on which the funds are mainly to be spent, are acceptable to us. We would be ready to contribute to Community finances only such sums as were fair in relation to what is paid and what is received by other member countries.

As stated earlier, we would reject any kind of international agreement which compelled us to accept increased unemployment for the sake of maintaining a fixed parity, as is required by current proposals for a European Economic and Monetary Union. We believe that the monetary problems of the European countries can be resolved only in a world-wide framework.

The retention by Parliament of those powers over the British economy needed to pursue effective regional, industrial and fiscal policies. Equally we need an agreement on capital movements which protects our balance of payments and full employment policies. The economic interests of the Commonwealth and the developing countries must be better safeguarded. This involves securing continued access to the British market and, more generally, the adoption by an enlarged Community of trade and aid policies designed to benefit not just 'associated overseas territories' in Africa, but developing countries throughout the world.

No harmonization of Value Added Tax which would require us to tax necessities.

If renegotiations are successful, it is the policy of the Labour Party that, in view of the unique importance of the decision, the people should have the right to decide the issue through a General Election or a Consultative Referendum. If these two tests are passed, a successful renegotiation and the expressed approval of the majority of the British people, then we shall be ready to play our full part in developing a new and wider Europe.

If renegotiations do not succeed, we shall not regard the Treaty obligations as binding upon us. We shall then put to the British people the reasons why we find the new terms unacceptable, and consult them on the advisability of negotiating our withdrawal from the Communities." [26]

The final threat - of no longer regarding the Treaty obligations as binding - did not materialize. The June 5 referendum produced a clear majority in favor of continued British membership, where after the Government definitively established its position. The solutions found were typical for the way the Communities would henceforward operate: Formal revisions

---

[26] Document E.1.8.

of the Treaties and the Acts of Accession were avoided; most demands entered the regular process of community decision-making; the most difficult issues were settled in the meetings of the Heads of State and Government, institutionalized since 1974 in the European Council; If no consensus could be reached Member States would still retain the right to opt out or refuse implementation as incompatible with the national interest. One could call this a Europe à la carte, or a Europe with different speeds; whatever one calls it is a European Community in which different states are allowed to make different commitments to the common cause.

In addition to the Gaullist challenge, this first British challenge would definitely change the character of the European Communities from a supranational institution into an interstate Union. As the British Government made clear in its definite position: *"The Government do not accept any commitment to any sort of federal structure in Europe."*[27] It took the Benelux countries until 1991 before they realized it.

Convergence and monetary questions

New and fairer methods of financing the Community budget as the principal item on the British demand for re-negotiation, were discussed seriously but not agreed upon to the satisfaction of the United Kingdom. From the British point of view the principal problem resided in the financing of the Common Agricultural Policy (CAP). CAP was the largest single item on the Community budget from which the British share of expenditure would be low and to which its net contribution would as a consequence be excessive. The Regulation setting up the financial mechanism, adopted by the Council of Ministers in January 1976, did not satisfy the British, nor did the

---

[27] Document E.1.9.

compensations to the United Kingdom. In his comments on the conclusions of the European Council of Paris in March 1979,

> "Mr. Callaghan, the British Prime Minister emphasized the need for the countries of Europe to work together to tackle current problems, but he restated the United Kingdom position, which on various issues differs from that of the other Member States. In particular he criticized the common agricultural policy on account of its wastefulness. With regard to the EMS, Mr. Callaghan recognized the need for a convergence of economic policies, but insisted that Member States' net payments to the Community budget should reflect more faithfully the specific circumstances of each country."[28]

Two months later he lost the elections and was succeeded by Conservative Prime Minister Margaret Thatcher, who would turn the budget issue into the principal make-or-break one in the European Community. As a consequence, the next European Council meeting of Dublin in November 1979 devoted almost all its time to it but could go no further than a procedural agreement on the next step. For well over four years, no agreement could be reached on the issue, nor on any other major issue facing the Community, that is until the European Council of Fontainebleau in June 1984. The political compromise reached under French leadership merits to be quoted:

> "1. Budgetary imbalances
>
> 1. Expenditure policy is ultimately the essential means of resolving the question of budgetary imbalances.
> However, it has been decided that any Member State

---

[28] Document E.1.10.

sustaining a budgetary burden which is excessive in relation to its relative prosperity may benefit from a correction at the appropriate time. The basis for the correction is the gap between the share of VAT payments and the share of expenditure allocated in accordance with the present criteria.

2. As far as the United Kingdom is concerned, the following arrangement is adopted:
(i) for 1984, a lump sum of 1 000 million ECU is fixed;
(ii) from 1985 the gap (base of the correction) as defined in paragraph 1 is, for the period referred to in paragraph 4, corrected annually at 66%.

3. The corrections foreseen in paragraph 2 will be deducted from the United Kingdom's normal VAT share in the budget year following the one in respect of which the correction is granted. The resulting cost for the other Member States will be shared among them according to their normal VAT share, adjusted to allow the Federal Republic of Germany's share to move to two thirds of its VAT share.

4. The correction formula foreseen in paragraph 2 (second indent) will be a part of the decision to increase the VAT ceiling to 1.4%, their durations being linked.
One year before the new ceiling is reached, the Commission will present to the Council a report setting out the state of play on:
(i) the result of the budgetary discipline;
(ii) the Community's financial needs;
(iii) the breakdown of the budgetary costs among Member States, having regard to their relative prosperity, and the consequences to be drawn from this for the application of the budgetary corrections.

> The Council will re-examine the question as a whole and will take the appropriate decisions ex novo.
>
> 6. Own resources and enlargement
> The maximum rate of mobilization of VAT will be 1.4% on 1 January 1986; this maximum rate applies to every Member State and will enter into force as soon as the ratification procedures are completed, and by 1 January 1986 at the latest. The maximum rate may be increased to 1.6% on 1 January 1988 by unanimous decision of the Council and after agreement has been given in accordance with national procedures." [29]

The principal points of the agreement are given emphasis: The essential means to deal with budgetary imbalances are on the side of expenditure policy. In apportioning costs, the Community must have regard for the relative prosperity of member countries - two clear principles in theory but extremely difficult to implement by consensus among member government, agreeing in the floodlights of publicity. Still the Fontainebleau Council did unblock decision-making and opened the road to further agreement on the membership of Portugal and Spain, on institutional changes and on the completion of the internal market.

Institutional Changes

In conformity with the "spirit" of the Hague Summit of December 1969, institutional changes during the period 1969-1986 moved along two tracks. *Along the first,* the Community track, efforts were made to further develop the supranational method of common action. *Along the second,* the intergovernmental cooperation track, the emphasis was on strengthening "Europe's identity"

---

[29] Document EC. 29

through political cooperation. President de Gaulle's Gaullist successors took a more realistic approach than their former leader by accepting to move along the two tracks concurrently rather than demanding reform along the second track only.

Along the first track, supported by the French to be assured of common financing of the CAP, progress had already been made in 1965 with the signing of the Merger Treaty. On 21 April 1970, the Council decided that: "The Communities shall be allocated resources of their own in accordance with the following Articles in order to ensure that their budget is in balance." The revenues were to come from the agricultural levies, from custom duties and from Member States in so far as necessary to balance the budget until the end of 1974. From 1975 onwards national contributions are to be replaced by "those accruing from the value added tax and obtained by applying a rate not exceeding 1 % to an assessment basis which is determined in a uniform manner for Member States according to Community rules." The next day the Council signed the "Treaty amending certain budgetary provisions of the Treaties establishing the European Communities and of the Treaty establishing a Single Council and a Single Commission of the European Communities." Following the entry into force of the agreements with respect to the Communities own resources, the Treaty of Luxemburg was revised by Treaty of 22 July 1975. The amended Treaty provided for an increase in the budgetary powers of the European Parliament and for the creation of a Court of Auditors. On 20 September 1976 the nine member governments adopted The Act of the Council of the Communities laying down procedures for direct elections to the European Parliament by universal suffrage. The first rounds of elections took place in June 1979 and 1984; uniform electoral procedures throughout the community/union are still to be agreed upon.[30]

---

30 EU. 7. and EU. 7A, Act Direct Elections.

Along the second track, the foreign ministers on 27 October 1970 adopted the Davignon Report stating:

> "The Ministers therefore felt that foreign policy concertation should be the object of the first practical endeavours to demonstrate to all that Europe has a political vocation. The Ministers are, in fact, convinced that progress here would be calculated to promote the development of the Communities and give Europeans a keener awareness of their common responsibility."[31]

To make progress towards political unification the governments decided to cooperate in foreign policy through regular meetings of their foreign ministers to be prepared by a political committee. Such political cooperation is to assert Europe's own identity as was stated in the "Document on The European Identity published by the Nine Foreign Ministers on 14 December 1973", in Copenhagen. According to this document, it was the objective to transform "the whole complex of their relations into a European Union before the end of the decade." The linkage between political cooperation and the European Identity was a product of the French drive, then supported by Britain's Prime Minister Edward Heath to clearly distinguish Europe from the United States of America and European political cooperation from NATO political consultation. It was an irony of history that the meeting of December 1973 in Copenhagen was visited uninvited by a delegation of Arab Foreign Ministers.[32] A further important step on the second track was set by the Summit of December 1974 in Paris in its decision to transform their meetings into regular (European) Council meetings:

---

31 See Chapter 5 below and Document E.5. 6.

32 Council Document (1973) EC/ES. 4.

> "3. The Heads of Government have therefore decided to meet, accompanied by the Ministers of Foreign Affairs, three times a year and, whenever necessary, in the Council of the Communities and in the context of political co-operation."

The Paris Summit inaugurated the institution of a European Council of Heads of State and governments, which henceforward would evolve into the supreme guiding body of the European Communities. The conclusions of its sessions three or four times a year offer an interesting documentary history of the European Community/Union since 1974. With the British challenge, the energy crisis and serious economic difficulties, the Council conclusions were meager except for their long statements on foreign policy issues. As Belgian Prime Minister Leo Tindemans wrote in his report to the Council:

> "Why has the European concept lost a lot of its force and initial impetus? I believe that over the years the European public has lost a guiding light, namely the political consensus between our countries on our reasons for undertaking this joint task and the characteristics with which we wish to endow it. We must first of all restore this common vision if we wish to have European Union."[33]

The report gave an interesting analysis but was hardly discussed in the Council. In the post-(British) renegotiation period there was no room for a common vision. With the British as the "odd-man-in", political leadership was exercised by the French-German duo of Giscard d'Estaing and Helmut Schmidt. Their principal contribution was the 1978 agreement on a European Monetary System (EMS). It was all that was left from the ambition to create

---

[33] Report makes interesting reading but disappeared in the archives. Document E.1.11.

Economic Monetary Union before the end of the decade - that was a decade of serious economic recession.

It was not until the early 1980s that the circumstances became more favorable for making some progress in institutional reforms. In November 1981 German Foreign Minister Genscher together with his Italian counterpart tabled a draft-treaty on European Union. Through a report of the Community Foreign Ministers, it ended up as the Stuttgart Summit "Solemn Declaration on European Union" of 1983.[34] In the meantime the new and directly elected European Parliament was drawing up a draft Treaty establishing the European Union on the initiative of Altiero Spinelli, Italian European of the first hour. Parliament adopted the draft on 14 February 1984, with the specific intention to have it approved by all (the nine) national parliaments. None of them did or even debated the draft. The draft, nevertheless inspired the European Council members to take action. The same European Council meeting (Fontainebleau) that finally solved the British budget issue, also decided to create an ad hoc committee of personal representatives of the Heads of State and Government to examine these institutional questions. The Dooge Committee - so called after its Irish chairman - made it clear that:

> "(it) is not enough to draw up a simple catalogue of measures to be taken - even if they are precise and concrete - since such exercises have often been attempted in the past without achieving results. We must now make a qualitative leap and present the various proposals in a global manner, thus demonstrating the common political will of the Member States. At the end of the day that will must be expressed by the formulation

[34] Document EC.26.

> of a genuine political entity among European States: i.e. a European Union:
>
> - with the power to take decisions in the name of all citizens, by a democratic process according to their common interest in political and social development, economic progress and security, and according to procedures which could vary depending on whether the framework is that of intergovernmental cooperation, the Community Treaties, or new instruments yet to be agreed;
>
> - in keeping with the personality of each of the constituent States."

The Committee clearly listed the economic policy priorities for the next decade and concluded with the proposal:

> "that a conference of the representatives of the governments of the Member States should be convened in the near future to negotiate a draft European Union Treaty based on the *acquis communautaire*, the present document and the Stuttgart Solemn Declaration on European Union and guided by the spirit and method of the draft Treaty voted by the European Parliament:
>
> - the parties to the conference will be the Member States;
>
> - Spain and Portugal will be invited to attend as full members on the assumption that the Treaties of accession have been signed prior to the opening of the conference;
>
> - the European Commission will participate in the negotiations;

- the European Parliament will be closely associated with the conference. Its outcome will be submitted to the European Parliament.

The very decision of the Heads of State or Government to convene such a conference would have great symbolic value and would represent the initial act of European Union."[35]

The Committee submitted its report to the Council on 30 March 1985.

Shortly thereafter on 14 June, the new European Commission headed by Jacques Delors submitted its White Paper on "Completing the Internal Market." According to its opening paragraphs:

"Unifying this market (of 320 million) presupposes that Member States will agree on the abolition of barriers of all kinds, harmonization of rules, approximation of legislation and tax structures, strengthening of monetary cooperation and the necessary flanking measures to encourage European firms to work together. It is a goal that is well within our reach provided we draw the lessons from the setbacks and delays of the past. The Commission will be asking the European Council to pledge itself to completion of a fully unified internal market by 1992 and to approve the necessary program together with a realistic and binding timetable."

2. In such terms did the Commission define its task in the "Programme of the Commission for 1985" which was presented to the European Parliament on 6 March.

---

[35] Dooge Report Document E.1.12.

> On 29 and 30 March, the European Council in Brussels broadly endorsed this view and "laid particular emphasis on ... action to achieve a single market by 1992 thereby creating a more favorable environment for stimulating enterprise, competition and trade; it called upon the Commission to draw up a detailed programme with a specific timetable before its next meeting".[36]

The White Paper was based on the program of the new Delors Commission and already endorsed by the European Council. Its principal objective was to complete the internal market within an agreed period of time by the removal of physical, technical and fiscal barriers to trade within the common market.

> "Delors entered office when eurosclerosis was at its height. The slow pace of enlargement, lack of democracy and economic problems caused that negative and apathetic attitudes to the Community were high. The preceding Thorn Commission was unable to exercise its authority to any meaningful extent in the face of the British vetoes on EU projects to force a more favourable agreement for it on the Community budget. Delors had previously been one of the architects of the agreement at Fontainebleau, which secured the UK rebate, and Delors intended that the settling of the budget issue should herald a new era of European integration".[37]

---

36 Document E.1.13. Commission's White Paper.

37 Dirk-Jan Eppink, *Life of a European Mandarin*: Inside the Commission, 2007.

In its meeting at Milan on 28 and 29 June 1985, the European Council agreed to convene an Inter Governmental Conference to draft a new treaty as proposed by the Dooge Committee. It was the unique combination of a new European German Chancellor in the person of the Christian Democrat Helmut Kohl, a new active European Commission and the transformation of François Mitterand to a European French President that enabled rapid progress towards agreement on the Single European Act of February 1986.

The Single European Act (SEA)

The entry into force of the Single European Act on 1 January 1987 paved the way to merging the European Communities and European Political Cooperation into the European Union.

The most important objective (article 8A) was to progressively complete the internal market over a period expiring on 31 December 1992. The Act extended the Communities' responsibilities to promoting economic and social cohesion, research and technological development and environmental policy cooperation. It contained additional articles on cooperation in economic and monetary policy and with respect to social policy. A special Title III of the Act dealt with cooperation in the sphere of foreign policy - without however adding new competences to the institutions.

The Act formalized the position of the European Council in article 2. It provided for increasing the number of cases in which the Council of Ministers can take decisions by qualified majority voting instead of unanimity. The Act enhanced the powers of the European Parliament with respect to association agreements and proposed legislation; it clarified and strengthened the powers of the Commission in the implementation of rules laid down by the Council.[38]

In reality the SEA marked some progress in an era characterized by grand declarations and modest achieve-ments. Instead of the Economic and Monetary Union - that should have been achieved before the end of the 1970's - there was the EMS. Despite the resounding declaration on democracy of 1978[39] - meant as a lesson to the three new South European Member States - democracy in the European Community had made modest gains, far short of solving the 'democratic deficit'. The free movement of persons was the subject of a special agreement - the Schengen agreement - as the United Kingdom and Ireland were not prepared as yet to abolish border controls. The SEA itself was not the European Union Treaty envisaged by the European Parliament, but, at best, a modest step towards that goal. The SEA paved the road to Maastricht, not so much by its institutional provisions as by the agreement to complete the internal market before the end of 1992, employing the well-known method of a system in permanent crisis.

TOWARDS EUROPEAN UNION (1987-1994)

"Conscious of the fact that Europe can be built only by concrete actions which create a real solidarity and by the establishment of common bases for economic development".

I am quoting this paragraph from the Preamble to the Treaty instituting the European Coal and Steel Community (ECSC) to re-emphasise the original assumptions and objectives of European Unification. Real solidarity within the limited scope of heavy industry and organised by common institutions under

---

[38] Text in Document. EU. 8 Single European Act.

[39] Text in Document EC. 32.

common rules was assumed to generate a threefold dynamics of unification:

- it would *widen* the scope of real solidarity to economic policies at large (and eventually to defence and foreign affairs);

- it would *deepen* solidarity through the transfer of real legislative, executive and judicial powers to common institutions;

- it would *enlarge* membership of the community, as other European states wanted to join.

These threefold dynamics were to prepare "Europe" for achieving the objective of federal unity. As we saw already, the objective was challenged by Charles de Gaulle in the 1960s. Contrary to the expectation of many, it ceased to be a realistic objective after the first enlargement in 1973. In a way the Single European Act definitely shelved the objective, when the intergovernmental European Council was legalised in article 2 of the Act. Wherever the scope of real solidarity was widened, it was through intergovernmental cooperation primarily. Deepening solidarity resulted from the dynamics of European economic integration and a number of landmark rulings delivered by the European Court of Justice. What brought Member States to the Maastricht Treaty on European Union (and beyond) was the process of completing the internal market within an agreed period of time. The Maastricht European Council primarily focused on further deepening solidarity and maintaining the economic dynamics of the integration process. Driven by the proposals of the European Commission, the emphasis was on completing the internal market, promoting the free movement of persons and transforming the internal market into a monetary and economic union. For each, deadlines had been or were agreed upon. The Hanover European Council in June 1988 entrusted a committee headed by Jacques Delors to propose concrete stages leading to Economic and Monetary Union. The Delors plan was endorsed in June. In the Strasbourg European Council (December 1989) it was decided to call an Intergovernmental Conference (IGC) to prepare a treaty on the Economic and Monetary Union (EMU). A year later, with much less agreement and preparation, the Rome European Council (October and December 1990) added the IGC on European Political Union.

Bypassed by the Spirit of 1989

The principal problem the 12 member states were facing, however, was that the external dynamics of the collapse of Europe's East-West division bypassed the internal dynamics of economic integration. By the time the heads of state and government of the European Communities assembled in Maastricht, Michael Gorbachev had resigned and the Soviet Union had disintegrated. The Central and East European states were free and wanted to join the West and Europe as soon as possible. Germany had celebrated its peaceful re-unification, despite French and British resistance. Yugoslavia was descending into civil war, finding European unity wanting at its finest moment.

All of this had caught EC's political leaders with complete surprise. The same Hanover European Council in June 1988 had this to say on the joint EC- COMECON Declaration issued a few days before:

> "The European Council welcomes the more outward-looking attitude now being shown by Eastern European countries in their economic contacts with the West,

> as witnessed by the establishment and development of relations with the Community. This should be encouraged as contributing to the wider opening up of their economies and societies. The East-West Economic Conference proposed by the Twelve at the Vienna CSCE follow-up meeting will also serve that purpose."

When the events of 1989 unfolded in the East, the strengthening of economic integration and political cooperation in the West became priority targets. In January Commission President Delors proposed a more structured relationship with the EFTA countries. It resulted in the agreement on a European Economic Area, signed on 2 May 1992 and entered into force on 1 January 1994. The agreement was meant to preclude further enlargement of the European Community before the imminent completion of EMU and European Union. Still, most EFTA member countries applied for Community membership well before EEA entered into force. At the time, the East and Central European countries were looked at primarily as objects for aid and association. Still, the IGC's and the Council in Maastricht had to deal with a re-united Germany as full member of the European Community; something that neither pleased the French nor the British leaders. Margaret Thatcher fell back on the idea of a large European free trade area. François Mitterrand briefly favoured a loose-knit European Confederation with the East and Central Europeans. At the same time he pushed for full Economic and Monetary Union with one common currency to contain the power of the Mark of united Germany. In April 1991 Luxembourg (than in the chair of the Council) submitted a draft treaty, based apparently on broad consensus. Nevertheless, Commission President Jacques Delors spoke out against the Luxembourg draft. In his opinion a federal Europe could be realised only on the basis of the Communities and not on reserving policy areas like foreign policy and justice for intergovernmental cooperation.

His remarks encouraged the Dutch government (taking over the Chair of the Council on 1 July 1991) to present its own draft-treaty for European Political Union in September 1991. According to the draft, foreign policy, justice and home affairs were to be included in the Community treaties; the powers of the Commission, European Parliament and European Court of Justice were to be strengthened accordingly. To their surprise and dismay, there was no support whatsoever during the 30 September informal meeting of the Ministers for Foreign Affairs. Even German Foreign Minister Genscher rejected it out of hand. It was a black Monday for the Dutch Government. In their preparation for the European Council session in December in Maaastricht, they fell back on the original Luxembourg draft-treaty for EPU. On the 10 December 1991, the European Council reached agreement on the Treaty on European Union to be formally signed by their foreign ministers on 7 February 1992. So began the somewhat rough and long ride to the entry into force of the European Union Treaty on 1 November 1993.[40]

A Treaty on European Union Finally

The road to European Union had been a long one; from the original French proposals in 1961, through the 1969 Hague Summit and the 1986 Single European Act to the Treaty of Maastricht. Nevertheless it was an unfinished Union as is recognised in the very first article of the Treaty:

> "Article A
>
> By this Treaty, the High Contracting Parties establish among themselves a European Union, hereinafter called 'the Union'.

---

40 Text in document EU. 9.

> *This Treaty marks a new stage in the process of creating an ever closer union among the peoples of Europe, in which decisions are taken as closely as possible to the citizen.*
>
> The Union shall be founded on the European Communities, supplemented by the policies and forms of cooperation established by this Treaty. Its task shall be to organize, in a manner demonstrating consistency and solidarity, relations between the Member States and between their peoples."

As is italicized, the Treaty marks a new stage in the process; several important institutional issues were still left open. The last paragraph together with article B already indicate the provisional structure of the Union as a roof over three pillars: the solid and strengthened pillar of the European Community; the shaky and unfinished pillar of a common foreign and security policy, and the new pillar under construction on justice and home affairs.

The first objective in article B includes the important strengthening of the European Community by the provisions (Title II, chapters 2-4, articles 105-109m) for achieving monetary union and one European currency in three stages.

> "Article B
>
> The Union shall set itself the following objectives:
> - to promote economic and social progress which is balanced and sustainable, in particular through the creation of an area without internal frontiers, through the strengthening of economic and social cohesion and through *the establishment of economic and monetary union*, ultimately including a single currency

in accordance with the provisions of this Treaty;

- to assert its identity on the international scene, in particular through the implementation of a common foreign and security policy including the eventual framing of a common defense policy, which might in time lead to a common defense;

- to strengthen the protection of the rights and interests of the nationals of its Member States through the introduction of a citizenship of the Union;

- to develop close cooperation on justice and home affairs;

- to maintain in full the *acquis communautaire* and build on it with a view to considering, through the procedure referred to in Article N(2), to what extent the policies and forms of cooperation introduced by this Treaty may need to be revised with the aim of ensuring the effectiveness of the mechanisms and the institutions of the Community.

The objectives of the Union shall be achieved as provided in this Treaty and in accordance with the conditions and the timetable set out therein while respecting the principle of subsidiarity as defined in Article 3b of the Treaty establishing the European Community."

New in the Treaty is the introduction of the principle of subsidiarity, a principle originally developed in the Encyclical *Quadragesimo Anno* of Pope Pius XI of 15 May 1931. As so often in *Eurospeak*, subsidiarity has been given a new meaning. In the Encyclical the principle was meant to protect intermediate societal organizations like trade unions against an overpowering (socialist) state. In *Eurospeak* its is meant to protect Member States against an over intrusive European Community (compare Title II, article 3b. of the Treaty.) The following three articles deal with the intended single institutional framework for the new Union:

> "Article C
>
> The Union shall be served by a single institutional framework which shall ensure the consistency and the continuity of the activities carried out in order to attain its objectives while respecting and building upon the 'acquis communautaire'.
>
> The Union shall in particular ensure the consistency of its external activities as a whole in the context of its external relations, security, economic and development policies. The Council and the Commission shall be responsible for ensuring such consistency. They shall ensure the implementation of these policies, each in accordance with its respective powers.
>
> Article D
>
> The European Council shall provide the Union with the necessary impetus for its development and shall define the general political guidelines thereof.
>
> The European Council shall bring together the Heads of State or of Government of the Member States and the President of the Commission. They shall be assisted by the Ministers for Foreign Affairs of the Member States and by a Member of the Commission. The European Council shall meet at least twice a year, under the chairmanship

of the Head of State or of Government of the Member State which holds the Presidency of the Council.

The European Council shall submit to the European Parliament a report after each of its meetings and a yearly written report on the progress achieved by the Union.

Article E

The European Parliament, the Council, the Commission and the Court of Justice shall exercise their powers under the conditions and for the purposes provided for, on the one hand, by the provisions of the Treaties establishing the European Communities and of the subsequent Treaties and Acts modifying and supplementing them and, on the other hand, by the other provisions of this Treaty."

In fact the single institutional framework - the roof - contains no more than the European Council in article D. The European Council, however, still maintains its character as originally envisaged by former French President Charles de Gaulle: a collective European Emperor, giving impetus and guidelines to their subjects, rather than having legal powers of its own (as a Council of Ministers in the composition of prime-ministers) placed under political and legal supervision by the European Parliament and the European Court of Justice. The European Council has not (yet) reached the status of an institution of the Union. Apart from article D, the European Council is referred to in Title II, article 103 and in Title V, articles J.3 and J.8. The European Council as the supreme body of the Union is to define the principles of and general guidelines for the common foreign and security policy and "shall discuss a conclusion on the broad guidelines of the economic policies of the Member States and of the Community."(art. 103.2).

The European Council, as befits an Emperor, issues mandatory conclusion, but stands itself above the law.

After the Dutch black Monday and the agreement on this Treaty on European Union, it should be clear that the process of creating an ever closer union is meant to be an ongoing process without a federal Europe as its final destination, underlined once more in the first paragraph of article F:

> "Article F
>
> 1. The Union shall respect the national identities of its Member States, whose systems of government are founded on the principles of democracy.
>
> 2. The Union shall respect fundamental rights, as guaranteed by the European Convention for the Protection of Human Rights and Fundamental Freedoms signed in Rome on 4 November 1950 and as they result from the constitutional traditions common to the Member States, as general principles of Community law.
>
> 3. The Union shall provide itself with the means necessary to attain its objectives and carry through its policies."

Respect for the national identities includes acceptance of 'variable geometry' within the Union. The right to opt out of e.g. common social policy, participation in the monetary union, "Schengen" (cases of Britain and Denmark), and of foreign policy and defense cooperation, has become one of the trademarks of European Union. Such rights can no longer be seen as examples of members moving at variable speeds towards the same goal. Variable geometry indicates the possibility for members to stay on board without moving in the same direction as others. It is one of the lasting outcomes of the British challenge since that country entered in 1973.

Finally the Treaty introduces the concept of a "citizenship of the Union" - in addition to but not instead of national citizenship - and its mission to respect fundamental human rights as guaranteed by the European Convention of November 1950. For both it concerns long standing intentions still to be realized.

The long road to entry into force

The ratification process in the 12 member-states took much longer than envisaged. In France and Denmark, the treaty required approval by popular referendum. In Germany the Treaty was subjected to constitutional review by the German Constitutional Court. The Danish voters rejected the Treaty on 2 June 1992 (50.7% No, 49.3% Yes). French voters accepted the Treaty on 20 September 1992 with a tiny majority (51.05% Yes, 48.95% No). The Danes had to go to the polls a second time on 18 May 1993 and accepted the slightly adapted question with a safe majority (56.7% Yes, 43.3% No). Germany could only deposit its instruments of ratification after the German Constitutional Court had pronounced itself on the Treaty in a ruling of 12 October 1993.[41] The Treaty finally entered into force on 1 November 1993.

In its ruling the German Constitutional Court defended the compatibility of the Treaty with the German Constitution by explaining that the Treaty institutes a *Staatenverbund* or confederation. The Treaty is an instrument of international

---

41 The verdict can be found in document E.1.14.

law and not the constitution of a *Bundesstaat* or federation.[42] According to the Ruling of the Court, the member states continue to be the "masters" of the treaty. Validity and implementation of European law in the German legal order depend on the provision of the law by which parliament approved the Treaty and are subject to the Court's power of review - a conditional acceptance of the primacy of European law at variance, possibly, with the case law of the European Court of Justice. The Ruling of the German Constitutional Court confirms the extent to which Germany is approaching the French and British views on the nature of the European Union.

The complaints that brought the German Constitutional Court to its Ruling reflected a much broader critical attitude to the European Union among the European citizens. The nice promise

---

42 "Der Vertrag begründet einen europäischen Staatenverbund, der von den Mitgliedstaaten getragen wird und deren nationale Identität achtet; er betrifft die Mitgliedschaft Deutschlands in supranationalen Organisationen, nicht eine Zugehörigkeit zu einem europäischen Staat (II.1). Die Aufgaben der Europäischen Union und die zu ihrer Wahrnehmung eingeräumten Befugnisse werden dadurch in einer hinreichend voraussehbaren Weise normiert, daß das Prinzip der begrenzten Einzelermächtigung eingehalten, keine Kompetenz- Kompetenz für die Europäische Union begründet und die Inanspruchnahme weiterer Aufgaben und Befugnisse durch Europäische Union und Europäische Gemeinschaften von Vertragsergänzungen und Vertragsänderungen abhängig gemacht, mithin der zustimmenden Entscheidung der nationalen Parlamente vorbehalten wird (II.2). Durch den Umfang der eingeräumten Aufgaben und Befugnisse und die im Vertrag geregelte Form der Willensbildung in der Europäischen Union und den Organen der Europäischen Gemeinschaften werden die Entscheidungs- und Kontrollzuständigkeiten des Deutschen Bundestages noch nicht in einer Weise entleert, die das Demokratieprinzip, soweit es Art. 79 Abs. 3 GG für unantastbar erklärt, verletzt (II.3.). "Bundesverfassungsgericht. Urteil verkundet am 12 Oktober 1993. DFR - BVerfGE 89, 155 - Maastricht.

to introduce a citizenship of the Union could not disguise the fact that European decision-making is clouded in mystery and far removed from the people. For them it was difficult to understand the relevance of 'Maastricht' for dealing with their problems of high unemployment and negative economic growth.

In addition, the concerns of the leaders in Maastricht seemed non responsive to the problems of the new post-1989 era. At least until 1993, admission of the former communist European countries was not on the agenda of either the European Community or NATO.[43] The twelve performed dismally and disunited in the Yugoslav civil war, despite the pretences of some that this crisis in Europe's backyard ought to be handled by the Europeans. Effective peace-making had to wait for America's active involvement in 1995. The long awaited free movement of persons within the Community could be solved only partially through the Schengen implementation agreement. Uncertainty about the feasibility of the EMU - the cornerstone of the Treaty on European Union - led to speculation against certain currencies in the Exchange Rate Mechanism. It resulted in the devaluations of the Italian Lira, the British Pound, the Spanish Peseta, the Portuguese escudo and the Irish Pound. The most serious blow to the ERM came when German-French disagreement on interest rates resulted in broadening the fluctuation margin to around 15%.

In 1993 both the United States and the Europeans realised that thoughts about a new architecture for a new era based on OSCE were leading nowhere. As Washington shifted to a new strategy of democratic enlargement, the European Council of Copenhagen in June 1993 took its first step in the direction of enlargement with the formulation of certain principles to be

---

43 Compare my *Western Cooperation,* Part II., Chapter 4.

observed in opening accession to the associated countries of East and Central Europe.[44]

Shortly after the entry into force of the Treaty on European Union, the agreement on the EEA entered into force on 1 January 1994 but for a short time only. Austria, Finland and Sweden entered on 1 January 1995. The road to further enlargement was now open.

FROM EUROPEAN UNION TO THE TREATY OF LISBON (1995-2009)

The latest period we are now entering in this survey begins with the European Union of the fifteen and is characterised by two major developments (1) the efforts to complete the Union and provide it with a solid constitutional foundation; and (2) the efforts to cope with a process of continuous enlargement. This final paragraph deals with the first; the second will be dealt with in the next chapter.

European Union: forever under construction?

The Maastricht Treaty on European Union clarified the new dynamics of the integration process since the Single European Act. The long road to its entry into force reflected a new public awareness of these dynamics, translating itself in growing opposition to its lack of transparency and democracy.

Among them was, *first* of all, the "ever widening scope of the legislative and policy agenda of the Community".[45] The widening scope was partly a consequence of the new

---

[44] Document EC.54.

[45] J.H.H. Weiler, *The Constitution of Europe,* Part I, Chapter 2, p. 65, Cambridge University Press 2004.

policy areas added in the SEA. The new policy areas blurred the distinctions between common policies as community policies or as coordinated national policies. It was even more the outcome of the gradual completion of the internal market. The European and national officials favoured an ever widening scope for common policies and the harmonisation of national legislations as presumably required for the sake of the free movement of persons, products and services within the internal market.

Among them was, *secondly*, the pressure from (and the fear for) the liberated countries from East and Central Europe for entry into the European Union.

Among them, *finally*, were the institutional dynamics created by the rising importance of the European Council together with the (unforeseen) effects of article 100A in the SEA. As Weiler made clear, article 100A had the opposite impact on decision-making in the Council than the 1966 Luxembourg compromise: "reaching consensus under the shadow of the vote is altogether different from reaching it under the shadow of the veto. The possibility of breaking deadlocks by voting drives the negotiators to break the deadlock without actually resorting to the vote."[46] In the shadow of the vote, agreement is reached more quickly and the role of the Commission is strengthened.

The European Union was still an edifice under construction. Further progress in construction had to be made before negotiations on enlargement to the East could begin. As can be read in the conclusions from the European Council meetings in Essen, Madrid and Turin, the opening of accession negotiations had to await agreement on an additional treaty.

---

46 *Op. cit.* p. 72.

Let us briefly look at the relevant conclusions:

> "*Essen December1994*
> The European Council has decided to boost and improve the process of further preparing the associated States of Central and Eastern Europe for accession. It is doing so in the knowledge that the institutional conditions for ensuring the proper functioning of the Union must be created at the 1996 Intergovernmental Conference, which for that reason must take place before accession negotiations begin.
>
> *Madrid December1995*
> Following the conclusion of the Intergovernmental Conference and in the light of its outcome and of all the opinions and reports from the Commission referred to above, the Council will, at the earliest opportunity, take the necessary decisions for launching the accession negotiations.
>
> *Turin March 1996*
> Moreover, future enlargement, which represents a historic mission and a great opportunity for Europe, is also a challenge for the Union in all its dimensions. In this perspective, institutions, as well as their functioning, and procedures have to be improved in order to preserve its capacity for action, while maintaining the *acquis communautaire* and developing it and also respecting the balance between the institutions. It is essential to sustain the very nature of European construction, which has to preserve and develop its features of democracy, efficiency, solidarity, cohesion, transparency and subsidiarity."

The applications of ten East and Central European states in the years 1994-1996, presented very different problems than the British application in 1961 and the Greek, Spanish and Portuguese applications in 1975 and 1977. In the perception of their new leaders, there was no alternative to joining the Western organizations as soon as possible. In their newly won independence from Soviet domination, membership of Western organizations was considered to be their best guarantee against a resurgent Russia. They hoped for Western responses comparable to the American Marshall-Plan in 1947.

Their applications put the European leaders in a quandary. By the very nature of the European Unification process (reaffirmed by article O of the TEU), they were obliged to open the door to their membership. Surprised as they had been by the events of 1989, they were not ready to deal with the applications for at least two reasons:

(1) all attention was focused on completing the Union, in particular the EMU and the preparations for the common currency; and

(2) conceptually, they continued to think of Europe in post cold war terms, that is how the "West" could help the "East" in Europe. When Washington changed from its "new architecture for a new era" to a strategy of democratic enlargement, the EU joined in with the Copenhagen Declaration of June 1993.

For the East and Central European leaders, the declaration was most disappointing. Instead of offering what they needed, the declaration erected the virtually insurmountable fence of full democracy, market-economy and the so called *acquis communautaire* as criteria for admission. It was not until the Revision Treaty of Amsterdam was signed on 2 October 1997, that enlargement negotiations became acceptable; the enlargement process was launched in 1999, ten years after the end to Europe's division. In reality it still had to wait for a compromise on the two most controversial issues left unresolved, namely the size of the European Commission and majority voting in the Council of Ministers. Those issues were dealt with in the Treaty of Nice, signed on 26 February 2001 and entered into force on 1 February 2003. Nice did not solve these issues satisfactorily and it was left to the Convention created by the Laeken Declaration to come up with a way out. The amendments made in the treaties of Amsterdam and Nice did at least give the impression that the fences against further enlargement were made higher rather than lower. Among them I consider first of all the addition of article F.1 in the Treaty of Amsterdam:

"Article F.1

1. The Council, meeting in the composition of the Heads of State or government and acting by unanimity on a proposal by one third of the Member States or by the Commission and after obtaining the assent of the European Parliament, may determine the existence of a serious and persistent breach by a Member State of principles mentioned in Article F(1), after inviting the government of the Member State in question to submit its observations.

2. Where such a determination has been made, the Council, acting by a qualified majority, may decide to suspend certain of the rights deriving from the application of this Treaty to the Member State in question, including the voting rights of the representative of the government of that Member State in the Council. In doing so, the Council shall take into account the possible consequences of such a suspension on the rights and obligations of natural and legal persons.
The obligations of the Member State in question under

this Treaty shall in any case continue to be binding on that State.

3. The Council, acting by a qualified majority, may decide subsequently to vary or revoke measures taken under paragraph 2 in response to changes in the situation which led to their being imposed.

4. For the purposes of this Article, the Council shall act without taking into account the by vote of the representative of the government of the Member State in question. Abstentions members present in person or represented shall not prevent the adoption of decisions referred to in paragraph 1. A qualified majority shall be defined as the same proportion of the weighted votes of the members of the Council concerned as laid down in Article 148(2) of the Treaty establishing the European Community. This paragraph shall also apply in the event of voting rights being suspended pursuant to paragraph 2.

5. For the purposes of this Article, the European Parliament shall act by a two thirds majority of the votes cast, representing a majority of its members."

This highly dubious extra-legal procedure reappears as article 7 in the Treaty of Lisbon, despite its problematic application once against Austria. It is in a way typical for the European Union, where the European Council, itself above the law, is gradually moved to centre stage. There should be no place for a political suspension of rights procedure in a Union pretending to be based on the rule of law and equipped with a European Court of Justice and a Charter of Fundamental Rights.

Other examples are the amendments with respect to asylum, the community charter of the fundamental social rights of workers and the amendments with respect to police and judicial cooperation in criminal matters.

The most important example of erecting higher fences were the decisions to prepare a Constitution for Europe and a Charter of Fundamental Human Rights of the European Union. The latter - meant to become part of a Constitution - was taken first in 1999. It resulted in a text drafted by a special body later called Convention, solemnly adopted by the European Council in 2001. The former, taken at the European Council at Laeken, Brussels in December 2001, resulted in a draft-constitution adopted by a special convention on 18 July 2003, and finalised by the Intergovernmental Conference on 29 October 2004. The Laeken Declaration listed a number of questions to be discussed in a special convention:

> "In order to pave the way for the next Intergovernmental Conference as broadly and openly as possible, the European Council has decided to convene a Convention composed of the main parties involved in the debate on the future of the Union. In the light of the foregoing, it will be the task of that Convention to consider the key issues arising for the Union's future development and try to identify the various possible responses."[47]

Eurospeak in the European Union

It is typical for *Eurospeak* in the post-1989 era, that key terms no longer mean what the knowledgeable reader would think they do. The term Convention was chosen to evoke the memory of the Philadelphia Convention that drafted the American Constitution. The body created by Laeken, however, was

---

47 See Document EC.89.

no Convention, neither by its composition, nor by its tasks. It finally did more than asked for. Under Giscard d'Estaing's authoritarian leadership, the so called Convention produced a five hundred page book and called it a Constitution for Europe. The text was adopted by consensus. That is to say, the Convention did not vote article by article of the draft as it ought to have done if it had acted as a constitutional convention. Adopting by consensus is *Eurospeak* for so much disagreement that delegates agree not to vote before going home! After the closure of the Convention, the IGC turned the draft into a constitutional treaty.

It was left to each Member States to choose its own method of approval of the Constitution. The majority opted for no more than parliamentary approval. Luxembourg, the Netherlands, Spain and Britain opted for a consultative referendum. Denmark, France, Ireland, Poland, Portugal and (maybe) the Czech Republic opted for a binding referendum. The parliaments dutifully adopted the Constitution. A clear majority in France and the Netherlands rejected the Constitution in a referendum in May and June 2005. Most likely, most parliamentarians and citizens and maybe some members of the Convention never read the full text. The French majority voted primarily against their president Jacques Chirac. The Dutch majority against the Constitution reflected anger and resistance against the procedures used. The Convention had not been a true convention. The Constitution was no Constitution at all. The referendum was just consultative. The government that had signed the Constitution first refused to defend it and at the last moment warned for a third world war if the Dutch would reject it!

The Caravan moves on nevertheless

The European politicians, however, had learned how to deal

with popular disagreement. In countries like Denmark and Ireland, people just need to vote again after having rejected a treaty in the first round. In the case of France and the Netherlands (and other countries where a referendum might have had the same results), a different method was required. Our European mandarins thus assembled again and gave the Constitution, with a few changes, the customary name again of an interstate treaty that for its ratification would only need parliamentary approval. On 13 December 2007 the Treaty of Lisbon was born and duly entered into force on 1 December 2009, of course after two referenda in Ireland. In France, the Netherlands, Britain, Denmark and other countries the citizens were told that the new Treaty bore no resemblance to a constitution and could be approved by parliament without further ado.

The Treaty of Lisbon, for the time being, completed the long process of transforming the three communities into one cohesive Union. Major issues such as enlargement, the ever growing needs of the common market, institutional reforms, foreign and security policies and human rights will be dealt with in the following chapters. The Treaty is a typical example of constructing Europe by political compromise in a body like the European Council. It is filled with non-binding intentions and surrounded with many protocols and declarations qualifying or postponing implementation of its provisions.

Where no agreement could be reached, new institutional arrangements were simply added to the existing ones. The Treaty of Lisbon gave birth to four presidencies: the Presidency of the European Council (*new*), the rotating Presidency of the Council of Ministers (*remaining*), the Presidency of the European Commission (*remaining*) and the presidency of the Council of Ministers for political affairs (who is vice-president of the Commission and high representative for foreign and security policy, *new*).

The serious problem laid bare by the process has two related aspects. The *one* is the growing gap between declared principles, values and policies, and actual progress towards a united Europe. The endless stream of resounding declarations is at variance with the increasing emphasis on national interests in actual negotiations. The *other*, related aspect is the growing gap between the European mandarins (community and national officials) - and the citizens of European Union member countries. Given the dynamics of economic and monetary integration, the scope of community legislation and policy continued to widen, while the declarations emphasized subsidiarity. Enlargement since the end of the twentieth century continues despite the fences erected in 1993; often by not applying the very principles of 1993. Deepening integration was repeatedly proclaimed. Opaque negotiation processes produced just a little bit more of the same.

The most important lesson to be drawn is that a Union directed by a collective Emperor in the garments of the European Council is undermining rather than solidifying the process begun with the Schuman Declaration in 1950. The European Union is in serious trouble, not only due to globalization and the world economic crisis. In the glare of television camera's the appearance of compromise too easily conceals lack of true progress.

The very Christian foundation on which Schuman, Monnet and Beyen and Spaak intended to rebuild Europe after the Second World War, may well crumble under the weight of political compromises and economic rules of the European Union of the Treaty of Lisbon.

CHAPTER 2

TWO —> MANY? THE ENLARGEMENTS OF THE EUROPEAN COMMUNITY/ UNION

COUNTRIES	Date of Request	Opening of Negotiations	Signature of Accession	Date of Entrance
United Kingdom	9 August 1961	30 June 1970	22 January 1972	1 January 1973
Denmark	9 August 1961	30 June 1970	22 January 1972	1 January 1973
Ireland	9 August 1961	30 June 1970	22 January 1972	1 January 1973
Norway	9 August 1961	30 June 1970	22 January 1972	*Rejected by Norway in referendum*
Greece	12 June 1975	27 July 1976	28 May 1979	1 January 1981
Portugal	28 March 1977	17 October 1978	12 June 1985	1 January 1986
Spain	28 July 1977	5 February 1979	12 June 1985	1 January 1986
Turkey	14 April 1987		*Still negotiating*	*Still negotiating*
Austria	14 July 1989	1 February 1993	24 June 1994	1 January 1995
Cyprus	3 July 1990	31 March 1998	16 April 2003	1 May 2004
Malta	16 July 1990	Request withdrawn on 25 November 1996.	16 April 2003	1 May 2004
Sweden	1 July 1991	1 February 1993	24 June 1994	1 January 1995
Finland	18 March 1992	1 February 1993	24 June 1994	1 January 1995
Norway (2nd)	1992	5 April 1993	24 June 1994	*Withdrawn*
Switzerland	20 May 1992		*Frozen due to public opinion*	*Frozen*
Hungary	31 March 1994	31 March 1998	16 April 2003	1 May 2004
Poland	5 April 1994	31 March 1998	16 April 2003	1 May 2004
Romania	22 June 1995	15 February 2000	25 April 2005	*1 July 2007*
Slovakia	27 June 1995	? March 2000	16 April 2003	1 May 2004
Latvia	13 October 1995	15 February 2000	16 April 2003	*1 May 2004*
Estonia	24 November 1995	31 March 1998	16 April 2003	1 May 2004
Lithuania	8 December 1995	15 February 2000	16 April 2003	1 May 2004
Bulgaria	14 December 1995	15 February 2000	25 April 2005	*1 July 2007*
Czech Rep.	17 January 1996	31 March 1998	16 April 2003	*1 May 2004*
Slovenia	10 June 1996	31 March 1998	16 April 2003	1 May 2004
Croatia	21 February 2003	12 June 2006	30 June 2011	1 July 2013

Schuman Declaration of 9 May 1950:

"If the nations of Europe are to join together, the centuries old antagonism between France and Germany must first be expunged. Our efforts must be primarily concerned with these two countries(...The French Government) proposes to bring the entire Franco-German production of coal and steel under a joint High Authority within an organization in which the other countries of Europe will be free to participate."

The primary purpose of the Schuman Plan was the reconciliation between France and the German Federal Republic - Western Germany in existence since May 1949. Robert Schuman was fully aware of the revolutionary nature of his proposal and thought it best to surprise everybody with it, including his own government.

West German Chancellor Konrad Adenauer was the only person informed in advance, that is to say the evening before its announcement, by Schuman's personal assistant sent to him with the proposal. Adenauer did not hesitate for a moment to accept it.[1] Neither the British Government, nor the US Administration were informed beforehand and much to their displeasure.[2] London's initial reaction was very negative:

---

1 Adenauer n'a pas hésité une seconde. Pour lui le plan du 9 mai était le signe concret d'un événement à ses yeux capital: la réconciliation franco-allemande. Je me souviens que lorsque je suis allé à Bonn huit à dix jours plus tard en compagnie de Jean Monnet le Chancelier nous accueillit avec des larmes dans les yeux. «Il y a vingt-cinq ans, nous dit-il, que j'attendais ce moment. Cette journée du 9 mai 1950 a été le plus beau jour de ma vie.» From an interview with Bernard Clappier as reproduced in European Navigator.

2 See Document E.2.1 . The quotation hereafter is from a meeting of the Cabinet on 10 May 1950.

> "There was general agreement that the French Government had behaved extremely badly in springing this proposal on the world at this juncture without any attempt at consultation with H. M. Government or the US Government. It was also agreed that until the proposal had been most carefully considered in all its aspects - economic, strategic and foreign political - by the various Departments and Ministers concerned, it was essential to adopt a very cautious and non-committal attitude."

As is recorded in the Confidential Document referred to, Dean Acheson's reaction was much less negative: "He admitted that the French announcement had embarrassed him personally because, though he was not a party to it, many people thought he must have been as he had been in Paris the previous day. He thought however that this was a contretemps which we ought to be able to live through." The negative British reaction not only concerned the procedure, they fundamentally disliked the very substance. "Our people are not going to hand to any supranational authority the right to close down our pits or steelworks. We will allow no supranational authority to put large masses of people out of work in Durham, in the Midlands, in South Wales, or in Scotland." Such was the reaction of Harold Macmillan to the Schuman Declaration.

The French proposal was communicated through diplomatic channels to the German Federal Republic, Great Britain, Italy, Belgium, Luxembourg and the Netherlands. The invitation to participate was extended on condition of accepting the principles formulated in the Schuman Declaration. The British Government refused, the others accepted.

FROM FRENCH-GERMAN RECONCILIATION TO THE COMMUNITY OF SIX ONLY

Negotiations between France, Germany, Italy, Belgium, Luxembourg and the Netherlands were opened on 21 June 1950. Reconciliation and supranational integration enlarged from two to six countries. In the negotiations leading up to the Treaty instituting the European Community for Coal and Steel (ECSC), the basic institutional framework was set up. The Convention Containing Transitional Provisions, signed together with the ECSC Treaty, specifically dealt with relations with Great Britain:

> "Section 14
> Upon the establishment of the High Authority, the member States shall undertake negotiations with the governments of third countries, and particularly with the British Government, on overall economic and commercial relations concerning coal and steel between the Community and such countries. The High Authority, acting upon instructions adopted unanimously by the Council, shall act for the member States as a group in these negotiations. Representatives of the member States may be present at these negotiations."

Preliminary talks between the High Authority and the British Mission in Luxembourg started as early as August 1952 and resulted in the Association Agreement of the ECSC with Great Britain of 18 December 1954. At that time, the French National Assembly had killed the Treaty Instituting a European Defense Community. London had taken the initiative to have Western Germany admitted to NATO through Western European Union.[3] It was hoped to associate Great Britain with the efforts

---

[3] Cf. my *Western Cooperation,* Second Revised Edition, pp. 154, 291.

to relaunch the integration process as it had taken the lead in solving the problem of Western defense through the Western European Union (WEU). For this reason, the six specifically invited Britain to participate in the negotiations leading to EEC and Euratom:

> In Messina:
> "The six Governments have decided to adopt the following procedure:
>
> (1) a conference or conferences will be convened for the purpose of drafting the relevant treaties or arrangements;
>
> (2) these conferences will be prepared by a Committee of government delegates assisted by experts under the chairmanship of a leading political figure whose task it will be to co-ordinate the work to be undertaken;
>
> (3) the Committee will call on the High Authority of the E.C.S.C. and on the Secretariats-General of the O.E.E.C., the Council of Europe and the European Conference of Ministers of Transport for any cooperation it may require;
>
> (4) the general report of the Committee will be submitted to the Foreign Ministers not later than October 1, 1955;
>
> (5) the Foreign Ministers will meet before that date in order to examine the interim reports prepared by the Committee and to give the necessary directives;

(6) the Government of the United Kingdom, as a State belonging to W.E.U. and associated with the E.C.S.C., will be invited to participate in this work;."[4]

The Government of the United Kingdom was invited and agreed to attend but in the person of an official of the Board of Trade. Before the end of the year, the official withdrew from the Spaak Committee. The British attitude to the Common Market negotiations in 1955-1958 was very similar to their attitude towards the Schuman Plan. They began by assuming that the negotiations would not succeed and ended up by actively working against a successful outcome. In the case of ECSC, they proposed to integrate a Coal and Steel authority into the existing machinery of the Council of Europe.

As Nora Beloff wrote: "Neither Macmillan nor anyone else in the Eden Government saw any reason to get excited over the *relance* at Messina which neither the British embassies nor most of the British press were inclined to take seriously. The only thing which did impinge on the British consciousness was that the Six were now talking about trade; the Board of Trade, it was felt, should try and find out what was happening." After the signature of the Treaties of Rome in March 1957, the attitude was not much different: "So in May 1957, after the Rome Treaty had been ratified, the Paymaster General, Mr. Reginald Maudling, was given the task of converting the Europeans to the Free Trade Area. He had no help from the Foreign Office. Selwyn Lloyd felt with some asperity that he had enough on his hands already, (others in the Foreign Office) considered

---

4 Resolution adopted by the Ministers of Foreign Affairs of the Member States of the E.C.S.C. at their meeting at Messina (June 1 to 3, 1955) Cf. Document E.2.2. Emphasis added.

Britain's European links far less important than her relations with the United States and the Commonwealth."[5]

He should try to convert at least some of the Six to such a free trade area before their ratification of the Treaties of Rome. An Intergovernmental Committee was formed by the OEEC Ministerial Council (the so-called Maudling Committee), to study the British proposals. The British efforts, first to have the entry into force of the Rome Treaties delayed, and second to agree on a free trade area, failed. The six and especially France rejected the proposals. The exchange of angry letters between British Prime Minister Harold Macmillan and French President Charles de Gaulle clearly shows the impossibility of reaching an agreement. The Report of the Maudling Committee and the meeting of the OEEC Council in December 1958 ascertained that no agreement could be reached before the beginning of the first stage in the transitional period to a common market on 1 January 1959.[6] On US initiative the OEEC was transformed into OECD. Britain joined the European Free Trade Association (EFTA) instituted by the Convention of Stockholm of 4 January 1960. Western Europe, much to Washington's regret, was split between the Six of the European Communities and the Outer Seven of EFTA.

From the outset British policy on European unification resisted "any supranational authority" and favored a free trade area over a common market. As we saw in the previous chapter, that policy has been continued after 1973, when the odd man out had been allowed to become the odd man in! Even after the entry into force of the Lisbon Treaty in December 2009, Britain is not yet a full member of the European Union. It opted

---

5 Nora Beloff, *The General Says No,* Penguin Special 1963, at pp.73 and 79.

6 Relevant documents can be found under Nr. E.2.3 and E.2.4.

out of the Monetary Union and the agreement on social policy, is not a party to the Schengen agreement, it does not recognize the jurisdiction of the European Court of Justice with respect to the Charter of Fundamental Rights.

The Six and the British problem

When the Six signed the Treaties instituting EEC and Euratom on 27 March 1957, they were still open to participating in an eventual European multilateral association as could be read in article 238 of the EEC Treaty. Their policy began to change after the failure of the negotiations in the Maudling Committee. They did so under the influence of the new Commission of the EEC and the policies of the new French Fifth Republic of Charles de Gaulle.[7] For them first priority should now be given to making the common market irreversible, reason for which it was decided a year later to accelerate the transition to the common market with one year and a half (1 July 1968 instead of 1 January 1970). In their opinion, EEC was, more than just a customs union, a new economic and political entity called upon to assume world responsibility together with the United States and Great Britain. Focusing on a regional West European solution would divert attention from that priority. Other OEEC Member States, in this line of thinking, were to be given the choice between entry into the EEC or a trade agreement with the EEC like any other third state. Exception could be made only to those states which were willing to join, but as yet unable to do so for economic reasons.

The results of these changes were the treaties of association concluded with Greece on 9 July 1961 (entered into force on 1 November 1962) and with Turkey on 12 September 1963

---

[7] Cf. my *Beyond the European Community,* Sythoff, Leiden 1969, pp. 106-114.

(entered into force on 1 December 1964). Both countries were members of NATO, OEEC and the Council of Europe, reason for which they both requested association in 1959. It would be politically difficult to accept Greece and refuse Turkey. As a consequence an agreement of association was concluded with both of them, but with a crucial difference: the agreement with Greece specifically provided for a transitional period of 22 years towards full membership and detailed the steps to be taken during that period. The agreement with Turkey was shorter and left that open, as one can read in article 28:

> "As soon as the operation of this Agreement has advanced far enough to justify envisaging full acceptance by Turkey of the obligations arising out of the Treaty establishing the Community, the Contracting Parties shall examine the possibility of the accession of Turkey to the Community."

As we shall see further on, Greece entered the Communities in 1981; the membership of Turkey is still pending.

FROM SIX TO NINE: BRITAIN AND THE EUROPEAN COMMUNITIES

As Prime Minister, Harold Macmillan informed the House of Commons on 3 July 1961 that her Majesty's Government had decided to open negotiations on British entry. These negotiations were abruptly terminated, after French President Charles de Gaulle said 'No' to British entry during his Press Conference on 14 January 1963.[8] A second bid for membership in 1967 was rejected even without negotiation.

---

8 See Document E.2.5.

It is useful to remind the reader that the story of Britain's road to membership was full of ironies and illusions. They existed on the British side, to begin with. For a long time Britain did not take the 'continental' idea of a common market seriously. During negotiations they did not expect agreement, thereafter they tried to undermine the common market. When they finally decided to apply, they did so with the illusion of recovering post war leadership. The 1961 decision "had two main grounds: the economic hope that the competitive stimulus of continental industry in a larger market would speed the modernization of British industry; and the political hope that, in the twilight of empire, Britain could find a new role of leadership in Europe."[9] Illusions also existed on the side of Washington and the Benelux Member States, especially the Netherlands. They pressed for British entry, assuming that the Common Market needed British membership to be able to form a true European political federation. President de Gaulle of France nurtured his own illusions. Ever since 1945, he dreamt of French leadership in post-war Europe and assumed that such leadership would be readily accepted, if only America could be kept at arms-length. The British decision to apply for membership coincided with de Gaulle's plans for replacing the Communities by a political union under his leadership. Like the British government, de Gaulle resisted supranational authority. His leadership was not accepted by the other EEC members. Political Union negotiations failed in 1962 and his 'No' to Britain in January 1963 only deepened the crisis in the EEC. De Gaulle nevertheless pursued his illusions with the bilateral treaty concluded with German Chancellor Konrad Adenauer on 23 January 1963. It would become the basis for close French-German cooperation thereafter except for foreign policy and defense, the two very domains in which de Gaulle wanted to

---

[9] Arthur M. Schlesinger, *A Thousand Days, John F. Kennedy in the White House,* Andre Deutsch 1965, p. 720.

oversee German policies. In final analysis it was a struggle for European leadership between France and Britain. Britain saw it in relation with a strong alliance with the US France conceived its leadership in continental terms; without the US and Britain, with control over Germany and in consultation with Russia. Both pursued an illusion.

Neither of them had given up their illusions, when Harold Wilson from Labor tried again in 1966/1967. This time de Gaulle answered immediately on the application of 10 May 1967, as was his custom in a press conference, only six days later. His arguments against Britain's admission were practically the same as those in his press conference of 13 January 1963.[10] The final irony of that episode can be read in the British memo to Luxembourg in December 1967. Now it was Britain to argue that it was to be full membership or nothing.[11] The principal lesson to be learned from this episode is that enlargement is and shall always be a matter of high politics rather than an issue of economic policies. European economic integration has always been a means to a political end.

The Hague Summit and the entry of Britain, Ireland and Denmark

As we saw already in our previous chapter, the convening of the Hague Summit in December 1969 was meant to be more than a formal occasion to celebrate the end of the transitional period of the common market. With Georges Pompidou as the new French President and Willy Brandt as the West German Chancellor of a new *Ostpolitik*, it was time for breaking the deadlocks of the 1960s. The three most important items for a new beginning were:

---

10 Compare the two in Document E.2.5.

11 Memo in Document E.2.6.

(1) Economic and Monetary Union;
(2) political cooperation; and
(3) enlargement.

According to the European Commission in her memorandum of November 1969: "Enlargement of the Community is an essential factor in the creation of Europe; the Commission thus feels that the Conference of Heads of State or Government should note the unanimous will to bring about this enlargement."

So short a time after de Gaulle's departure, President George Pompidou could not yet agree openly to re-opening negotiations with Britain. The Communiqué of the Hague Summit was deliberately vague on enlargement.[12] Actual negotiations with Britain, Norway, Denmark and Ireland could start on 30 June 1970 after some of the French conditions had been fulfilled.

The communiqué issued by President Pompidou and British Prime Minister Edward Heath sealed the agreement on British entry. As their communiqué and the declarations on the French-British Summit of 20-21 May 1971 made clear, the meeting was the political breakthrough to the enlargement.[13] To Georges Pompidou, Edward Heath had given sufficient proof of being a European rather than an American Trojan Horse; to Edward Heath, Georges Pompidou had given sufficient proof of favoring a less supranational community. The first enlargement of the communities with Britain, Denmark and Ireland on 1 January 1973 did not end the story of British accession. Following the election of a new Labor government, Britain demanded renegotiation of the accession treaty affording it more equitable conditions relating to the

---

[12] Cf. Part II, Chapter 1 and Document EC.H.
[13] See Document E.2.7.

conditions of financing the Community budget, the reform of agricultural policy, relations with the Commonwealth, regional and industrial policy and harmonization of the Value Added Tax. Agreement could be reached in 1975 without a formal revision of the Treaties.[14] Denmark, Ireland and Norway were member states of EFTA. Entry negotiations with them followed those with Britain and posed no additional problems.

As these developments made clear, membership of the European Community/Union also was and continues to be a hot issue in internal British politics. Socialist Harold Wilson had to ask for renegotiation because Edward Heath not only was too European but also a Conservative. 'Europe' is a controversial issue between Britain's political parties and within them - contrary to the situation in the original six, where all major political parties were in favor of Europe.

FROM NINE TO TWELVE: SOUTHERN ENLARGEMENT

By all accounts, the new European Communities of the Nine had a bad start. The Middle-East War of October was followed by the first oil crisis. Elections in Britain brought a new Labor government to power. Her Majesty's new government immediately required re-negotiation of the accession treaties. The follow-up to the new West German *Ostpolitik* focused attention on East West relations. In addition the 1970s were to be an era of economic recession.

---

14 Cf. Part II, Chapter 1, for the renegotiation after accession. Norway did not join following a negative outcome of the referendum on membership.

Three Democratic Revolutions in Southern Europe

Developments in Southern Europe came as a surprise to the EC Member States.

In Greece there were demonstrations in April 1973 against the military junta that had come to power in 1967. Four retired generals called for the restoration of democracy. Following a dubious referendum on 1 June 1973, Junta leader Giorgios Papadopoulos abolished the monarchy - King Constantin II had been in exile since his abortive counter coup in December 1967. After new demonstrations in November, Papadopoulos was deposed by another military coup. With their support Bishop Makarios of Cyprus was overthrown on 15 July 1974 and Turkey invaded the island five days later. The Greek Junta collapsed and democracy was restored on 25 July 1974. It enabled the European Community to reactivate the Association Treaty that had been frozen in 1967. On 12 June 1975 the Greek Government applied for membership of the European Communities.

In Portugal, the Carnation Revolution, a bloodless left-wing military coup, in April 1974 ended the long fascist rule of the Salazar regime in the country and colonial rule in Angola and Mozambique. After a revolutionary transitional period of more than a year, democratic elections were held in 1975. Legislative elections followed on 26 April 1976, won by the Socialist Party. Mario Soares became Prime Minister of the first government under the new democratic Constitution on 23 July 1976. On 28 March 1977, Portugal applied for membership of the European Communities.

On 20 November 1975, Spanish Dictator Franco died and two days later Juan Carlos was sworn in as king of Spain in accordance with Franco's law of succession. The new king successfully oversaw the transition of Spain to democratic rule.

A new democratic Constitution was adopted by referendum on 6 December 1978. Already on 28 July 1977 Spain applied for membership of the European Communities.

Enlargement: a political process

Their applications did not produce great enthusiasm in Brussels, despite the fact that all three countries belonged to the West. Enlargement, wrote the Commission, "presents economic difficulties and poses problems of an institutional nature. Enlargement might therefore weaken it to such an extent that its fundamental objectives would be called into question."[15] In its first opinion on the application of Greece, the Commission in addition had raised the problem of balancing relations with Turkey; relations with this associated country should no be affected by negotiations on Greek admission. We now know that the problem has not as yet been solved. Turkey is not a member; Cyprus in the meantime was admitted despite continued Turkish occupation of half of its territory.

The Commission also saw other problems. "In the case of Greece, where structural changes of a considerable magnitude are needed, it would seem desirable to envisage a period of time before the obligations of membership, even subject to transitional arrangements, are undertaken. During this period, which will in any case need to be limited, it would be necessary to do much more than simply press ahead with the final stages of the development of the Association. In the Commission's view what is needed is on the one hand a substantial economic program which would enable Greece to accelerate the necessary structural reforms, and on the other, measures to bring Greece into a closer working relationship

---

15 See Document E.2.8. Report of the Commission on the Conditions for Enlargement.

with the Community's institutions."[16] Despite these serious doubts expressed by the Commission and differences of opinion among its nine members, it was nevertheless decided to open negotiations with Greece without delay. The overriding political argument appeared to be the defense of democratic values. European integration had come to be identified with the defense of democratic values and admission therefore had to be accepted "as a political responsibility which it (the Community) cannot refuse, except at the price of denying the principles in which it is itself grounded." The political argument in favor of enlargement would henceforward prevail over economic or financial arguments of caution against rapid enlargement. As Emanuele Gazzo, Director and Editor in Chief of Agence Europe at the time, wrote: "Thus we saw the very interesting phenomenon in the development of contemporary history emerging where *the process of European integration was identified with the defense of democratic values.* Once more, the image of Europe was seen, in some measure, to be molded by outside influences. It was inevitable from this time on that the democratic forces, having once come to power in these countries, considered their participation in the European venture to be a matter of course."[17] It applied to Greece, to Portugal and to Spain. After 1989, it would also apply to the democratic forces in East and Central Europe.

Southern enlargement in a period of economic recession and political difficulty, was no easy task. It would also take longer.

---

16 See Document E.2.9. Opinion of the Commission on Greek Application for Membership, 29 January 1976, and Position of the Council of February 1976.

17 From his Chapter 1, Enlargement of the Community: Attitudes of Member States, in J.W. Schneider (editor), *From Nine to Twelve: Europe's Destiny?,* Sythoff & Noordhoff, 1980, A Publication of the John F. Kennedy Institute, Center for International Studies, Tilburg the Netherlands.

Negotiations with Greece were opened on 27 July 1976 and concluded with the signing of the Accession documents on 28 May 1979. Greece entered the Communities on 1 January 1981. With Spain and Portugal negotiations opened on 5 February 1979 and 17 October 1978 and were concluded on 12 June 1985. The two countries joined the Communities on 1 January 1986, just in time to sign the Single European Act.

The structures of the enlargement instruments were very similar. They consisted of a final positive opinion of the Commission, a decision of the Council of Ministers, two formal accession treaties (one for the ECSC, the other for the EEC and Euratom), the Act of Accession and annexes, protocols and declarations.[18] Among them, the Act was the most important document. The Acts contained the adjustments to the institutions, adaptations to the Acts adopted before entry, transitional measures and Implementation provisions. The Accession Act with Greece provided for a transitional period of 5 years. The Accession Act with Spain and Portugal provided for a transitional period of 7 years with the exception of full integration into the agricultural policy for which there was a transitional period of 11 years.

FROM TWELVE TO FIFTEEN: WHEN NEUTRALITY NO LONGER AN ISSUE

The collapse of the Soviet system and the end of Europe's post-war division faced the European Community of the Twelve with an entirely new situation and a large number of applications for membership. It caught Community Member States in a difficult dilemma. On the one side, it was necessary to strengthen the fragile, internal cohesion of the twelve and to uphold the internal dynamics of economic integration as envisaged by the Single European Act and by renewed efforts

---

[18] The Documents of Accession can be found under Nr. E.2.10-12.

to deepen the communities. On the other side, it became necessary to respond to the external dynamics of the collapse of the Soviet totalitarian system.

Priority was given to deepening the communities. The concept for a European Economic Area, presented in January 1989 as a proposal for a new partnership with the member states of EFTA, was meant to avoid a new round of enlargement. The idea of a European Economic Area, however, did not satisfy Austria, Finland, Norway and Sweden. Austria applied for full membership on 14 July 1989; Sweden on 1 July 1991, Finland on 18 March 1992 and Norway the same year. As there were no valid arguments any longer against their admission - the three applicant states had highly developed economies and their neutrality was no longer an issue - negotiations were opened on 1 February 1993. The Instruments of Accession were signed on 24 June 1994 and the three neutral states entered on 1 January 1995, less than a year after the entry into force of the EEA Treaty.[19]

The neutrality of Austria, Sweden and Finland was linked to the Cold War. Austria's neutrality was based on national and international law, Sweden's neutrality on internal political consensus and Finland's neutrality on geopolitical reality. [20] At the time of publishing its opinion, the Treaty of Maastricht on European Union had been signed already. The strictly intergovernmental (and provisional) character of the articles with respect to a common foreign and defense policy were not considered to be incompatible with the neutrality of the

---

19 See Document E.2.14. for the Documents of Accession. Following a second negative referendum, Norway did not enter.

20 Compare the Opinion of the European Commission on their application: E.2.13. On Austria, 31 July 1991, On Sweden 31 July 1992, On Finland 4 November 1992.

three applicants. By 1991 the political situation in Europe had changed fundamentally. In Sweden and Finland the governments made a reassessment of their neutrality in this new situation and decided to apply for membership. After the peaceful re-unification of Germany, the Austrian coalition government considered European Union membership to be compatible with its status of permanent neutrality. In their view, the constitutional law on neutrality no longer prohibits accession as the EU, unlike NATO, is not a military alliance.

FROM FIFTEEN TO TWENTY-SEVEN: EUROPE'S REUNIFICATION

THE ADMISSION OF THE CENTRAL AND EAST EUROPEAN COUNTRIES (CEEC)

The peaceful revolutions in Central and Eastern Europe ended the post-war division of Europe. For the liberated countries joining Europe and the West was their first priority. The immediate problem to be solved, however, was the reunification of Germany after the opening of the Berlin Wall on 9 November 1989. It happened far more quickly than anybody had envisaged. At the Dublin meeting of the European Council in June 1990, the President concluded in par. I. 12:

> "The European Council heard a report from the German Federal Chancellor on the progress towards German unification. It welcomed the conclusion of the inter-German State Treaty which will promote and accelerate the integration of the territory of the German Democratic Republic into the Community."

German re-unification as enlargement

This rather terse statement was the outcome of a major political agreement. All Member States agreed to a *European*

Community enlargement without accession. The inclusion of the GDR in the German Federal Republic was accepted without a revision of the Community Treaties. German reunification within the European Community also triggered the establishment of the intergovernmental conference to prepare the Economic and Monetary Union. The increased power of a united Germany was to be checked by a common European currency. As Carlo Trojan, chief negotiator of the European Commission for German unification, said:

> "German unification was the trigger of the European Monetary Union and strengthening integration in Europe. Without it we wouldn't have had the euro. Without Helmut Kohl we wouldn't have had the euro either. Against rather negative German public opinion on that issue, he won the elections and won the acceptance of Monetary Union. I think the fall of the Wall and the subsequent German unification has been a watershed in post-war history and by far the most important event after the war."[21]

Accession of the Central and East European Countries (CEEC)

The speed of the Eastern enlargement of the German Community member was in sharp contrast to the long time it took to achieve the accession of the ten other Central and East European States seeking membership. The admission of these states of the former Soviet system, of course, posed much greater problems. The European Community initially offered a program of assistance towards political and economic reform, the so called PHARE program in the framework of

---

21 Interview in Document E.2.15., Presidency Conclusion of the Dublin Council in document EC.45.,Compare Jean-Paul Jacqué, German *Unification and the European Community, 2 EJIL (1991) 1.*

agreement reached in the Economic Summit of the G-7.[22] In the Communication of the Commission of 27 August 1990, relations with the CEEC were seen in the framework of the so-called new European architecture to be built on the CSCE, a kind of continuation of the former Cold War structure in which former enemies cooperate as new friends.

The next step towards the CEEC was the conclusion of so called *Europe Agreements*; proposed by the Commission in the same Communication. They were in fact association agreements concluded on the basis of article 238 of the EEC Treaty. The willingness to conclude such agreements always was based on a political agreement reached in the European Council. As the Commission made clear:

> "Several governments have referred to their ' interest in eventual membership for their countries in the Community. This, however, is not among the objectives of the association agreements discussed in this Communication."[23]

With Poland, Czechoslovakia and Hungary such agreements were concluded on 16 December 1991 (with Slovakia on 4 October 1993 after the separation of 1992); with Bulgaria and Romania on 8 March 1993; with Estonia, Latvia and Lithuania on 15 June 1995 and with Slovenia on 10 June 1996.

The Europe Agreements stopped short of a commitment to membership, aiming at providing an appropriate framework for gradual integration into the Community. Membership was

---

22 Cf. Document I.6.3 linked to my *Western Cooperation,* Second Revised Edition, documents to Part I, Chapter 6.

23 Communication of the Commission of 27 August 1990. Text in Document E.2.16.

not among the aims of the Europe agreements. As article 2 (in the Europe agreement with Poland) provides:

> "The aim of this Agreement is:
>
> - to provide an appropriate framework for the political dialogue, allowing the development of close political relations between the parties,
>
> - to promote the expansion of trade and the harmonious economic relations between the parties and so to foster the dynamic economic development and prosperity in Poland,
>
> - to provide a basis for the Community's financial and technical assistance to Poland,
>
> - to provide an appropriate framework for Poland's gradual integration into the Community. To this end, Poland shall work towards fulfilling the necessary conditions,
>
> - to promote cooperation in cultural matters."

According to article 117, the agreement was concluded for an unlimited period. Reference to future membership was made in the preamble only and in the following terms:

> "*Recognizing* the fact that the final objective of Poland is to become a member of the Community and that this association, in the view of the Parties, will help to achieve this objective...[24]

---

[24] From the agreement with Poland. See Document. E.2.17.

The Europe Agreements concluded with Romania and Bulgaria were not different.

After the signing of the first slate of Europe Agreements in December 1991, the Commission maintained its reluctance in the communication on "Europe and the Challenge of Enlargement". The Commission was prepared to initiate entry negotiations with Turkey, Cyprus and Malta, but on the CEEC it wrote:

> "35. However, the countries which are not yet in a position to accept the obligations of membership have political needs which go beyond the possibilities of existing agreements. They desire the reassurance that they will be treated as equal partners in the dialogue concerning Europe s future. They wish to increase their security by strengthening their political links with Western Europe. The Commission believes that new means should be created for this purpose, building upon the existing ' architecture' of European organizations, so as to create a ' European political area".[25]

As the post-1989 dynamics continued, the Community could no longer avoid such a commitment. The Copenhagen Summit in June 1993 formally accepted enlargement and decided on the general criteria for admission in the following terms:

> "The European Council today agreed that the associated countries in Central and Eastern Europe that so desire shall become members of the European Union. Accession will take place as soon as an associated country is able to assume the obligations of

25 Communication of the Commission of 24 June 1992, see Document E.2.18.

> membership by satisfying the economic and political conditions required. Membership requires that the candidate country has achieved stability of institutions guaranteeing democracy, the rule of law, human rights and respect for and protection of minorities, the existence of a functioning market economy as well as the capacity to cope with competitive pressure and market forces within the Union. Membership presupposes the candidates' ability to take on the obligations of membership including adherence to the aims of political economic and monetary union."[26]

It was only after this political agreement in the European Council that the CEEC formally applied for membership. On the side of the European Union, the Commission outlined its views on pre-accession in its strategy document of 13 July 1994,[27] written on the specific request of the European Council session of Corfu. The reader should be reminded that this change of objectives followed the new American strategy of democratic enlargement. Henceforward, the talk on a new European architecture vanished in favor of a policy of enlargement of the Western institutions.

As we saw already in the previous chapter, the European Council of December 1994 agreed with the strategy of further preparing the associated states of Central and Eastern Europe, as proposed by the Commission. The next step was the White Paper of the Commission of 3 May 1995, "Preparation of the Associated Countries of Central and Eastern Europe for integration into the

---

[26] European Council Copenhagen 1993, see Document EC.54.

[27] The Europe Agreements and Beyond: A strategy to prepare the CEEC for Accession. See Document E.2.19.

internal market of the Union," essentially outlining the technical assistance required for preparing their accession.[28]

Accession negotiations, however, had to wait for ensuring the proper functioning of the Union: that took several more years. The Commission gave her opinion on the applications on 15 July 1997 - at the same time for all ten of them. The opening of negotiations was to depend on the progress made - according to the Commission - towards meeting the criteria of Copenhagen. Negotiations with Hungary, Poland, Slovenia, the Czech Republic and Estonia were opened on 31 March 1998; and with Latvia, Lithuania and Slovakia on 15 February 2000. As Peter Ludlow wrote, it was not until 1999 that accession negotiations finally gathered speed. Under Prodi's presidency with Commissioner Günther Verheugen for enlargement, the Commission's attitude towards Eastern enlargement changed from somewhat lukewarm support to becoming the most vigorous champion of admitting the CEEC. Under the Danish presidency (Anders Fogh Rasmussen Prime Minister), the European Councils of Brussels and Copenhagen in 2002 determined their admission for 1 May 2004.[29] With those eight countries (and with Cyprus and Malta) the instruments of accession were signed only on 16 April 2003. The ten countries acceded on 1 May 2004.

Negotiations with Bulgaria and Romania could not start until after that date. For a number of reasons, these two countries

---

28 See document E.2.20.

29 European Council, Cf. Documents EC.92 and EC.93. Peter Ludlow, *The Making of the new Europe; The European Councils in Brussels and Copenhagen 2002,* EuroComment, Brussels 2004. See also: ESI, *Rethinking Enlargement,* www.esiweb.org/enlargement/?cat=3#awp::?cat=3

needed an extended pre-accession treatment.[30] In its conclusions on enlargement, the European Council of Brussels in December 2004, stated:

> *Bulgaria*
>
> 6. The European Council recalled that all of the outstanding chapters in the accession negotiations with Bulgaria had been provisionally closed earlier in 2004. It welcomed the successful completion of these negotiations with Bulgaria on 14 December 2004 and accordingly looked forward to welcoming it as a member from January 2007.
>
> 7. Taking due note of the relevant assessments and recommendations by the Commission, the European Council considered that Bulgaria will be able to assume all the obligations of membership at the envisaged time of its accession, provided that it continues its efforts to that end and completes in a successful and timely way all necessary reforms and commitments undertaken in all areas of the acquis. Safeguard clauses will provide for measures to address serious problems that may arise before accession or in the three years after accession.
>
> 8. *The European Union will continue to monitor closely Bulgaria's preparations and achievements, including the effective implementation of the commitments undertaken in all areas of the acquis and in particular Justice and Home Affairs; to this end the Commission will continue to submit annual reports on Bulgaria's progress*

---

[30] Cf. Milada Anna Vachudova, *Europe Undivided; Democracy, Leverage, & Integration After Communism,* Oxford University Press 2005.

towards accession, together with recommendations if appropriate.

9. Anticipating the successful completion by Bulgaria of its preparations for accession to the Union, the European Council called for the finalisation of the Accession Treaty with Bulgaria and Romania with a view to its signing in April 2005 on the occasion of the meeting of the General Affairs and External Relations Council, provided the European Parliament has given its assent.

Romania

10. The European Council noted with satisfaction that progress made by Romania in implementing the acquis and commitments entered into as regards, in particular, Justice and Home Affairs and Competition, has made it possible to close formally all of the outstanding chapters with this candidate on 14 December 2004 and accordingly looked forward to welcoming it as a member from January 2007.

11. Taking due note of the relevant assessments and recom-mendations by the Commission, the European Council considered that Romania will be able to assume all the obligations of membership at the envisaged time of its accession, provided that it continues its efforts to that end and completes in a successful and timely way all necessary reforms and commitments undertaken in all areas of the acquis, in particular the important commitments regarding Justice and Home Affairs, Competition and Environment. Safeguard clauses will provide for measures to address serious problems that may arise, as the case may be, before accession or in the three years after accession, in particular in the areas

of Justice and Home Affairs and Competition as well as Environment.

12. *The European Union will continue to monitor closely Romania's preparations and achievements, including the effective implementation of the commitments undertaken in all areas of the acquis, and in particular in the areas of Justice and Home Affairs, Competition and Environment; to this end the Commission will continue to submit annual reports on Romania's progress towards accession, together with recommendations if appropriate.*

13. Anticipating the successful completion by Romania of its preparations for accession to the Union, the European Council called for the finalization of the Accession Treaty with Bulgaria and Romania with a view to its signing in April 2005 on the occasion of the meeting of the General Affairs and External Relations Council, provided the European Parliament has given its assent."

Instruments of accession with the two were signed on 25 April 2005 and they acceded on 1 January 2007.[31] As Bulgaria and Romania were not fully ready for accession, the Council agreed that the two countries' progress needed continuing

---

31 For the Acts of Accession see Documents E.2.21-23. Since the Treaty of Amsterdam, the instruments of accession include the opinion of the European Parliament in addition to the (final) opinion of the Commission, the decision of the Council and the formal Treaty of Accession. With Bulgaria and Romania, the Europe Agreements remain in force until completion of the necessary transition to full membership. For the quotations from the European Council of December 2004, Cf. Document EC.104.

supervision after accession as provided in paragraphs 8 and 12 (italicized) above.

Eastern Enlargement: More than just a larger market

Prior to the formal entry of the eight CEEC on 1 May 2004, COMECE[32] took the European Bishops of the twenty-five member countries of the EU on a pilgrimage to Santiago de Compostella. "Europe is born in pilgrimage and Christianity is her mother tongue", a quotation, we pilgrims were told, from German poet Goethe.[33] Following the entry of Bulgaria and Romania, COMECE called a Congress on "*Values and Perspectives for Europe. 50 Years of the Treaties of Rome*" on 23-25 March 2007 in Rome.

The enlargement of the European Union this century should be seen as a major event in the spiritual realm rather than just inevitability in the economic realm. As Norman Davies rightly emphasized in a recent book[34] there is a long history of misunderstanding, neglect, sense of superiority and ignorance of Western Europe towards East and Central Europe. As a result of the Cold War, "the East" was something like a black hole to most in the West. Worse than the hostile image of Eastern Europe was the well-established convention of ignoring Eastern Europe completely writes Norman Davies. Few of us in the Western part of Europe understood the profound significance of the spirit of 1989; because few of us really understand how different the Eastern experience with totalitarianism has

---

32 Commission of the National Conferences of Bishops (in the Roman Catholic Church) of the European Community.

33 *Les Chemins de Saint-Jacques de Compostelle,* In Situ Thèmes, MSM 1999, p. 107. This quotation was attributed to Goethe in 1980 by Pope John-Paul II. This author never found it in Goethe's works!

34 Norman Davies, *Europe East & West,* Jonathan Cape 2006.

been from our Western experience. The majority of the new Member States were squeezed between the two ideologies of evil for most of their national life in the twentieth century.[35] In all these countries, people have great difficulty to deal with the moral heritage of these ideologies and the superficial and materialist view on economic progress brought in from the West. In a "debased moral environment" (Vaclav Havel) it is difficult to resist the Western dictatorship of economic values. The inability to come to grips with the communist past and the new dictatorship is proving to be a poisonous mixture. Judging by political developments in the new Member States and the sometimes arrogant comments on them in the West, there still is a long way to go. The original EU Member States have their own past to come to grip with; from the Nazi-Soviet partnership and the Grand Alliance (1939, 1941)[36] to their détente policies of the 1980's; and from their fellow-travelers in the 1930's to their neo-Marxists and appeasers of the détente era. The longevity of totalitarianism in the East had a lot to do with Western acquiescence, indifference, neglect and ignorance. The new Member States need support and understanding in the difficult process of transitional justice and reconciliation.

If the European Union continues to give priority to the process of economic integration, it is heading nowhere according to Norman Davies. It is a nice irony, he writes, that the peoples of the new Member States may well have a more rounded vision of the Europe to which they wish to return than the often arrogant West Europeans who reluctantly let them in.[37]

---

35 Cf. Timothy Snyder, *Bloodlands, Europe between Hitler and Stalin,*Basic Books 2010.

36 Compare my*Western Cooperation: Origins and History,* Wolf Legal Publishers 2002, Part I, Chapter 4.

37 *Op.cit.* p.42.

Europe's re-unification today like the initiation of its post-war unification needs the living sources tapped by the founding fathers in the 1950's in the West and in the 1980's in Central Europe.[38]

Undivided Europe

The peaceful enlargement of the European Union to the borders of Belorussia, Ukraine, Russia and Turkey has been an achievement of historic proportions without precedent. For the ten new member countries, the road to membership was long and crooked, often exasperating and humiliating. With limited financial assistance and too many consultants and counselors, their economies had to make the transition from a socialist command economy to a European market economy with a staggering number of common rules, called the *acquis communautaire.*[39]

Still it should be kept in mind that the eight CEEC's had to achieve a threefold and fundamental transition:

(1) from a totalitarian one–party state to a parliamentary democracy under the rule of law;

(2) from a poorly performing command economy to a competitive and open market-economy; and

---

38 The full text of my contribution to the Congress can be found on my website under European Union. The Congress read a report of wise men to the Bishops on "A Europe of Values. The ethical Dimension of the European Union", and concluded with the text of a contribution to the Declaration of Berlin (of the Heads of State and Government) of the European Union on Common Values as a living source of the European Project. Cf. Part I, Chapter 3 above.

39 For the 35 chapters to be negotiated, compare the list in Document E.2.24.

(3) from "limited sovereignty" as Soviet satellite states to "shared sovereignty" as European Union Member States. This threefold transformation process had to be realized in an age of rapid globalization and (often) criminal privatization. The principal political actors available for managing the process were inexperienced former dissidents, reconstructed former communist leaders or *apparatchiks,* and young business graduates.

Conditionality

Whereas all political actors agreed on the necessity to enter the European Union at the earliest possible date, the initial reluctance on the part of the EU, resulted in a pre-accession strategy - as we saw already - to prepare the candidate CEEC's for the ability in economic, financial and political respect to exercise the rights and obligations of membership. The Europe Agreements provided the tools for guiding and monitoring the pre-accession adaptation to membership. In retrospect the process could be characterized as "positive conditionality". The threefold transition through conditionality was managed by functional cooperation, pre-accessional integration into the internal market under the guidance of strict rules meant to effect convergence with the EU, and support towards modernization.[40] As Heather Grabbe emphasized, the scope of the EU's agenda for transition in the candidate states went far beyond the requirements of membership for the existing Member States. The prospect of membership at the end of the

---

40 Cf. Heather Grabbe, *Europeanisation Goes East: Power and Uncertainty in the EU Accession Process* In: K. Featherstone and C. Radaelli (ed), *The Politics of Europeanisation,* Oxford University Press 2004; Heather Grabbe, *The European Union's Transformative Power; Europeanization through Conditionality in Central and Eastern Europe,* Palgrave Macmillan 2006.

road gave the European Union coercive power she did not have towards their current members.

The "great transformation of Central and Eastern Europe" was an exceptional success story according to János Kornai in history. Integration with the European Union acted as a stabilizing force in the economy and facilitated the creation of democracy and above all it took place peacefully and without violence. At the same time, he writes, the transformation was a failure from the perspective of everyday life, as it caused pain, bitterness and disappointment for so many people through unemployment, corruption, growing inequality and immorality.[41]

ANY EUROPEAN STATE?

According to Article 49 in the Treaty on European Union:

> "Any European State which respects the values referred to in Article 2 and is committed to promoting them may apply to become a member of the Union. The European Parliament and national Parliaments shall be notified of this application. The applicant State shall address its application to the Council, which shall act unanimously after consulting the Commission and after receiving the consent of the European Parliament, which shall act by a majority of its component members.

---

41 Janos Kornai, *The Great Transformation of Central Eastern Europe, Success and Disappointment,* Presidential Address delivered at the 14th World Congress of the International Economic Association on 29 August 2006, as published by the European Bank for Reconstruction and Development, with Blackwell Publishing.2006

The conditions of eligibility agreed upon by the European Council shall be taken into account. The conditions of admission and the adjustments to the Treaties on which the Union is founded, which such admission entails, shall be the subject of an agreement between the Member States and the applicant State. This agreement shall be submitted for ratification by all the contracting States in accordance with their respective constitutional requirements."[42]

Partners only

So far, Switzerland and Norway once and twice applied but withdrew, following the negative outcome of referenda. With Russia, Ukraine and Belorussia, Moldavia and the other former Soviet Republics in the Caucasus and Central Asia, the European Union concluded Partnership and Cooperation Agreements in 1994, a clear indication that the former Soviet Republics are not as yet considered eligible for or interested in membership.

On the initiative of Poland and Sweden, the European Union launched a new Eastern Partnership at the Prague Summit in May 2009.[43] The Declaration makes it quite clear that Eastern Partnership is to be seen as good neighborhood policy, not as a step towards accession. The list of participants does not include Russia; the low level of EU Member States representation indicates the limited interest for such a partnership.[44]

---

42 Text as from the entry into force on 1 December 2009 of the Treaty of Lisbon. The second paragraph of this article is new.

43 Text of the Summit Declaration in Document E.2.25.

44 Cf. Nico Popescu & Andrew Wilson, *The Limits of Enlargement-Lite: European and Russian Power in the Troubled Neighbourhood,* June 2009, a publication of the European Council for Foreign Relations; www.ecfr.eu

Russia

Relations with Russia must be mentioned separately.

Ever since Czar Peter the Great made Russia a major player in European power politics, the Russian debate about Europe focused on Russia itself and on Europe as the other world. Should Russia modernize by following European models? Should Russia turn away from a Europe that had failed in maintaining its past values? Or should Russia, mindful of its universal mission, assume a leading and guiding role in Europe?

Does Russia belong to Europe and can Europe not be made without Russia? The question whether Europe can unify without sorting out its relations with Russia, or whether Russia can be transformed into a democracy, need new and serious reflection. Europe, as we saw already, is the work of men rather than of nature. It is a construction of the human mind based on a poorly delimited geography. Today, it no longer satisfies to identify Europe with the West and to draw Europe's borders along the former borders of the defunct Soviet Union, thus excluding Russia, Belorussia, Ukraïne and Moldavia - borders close to the old fault line between Eastern and Western Christendom in 1054, the year of the consummation of the Great Schism. Looking at Europe as a civilization and to its spiritual genealogy, Russia cannot simply be excluded.

Russia's relations with the European Union, however are highly ambivalent.

Russia knows that adherence to the Council of Europe and the European Convention on Human Rights - since 1997 - requires progress towards democracy, the rule of law and respect for human rights. At the same time, such adherence is presented and justified as a means to restore Russia's role as a great power, but without making much progress towards democracy. Russia resents the enlargement of NATO and questions the willingness of Europeans to accept its rightful place in European and world politics. At the same time, Russia deals with the European Union in terms of traditional power politics, rather than as a partner in restoring democracy and unity in Europe. Russia also resents the Eastern Partnership launched in 2009 as the Eastern leg of the European Good Neighborhoodpolicy, warning the EU that its structural relationships should not overlap relationships in the post-Soviet area. At the same time Russia wants a strategic relationship with the EU. Russian European policy under Putin and Medvedev is surprisingly similar to the power plays from Czar Peter onwards. The post-Soviet area should remain the "near abroad" that is Moscow's sphere of domination. The EU should stay out of the area and otherwise accept Russia's leading role in Europe at large.

The European attitude towards relations with Russia is just as ambivalent in response. The EU followed NATO in accepting the three Baltic Republics as EU members, but limit relations with the former Soviet republics to partnership and cooperation agreements - all of them, including Russia. EU's Eastern Partnership excludes Russia and the Central Asian Republics, but includes the European and Caucasian Republics. With Russia the EU concluded a strategic partnership - that is a very special relationship in name but not in substance.

It would be wrong to conclude that the European Union is drawing new borders in Europe, excluding Russia. Putin's Russia wants to be restored in its position as world power equal to the United States of America, to recover its lost territories and be accepted as a leading power in Europe. Member states of the European Union are deeply divided on the relationship. Germany, France and Britain like their own, special and bilateral relationships with Russia, who-ever is in power. The new member-states from Central and Eastern Europe prefer to keep Russia at arms length.

The Western Balkans

Article 49 leaves the possibility for "any European State to apply" to the remaining countries in the Western Balkans, that is Albania and the former Yugoslav Republics in addition to Slovenia, a member already since 2004. According to the (same) Brussels European Council (on 16 and 17 December 2004) on Enlargement: (...)

> "5. With the accession of ten new Member States to the European Union successfully accomplished, the European Council expressed its determination to continue the process it has engaged in with the candidate countries, thus contributing to Europe's prosperity, stability, security and unity. In this connection, it recalled that the Union's capacity to absorb new members, while maintaining the momentum of European integration, is an important consideration in the general interest of both the Union and the candidate countries."
>
> *Croatia*
>
> 14. The European Council noted with satisfaction the progress made by Croatia in preparation for the opening of accession negotiations.
>
> 15. Reaffirming its conclusions of June 2004, it urged Croatia to take the necessary steps for full cooperation with ICTY and reiterated that the remaining indicted must be located and transferred to the Hague as soon as possible.

16. It invited the Commission to present to the Council a proposal for a framework for negotiations with Croatia, taking full account of the experience of the fifth enlargement. It requested the Council to agree on that framework with a view to opening the accession negotiations on 17 March 2005 provided that there is full cooperation with ICTY."
(...)

"Framework for negotiations

23. The European Council agreed that accession negotiations with individual candidate states will be based on a framework for negotiations. Each framework, which will be established by the Council on a proposal by the Commission, taking account of the experience of the fifth enlargement process and of the evolving *acquis*, will address the following elements, according to own merits and specific situations and characteristics of each candidate state:

- As in previous negotiations, the substance of the negotiations, which will be conducted in an Intergovernmental Conference with the participation of all Member States on the one hand and the candidate State concerned on the other, where decisions require unanimity, will be broken down into a number of chapters, each covering a specific policy area. The Council, acting by unanimity on a proposal by the Commission, will lay down benchmarks for the provisional closure and, where appropriate, for the opening of each chapter; depending on the chapter concerned, these benchmarks will refer to legislative alignment and a satisfactory track record of implementation of the *acquis* as well as obligations deriving from contractual relations with the European Union.

- Long transition periods, derogations, specific arrangements or permanent safeguard clauses, i.e. clauses which are permanently available as a basis for safeguard measures, may be considered. The Commission will include these, as appropriate, in its proposals for each framework, for areas such as freedom of movement of persons, structural policies or agriculture. Furthermore, the decision-taking process regarding the eventual establishment of freedom of movement of persons should allow for a maximum role of individual Member States. Transitional arrangements or safeguards should be reviewed regarding their impact on competition or the functioning of the internal market.

- The financial aspects of accession of a candidate state must be allowed for in the applicable Financial Framework. Hence, accession negotiations yet to be opened with candidates whose accession could have substantial financial consequences can only be concluded after the establishment of the Financial Framework for the period from 2014 together with possible consequential financial reforms.

- The shared objective of the negotiations is accession. These negotiations are an open-ended process, the outcome of which cannot be guaranteed beforehand.

While taking account of all Copenhagen criteria, if the Candidate State is not in a position to assume in full all the obligations of membership it must be ensured that the Candidate State concerned is fully anchored in the European structures through the strongest possible bond.

- In the case of a serious and persistent breach in a candidate state of the principles of liberty, democracy, respect for human rights and fundamental freedoms and the rule of law on which the Union is founded, the Commission will, on its own initiative or on the request of one third of the Member States, recommend the suspension of negotiations and propose the conditions for eventual resumption. The Council will decide by qualified majority on such a recommendation, after having heard the candidate state, whether to suspend the negotiations and on the conditions for their resumption. The Member States will act in the IGC in accordance with the Council decision, without prejudice to the general requirement for unanimity in the IGC. The European Parliament will be informed.

- Parallel to accession negotiations, the Union will engage with every candidate state in an intensive political and cultural dialogue. With the aim of enhancing mutual understanding by bringing people together, this inclusive dialogue also will involve civil society."

The above framework is to be seen as an addition to the criteria for admission formulated by the European Council of Copenhagen in 1993. It is the outcome of the experiences gained in the accession negotiations since 1993 and should be applicable to negotiations with Turkey (see next paragraph) and with the Western Balkan states."

Two years later (December 2006) the European Council had another in-depth discussion on enlargement:

> "As agreed at the June 2006 European Council and on the basis of the Commission communication on the enlargement strategy and its special report on the EU's capacity to integrate new members, the European Council held an in-depth debate on enlargement. The European Council agrees that the enlargement strategy based on consolidation, conditionality and communication, combined with the EU's capacity to integrate new members, forms the basis for a renewed consensus on enlargement. The EU keeps its commitments towards the countries that are in the enlargement process."

Reflecting the growing resistance to on-going enlargement, the Council added "the capacity to integrate new members" to the three c's already considered to be the basis for further enlargement. With respect to the accession of the Western Balkan States, the European Council re-affirmed, nevertheless:

> "The European Council reaffirms that the future of the Western Balkans lies in the European Union. It reiterates that each country's progress towards the European Union depends on its individual efforts to comply with the Copenhagen criteria and the conditionality of the Stabilisation and Association Process. A country's satisfactory track-record in implementing its obligations under a Stabilisation and Association Agreement (SAA), including trade related provisions, is an essential element for the EU to consider any membership application."[45]

---

[45] Cf. Document EC 116, par. 4 and 6.

Contrary to the previous Eastern enlargement, accession is to be negotiated with each applicant individually. Such is easier stated as a principle than carried out in practice. With the exception of Albania, the applicant states Croatia, Macedonia, Montenegro and Serbia, and the prospective applicants Bosnia-Herzegovina and Kosovo are the broken pieces from the violent collapse of Yugoslavia.[46] Unlike developments in the CEEC - where the threefold transition happened peacefully - in Yugoslavia the ghost of nationalism in its new shape of the ethnic-nationalist warrior emerged from under the rubble of communism. Focused as European politicians were on what happened in Moscow, they turned a blind eye to what unfolded in Yugoslavia. Tito's Yugoslavia after all had been conceived as the model for the peaceful liberation of Eastern Europe from Soviet domination. When they finally turned their attention to the violent collapse of Yugoslavia, it was too late. Even worse, the European politicians at the time of the conclusion of the first European Union Treaty , saw the crisis as an opportunity to assert the Union's new role in crisis management. It became a cumulative record of failure. The EU lacked the tools to deal with the crisis. Member states were in profound disagreement among themselves on how to deal with the crisis. It required the United States and NATO in 1995 and 1999 to reach a shaky settlement, and NATO (later EU) military presence to maintain a modicum of peace.

Currently, EU Member States are hardly more united in their approach to the broken pieces of Yugoslavia - for instance on the recognition of Kosovo's independence. Progress towards peace and reconciliation inside and between the republics is minimal, if not completely absent. The piecemeal approach agreed upon is based on a twofold circumvention of the political problem of enlargement into the Western Balkans. It

---

[46] Cf. E.2. 26: Chronology "Collapse of Yugoslavia".

tries to circumvent the requirement of unity inside the EU and the need to reconcile the parties inside and between the broken pieces of former Yugoslavia.

Currently, negotiations with Croatia only were concluded and admission is foreseen for 2013. They could have been conducted with Macedonia, were it not for the silly problem of the name of the republic; the only reason why Greece is blocking the beginning of negotiations. Serbia and Montenegro applied and received candidate status like Albania. All of them together with Bosnia-Herzegovina are linked to the European Union by an association agreement (SAA).

To this author it appears at least doubtful that the "Success Story of Enlargement" can extend to the Western Balkans. Too many fundamental problems remain unsolved. The ghost of the ethnic-nationalist warrior is still alive and kicking. Convicted war criminals (by the International Criminal Tribunal for the former Yugoslavia) are still heros in their own country.

MEDITERRANEAN ENLARGEMENT AND GOOD NEIGHBOURHOOD POLICY

While urged to look East, the European Union also had to deal with the applications for membership submitted by Turkey, Cyprus and Malta and with the long standing interest of the Northern-Mediterranean Member States to develop special relations with the Southern and Eastern Mediterranean countries.

Malta and half of divided Cyprus applied in July 1990, when their non-alignment policy presumably was no longer deemed to be incompatible with EU membership. Malta withdrew in 1996 and restored its application two years later. The EU decided to negotiate with them together with the eight CEE applicants. They entered the EU together with them on 1 May

2004. In the case of Cyprus, Protocols 3 and 10[47] deal with the status of the British sovereign base area on the island and the issue of applying the *acquis* to the non-recognized Turkish Cypriote Republic on half of the island. It was the intention to postpone Cyprus membership until agreement had been reached on its re-unification. As such agreement was again impossible, protocol 10 is to conceal the reality of truncated membership.

The failure to resolve the Cyprus conflict is one of the reasons for the continuing difficulties in dealing with the application of Turkey.

Recognizable illusions

The year 2011 may well enter the history of EU's Mediterranean good neighbourhood policy alongside the history of the European Community's East European policy in the era of East-West détente. In both cases, European external relations policy was based on illusions. Among them were: *that* the economic attraction could produce political change; *that* political dialogue could soften dictators and turn them into benign rulers; *that* the soft power of Europe could promote democracy from above in the partner countries. Wrapped inside those illusions has been the most dangerous illusion about Turkey deemed to have converted from Ottoman Empire to a Western style secular and democratic republic - comparable also to the illusion about the Soviet Union in the era of détente.

At this time in the history of European unification, European politicians and scholars could have learned from the year 1989, that all three assumptions underlying West European *Ostpolitik* had turned out to be illusions. True change in the

---

[47] See Documents E.2. 28-29. For Malta see Document E. 2. 27.

CEEC came from below and overthrew the communist leaders - it all happened peacefully as we saw, due to the extraordinarily moral content of the CEE revolutionary spirit. Despite the West European illusions, three circumstances made CEEC membership possible:
(1) the peaceful nature of the revolution and the transition to democracy;
(2) the policy of a weakened Russia; and
(3) the reality of a shared Christian European culture.

Very different neighbors to the South

It is important to make the comparison, but also to be reminded of the modern history of the Southern Mediterranean and the Middle East. It is less than a hundred years ago that all countries concerned - with the exception of Morocco, Algeria and Egypt - belonged to the Ottoman Empire. In the first World War of the twentieth century, Turkey fought on the side of the German Empire and lost with the Central Powers.

At the end of the First World War, the Ottoman Empire collapsed and Turkey lost Iraq, Syria, Lebanon, Jordan, Palestine, the Arab peninsula and Libya, to France, Britain and the League of Nations Mandate arrangement. After a French and British interregnum period, these countries emerged as new states with the exception of Palestine that became British Mandate. After the Second World War, the United Nations tried (so far in vain) to partition the area into Israel and an Arab/Palestinian state.[48] The harsh treatment of Turkey in the Treaty of Sèvres had a lot to do with the extermination of the Armenian population during the war. Turkey's new leader could turn the tide after Greece lost its war against Turkey in 1920; in the new Treaty of

---

48 For the peace treaties with Turkey after the First World War, see my *Western Cooperation, Origins and History,* Part I, Chapter 1.

Lausanne, Armenia and Kurdistan were no longer mentioned and Turkey received (almost) ally treatment.

In the Second World War, Turkey began as an ally of Hitler Germany, but changed in time to emerge, with Greece, as the recipient of US aid under the Truman doctrine in 1947.[49]

In the new constellation of power created by the Cold War, Turkey's control over the straits turned the country into a strategic asset against the Soviet Union. Just as the Grand Alliance in 1941 made from cruel dictator Stalin a benign Uncle Joe, did the Cold War make from young Turk Kemal Atatürk a democratic leader of a Western secular and democratic republic. So called strategic interests turned Turkey into an ally and a European democracy. As none of the serious conflicts between Greece and Turkey had been solved, Washington's solution was to treat them as equals within a Western Alliance. Both states became member of the Council of Europe and the North Atlantic Alliance. Both states could become associated with the European Economic Community in the 1960's as we saw already above.

Equal treatment of Greece and Turkey was based on strategic arguments and American pressure, but not on political reality. The evolution of their relations with the European Community/ Union would diverge more and more. Greece, despite a seven year military dictatorship, could become a full member in 1981. Turkey could only apply on 14 April 1987. It took another twelve years until Turkey was granted candidate status and another six years before accession negotiations could formally start on 3 October 2005. Negotiations since that date are not making much progress. The unsolved Cyprus issue remains a major stumbling block.

---

[49] Cf. my *Western Cooperation. Op.cit.* Part I, Chapter 5.

On the side of the European Union, there is no clear commitment to enlargement with Turkey. Britain, Sweden and Italy might agree with the US that Turkish membership continues to be of strategic importance, although its importance against Russia has lost its relevance. They might also argue in favor of admission on the basis of promises to Turkey since the Treaty of Association. Another argument in favor would be Turkey's bridge-function between Europe and the Islamic countries. France, Germany and Austria are on record as opponents to Turkish membership. In terms of history and culture, Turkey's "European" identity is a topic of much debate and controversy. Once across the bridge over the Dardanelles, one enters Asia. Istanbul might still be European, Ankara definitely is Asia. In terms of demography and geography, a European Union with Turkey would be a very different Union.

The 2011 revolts in the Arab countries belonging to the Ottoman Empire until the First World War, are bound to draw Ankara's attention towards them. The European Union shall have to reconsider its Mediterranean policies, including further enlargement, in terms of an agonizing reappraisal of the illusions on which these policies had been based before the 2011 upheavals.

CHAPTER 3

REAL SOLIDARITY? FROM COMMON MARKET TO €

> "*Conscious* of the fact that Europe can be built only by concrete actions which create a real solidarity and by the establishment of common bases for economic development"

This phrase, from the Preamble to the ECSC Treaty, clearly expresses the idea behind the Schuman plan and the Coal and Steel Community. The text almost literally comes from the Schuman Declaration:

> "L'Europe ne se fera pas d'un coup, ni dans une construction d'ensemble: elle se fera par des realisation concretes créant d'abord *une solidarité de fait.*" [1]

Reconciliation and European political unity, in Schuman's philosophy are the outcome of a long term process, requiring concrete actions through which real solidarity can be achieved. "Real solidarity" expresses a virtue to be learned and practiced rather than just a principle or a value to be written in a treaty. As it is the case with virtues, the more they are being practiced, the better their effect and the better their meaning and significance will be understood. Common rules and common institutions are set up to keep the memory

---

[1] For a proper understanding of the original ideas and their writing into law, read Paul Reuter, *La Communauté Européenne du Charbon et de L'Acier,* Paris 1953; Avec une préface de M. Robert Schuman. Paul Reuter was close to Robert Schuman and the principal drafter of the Treaty.

of good practice and thus the practice itself alive. The longer the duration of the process, the more important are these rules and institutions to fall back on, whenever vice derails the process.

Learning from the ECSC's first years and the first 1954 crisis, the six understood, that setting up a common market would take a long time. According to the EEC Treaty, it would take a transitional period of twelve years to establish a common market. The concrete actions to be undertaken during this period were written in article 3 of the Treaty:

> "*Article 3*
>
> For the purposes set out in the preceding Article, the activities of the Community shall include, under the conditions and with the timing provided for in this Treaty:
>
> (a) the elimination, as between Member States, of customs duties and of quantitative restrictions in regard to the importation and exportation of goods, as well as of all other measures with equivalent effect;
>
> (b) the establishment of a common customs tariff and a common commercial policy towards third countries;
>
> (c) the abolition, as between Member States, of the obstacles to the free movement of persons, services and capital;
>
> (d) the inauguration of a common agricultural policy;
>
> (e) the inauguration of a common transport policy;
>
> (f) the establishment of a system ensuring that

competition shall not be distorted in the Common Market;

(g) the application of procedures which shall make it possible to co-ordinate the economic policies of Member States and to remedy disequilibria in their balances of payments;

(h) the approximation of their respective municipal law to the extent necessary for the functioning of the Common Market;

(i) the creation of a European Social Fund in order to improve the possibilities of employment for workers and to contribute to the raising of their standard of living;

(j) the establishment of a European Investment Bank intended to facilitate the economic expansion of the Community through the creation of new resources; and

(k) the association of overseas countries and territories with the Community with a view to increasing trade and to pursuing jointly their effort towards economic and social development."[2]

The Transitional Period to the Common Market (1958-1970)

These concrete actions were to be taken during the transitional period in order to create the real solidarity needed to achieve political unity and contribute to world peace. They were to be taken by the Institutions of the Community in close cooperation with the governments of Member States represented in the

---

2 Full original text of the EEC Treaty in Document EU. 3. Compare with article 3 in the TEU of Lisbon, in Document EU. 15.

Council of Ministers. The important common denominator for the Institutions resided in their task to pursue the common good of the Community.

It is important to be reminded of this task, underlying the Schuman plan. Real solidarity cannot be created by market forces alone, nor by the pooling of national interests. The common good to be pursued goes beyond a common or even a global market and beyond a European (super)state, with the power to play a world role. This idea was very strong in the years following the Second World War, in which the spectacle of the ruins of the war had aroused European conscience. It is more and more forgotten or dismissed at present. Early twenty-first century European conscience is shaped by the economics of globalization and the fear for terrorism.

As Jonathan Sacks rightly observed: "Enthusiasts of the global market are the latest in the line of those who have been held captive by possibly the single most influential idea of modernity: that competition is the driving force of progress." That idea in turn led to the question: "How can the destructive passions to which human beings are prone, be turned to collective advantage?" Competition for power - in politics as in the marketplace - can become a destructive passion and the answer to the question became that "Private vice would become public virtue when society was so organized as to turn passions into interests. Thus was economics born."[3] The answer does not hold and the idea does not work. On the contrary. Global society is not organized to turn the private passion for wealth into an interest to share wealth with others. Nor does it turn the private passion of politicians for power and prestige into a common commitment to the common good of order

---

3 Jonathan Sachs, *The Dignity of Difference, How to avoid the clash of civilizations,* London 2002, pp. 42-44

and justice. Public virtue can only be practiced by those who have learnt to practice virtue in personal life. Private vice is more prone to turn into destructive public vice.

There is more, however. The single most important idea of modernity, referred to by Sachs, has one major shortcoming. The "progress" talked about is no more than economic growth. And indeed, economics was born and economic values were formulated. In economics, growth is a valid objective and competition an important value, but it is not (yet) the common good of order and justice. The pursuance of the common good requires more than individual strength through competition. It needs cooperation and trust. As Sachs rightly observes: "markets depend on virtues not produced by the market, just as states depend on virtues not created by the states."[4] The *"solidarité de fait"* Schuman intended to create was one of the virtues not produced by the market. Whenever that perspective was lost, by the magnitude of economic tasks along the way, European unification would be in trouble, and that is exactly what is happening in the European integration process since the entry into force of the Single European Act.

The list of activities to be performed according to article 3 of the EEC Treaty was an ambitious one and the result of the actions taken was not as good as the 1969 Hague Summit declared it be. During the transitional period the initial commitment to real solidarity had seriously been weakened. The most important internal cause was the new French policy conducted by Charles de Gaulle. His passion for power and prestige returned community decision-making to the pursuance of national interests and not only in France. Even inside the supranational institutions, the national spirits were revived. A telling example was the organization of the

4 *Op. cit.* p. 152.

common agricultural policy. It would be managed in the relevant agricultural committees, by a symbiosis of European and national officials. Two external causes during the sixties for the weakening of the initial commitment must be added. One of them was the emergence of East-West détente; the other the revolt of the intellectuals, beginning in the United States, followed by the student revolt of May 1968 in Paris and spreading throughout Europe thereafter. They seriously weakened the initial commitment to real solidarity inside the community of the six and as a pilot project within the Western Alliance of free nations.[5]

ECONOMIC AND MONETARY UNION

The outcome of the Hague Summit of December 1969 was a compromise after the crisis years of the sixties. According to its communiqué the transitional period towards a common market had been completed. The Summit thereby launched the fourfold development towards:

(1) Economic and Monetary Union;

(2) Enlargement of the Communities;

(3) a reformed social policy and

(4) European Political Cooperation. Paragraph 8 had this to declare on the first item:

> "8 . They have reaffirmed their readiness to expedite the further action needed to strengthen the Community and promote its development into economic union. They

---

5 Cf. my *Beyond the European Community, Op.cit.* and *The Illusions of Détente, Op.cit.*

are of the opinion that the integration process should result in a Community of stability and growth. To this end they agreed that within the Council, on the basis of the memorandum presented by the Commission on 12 February 1969, and in close collaboration with the latter, a plan in stages will be worked out during 1970 with a view to the creation of an economic and monetary union. The development of monetary co-operation should be based on the harmonization of economic policies. They agreed to arrange for the investigation of the possibility of setting up a European reserve fund which should be the outcome of a joint economic and monetary policy."[6]

The creation of Economic and Monetary Union was no new idea.[7] There was general agreement on the need for monetary unity after the completion of the common market. It received prominent attention in 1969 as part of the effort to overcome the crisis of the 1960s and it was strongly advocated by French President Pompidou. In line with his Gaullist background, he preferred a *union* controlled by member state governments. Monetary Union also could better constrain West German prominence, at the time increased by Chancellor Brandt's new *Ostpolitik.* The federalists urged rapid progress, though for different reasons. In their view monetary unity was a major step towards political unity. The Commission Halstein had proposed action as early as 1962. Following the Hague Summit the so called Committee Werner formulated plans to create Economic and Monetary Union in two stages: the first one to

---

6 Document ES. 3 . For enlargement and political cooperation, see Chapters II. 2 and II. 5.

7 A survey of the history of such union can be found in Document E. 3. 1.

begin on 1 January 1971 and the second one to be completed before the end of the decade.

The report makes interesting reading, but its plans were not realized. Among the reasons are the American decision in August 1971 to decouple the dollar from the gold-price - creating a period of world monetary instability; the energy crises of the seventies, following the steep rise in oil prices in 1973; and serious disagreements among the EEC Member States, especially over the British contribution to the budget.[8]

French-German agreement, nevertheless resulted in the first step towards monetary stability in the EEC, at least among some member-states: the creation of the European Monetary System and the European Currency Unit (ECU) in 1979.[9]

A new transitional period to the Internal Market (1986-1992)

The solution of the British budget problem and the appointment of Jacques Delors as president of the Commission enabled the Commission to launch its White Paper envisaging a new transitional period towards completing the internal market,[10] to be followed by Monetary Union.

Such a new transitional period was necessary as the difficult intervening years had seriously eroded the common market by the adoption in member states of measures amounting to non-tariff barriers to free trade. The Single European Act embodied agreement on the transitional period towards completing the internal market. Shortly after the entry into force of the Single

---

8 The relevant Documents can be found in E. 3. 2-4.

9 As decided by the European Council meetings of Bremen and Brussels in 1978, See Documents EC. 11-12.

10 Text of the 1985 White Paper in Document E. 1. 13.

European Act, the European Council in Hannover:

> "... recalls that, in adopting the Single Act, the Member States confirmed the objective of progressive realization of economic and monetary union.
> They therefore decided to examine at the European Council meeting in Madrid in June 1989 the means of achieving this union. To that end they decided to entrust to a Committee the task of studying and proposing concrete stages leading towards this union. The Committee will be chaired by Mr Jacques Delors, President of the European Commission."[11]

In June 1989, the European Council of Madrid adopted the report of the Delors Committee, in the following terms:

> "B. *Economic and Monetary Union*
> The European Council restated its determination to progressively achieve Economic and Monetary Union as provided for in the Single Act and confirmed at the European Council meeting in Hanover. Economic and Monetary Union must be seen in the perspective of the completion of the Internal Market and in the context of economic and social cohesion.
> (...)
>
> The European Council considered that the report by the committee chaired by Jacques Delors, which defines a process designed to lead by stages to Economic and Monetary Union fulfilled the mandate given in Hanover. The European Council felt that its realization would have to take account of the parallelism between economic and monetary aspects, respect the principle

[11] Document EC. 39.

of "subsidiarity" and allow for the diversity of specific situations.

The European Council decided that the first stage of the realization of Economic and Monetary Union would begin on July 1, 1990.

The European Council asked the competent bodies (the Economic and Financial and General Affairs Councils of Ministers, the Commission, the Committee of Central Bank Governors and the Monetary Committee):

(a) to adopt the provisions necessary for the launch of the first stage on 1 July 1990;

(b) to carry out the preparatory work for the organization of an intergovernmental conference to lay down the subsequent stages; that conference would meet once the first stage had begun and would be preceded by full and adequate preparation."[12]

The results of the Intergovernmental Conference (IGC) are written in the TEU of Maastricht, Title VI, articles 102A-109M.[13]

---

12 Text of the Delors report in Document E. 3. 6. Text of the Conclusions of the European Council: EC. 41. See also Chapter II. 1 above.

13 Document EU. 9 Since the Treaty of Amsterdam, the relevant articles were renumbered: Title VII, articles 98-124. See Document EU. 12 and EU. 12A for the table of equivalences. In the Lisbon TFEU, economic and monetary union are under Title VIII, articles 119-133.

The second stage was to begin on 1 January 1994; the third began on 1 January1999.[14]

Completion of the first stage comprised achieving the internal market, reinforcing the EC's regional and structural policies, new procedures for supervising national economic policies, liberalization of capital transactions, participation in the EMS and no more barriers to the private use of the ECU. It is important to keep in mind, what the abolition of non-tariff barriers implied and the sheer number of intrusive and detailed issues that were going to be regulated by "Brussels." The Commission's interpretation of what was needed to achieve the free movement of persons, goods, services and capital went much further than had been realized.

The specific requirements for the completion of the second stage are written in TEU article 109E/116(1). On 1 January 1999, the third and final stage began for the eleven Member States which had satisfied the conditions for adopting a single currency: Austria, Belgium, Finland, France, Germany, Ireland, Italy, Luxembourg, Netherlands, Spain and Portugal. For them and for Greece Euro notes and coins were introduced on January 1, 2002. Since then five more member countries introduced the Euro: Slovenia in 2007, Cyprus and Malta in 2008, Slovakia in 2009 and Estonia in 2011.

These seventeen countries have transferred to the Union the exclusive competence to conduct monetary policy (Lisbon TFEU, art.3). According to Lisbon TFEU, art. 127(2):

> "The basic tasks to be carried out through the ESCB shall be:

---

14 The Compendium on EMU in document E. 3. 7 contains all relevant documents from 1992-2007.

- to define and implement the monetary policy of the Union,
- to conduct foreign-exchange operations consistent with the provisions of Article 219,
- to hold and manage the official foreign reserves of the Member States,
- to promote the smooth operation of payment systems."[15]

Technically, the operation towards one currency for (currently) seventeen EU Member States was most successful. The mostly technical exclusive competence transferred to the EU is not anchored in an equally exclusive competence to conduct the economic policy of the EU. That conduct is left to the Member States, although with a growing number of provisions providing for coordination, monitoring and supervision of national policies.

There is serious discussion on the question whether monetary policy can be so conducted without at the same time transferring fiscal and economic policies.[16] Due to the global credit crisis, the question is no longer academic but addressed directly and urgently to the EU political leaders.

IN TIME OF CRISIS

At the time of writing, we are still in the midst of the global financial crisis. It began in 2007, seriously affected the stock market since 2008 and was transformed into a sovereign

---

15 Lisbon TFEU in Document EU. 15B.

16 Cf. Jacques Pelkmans, *European Integration, Methods and Economic Analysis,* Longman Third Edition 2006.

debt crisis in the Euro-area.[17] There is ample evidence that the European Union has so far been unable to effectively manage the crisis. It responded reluctantly and too late, waiting for the German Chancellor to make up her mind. Real solidarity as envisaged by the founding fathers no longer appeared to be the guiding principle in the EU.

The first reason - as in other fields - is the dominance of the (intergovernmental) European Council over the supranational institutions. The story of the initial failure in the 1970's, the partial success since the SEA and the first TEU of Maastricht can be followed entirely through the conclusions of the European Council meetings.

European Council meetings are dominated by politics and the need to show results on paper, rather than by expertise and logic thinking. German reunification in 1990 was a primary motive for accelerating the transition to the Euro. The required transfer of competences to the common institutions in economic and monetary policy-making did not take place, neither in the Treaties of Maastricht, Amsterdam, Nice and Lisbon; nor for that matter in the abortive Constitution for Europe.

Conclusions of the European Council meetings offer, more often than not, attractive illusions and false promises. Among the many examples, the clearest one is given by the so called Lisbon 2000 strategy, reading in its fifth paragraph:

> "The Union has today set itself *a new strategic goal* for the next decade: *to become the most competitive and dynamic knowledge-based economy in the world*

---

17 Cf. Document E. 3. 8. An economic paper on the sovereign debt crisis published by the European Commission.

capable of sustainable economic growth with more and better jobs and greater social cohesion."[18]

The principal message the French in the Council wanted to publicize was the intention to catch up with the United States economy and bypass them. A similar message was publicized some fifty years earlier by Soviet leader Nikita Khrushchev! The intention to form EMU before the end of the 1970's was another such example.

A more important reason lies in the direction the EC took with the adoption of the 1985 White Paper on completing the internal market as the first stage to the EMU. The sheer magnitude of the tasks and the intrusive character of the measures taken, pushed the unification of Europe towards economic unity as the final objective. Continuing economic growth has become the central objective; competition the highest value. The 35 Chapters of the *acquis communautaire* represent some 30 000 legal documents, filled with detailed economic rules affecting daily life of all citizens. Their sheer number makes it difficult even to observe, even more to ensure implementation throughout the Union.[19] Creating real solidarity moved out of sight. European solidarity is still preached but no longer practiced. Subsidiarity - which in Eurospeak means protecting national sovereignty against European regulation - has taken its place.

The process of completing the three stages to an EMU predominantly coincided with the post-cold war era. It was, and is, the era of globalization, a phenomenon by the way of the American era in international relations. Globalization means of course the exponential growth of means of

---

18 Document EC. 81.

19 Cf. Documents E. 2. 24-24A; E. 3. 9 on the *acquis communautaire.*

communication, of internet, email, mobile telephone etc. It also means open borders, market economy and free trade, liberalization of capital transactions, large scale privatization and exponential growth of drug trade, human trafficking and international crime. Instead of protecting European citizens more effectively against the excesses of globalization, the European Union has opted for competing for prominence in the global market. Instead of creating more solidarity, the EU has been going along with the ideologies of globalization. National railways, postal services and utilities are being split up and privatized. Good profit (for the shareholders) has become more important than good public service for the citizens. (European) Council of Ministers meetings are becoming very similar to big company board meetings.

During the sovereign debt crisis, Europe is realizing that real solidarity between Member States of the Union is in serious disrepair. In a European Union with at least four presidents, there is no leadership when required in serious crises. As a consequence, the only responses left to the Member States are massive spending cuts and high levels of unemployment, preventing the needed economic growth to overcome the debt crisis.

As the original objectives began to disappear behind the horizon after the SEA, popular support for European unification has substantially diminished since the TEU of Maastricht. The repeated promises to deepen integration were not fulfilled, whereas the enlargement of the EU continued despite serious reluctance and misgivings. "Maastricht" also introduced the practice of variable geometry - not different speeds! - allowing some member countries to opt out of crucial policies. Seventeen and not twenty-seven Member States have introduced the Euro; the readiness to be in the Euro zone for some of them is doubtful at best. Maastricht finally initiated the Union era of complexity and opacity. European Council conclusions are political statements, difficult to decipher and even more difficult to follow in their implementation; that process disappears behind the walls of the European and national bureaucracies of decision-making. No wonder that a majority of citizens in France and the Netherlands voted against the Constitution for Europe. The same European Council, nevertheless, decided in 2007 to present a little remake of the Constitution as the Reform Treaty of Lisbon. The European Union now dressed up as an Economic and Monetary Union goes through a serious crisis. Beneath the financial and sovereign debt crisis is the lack of purpose and the lack of agreement on the road to follow. Real solidarity is no longer in view and common rules and institutions no longer keep the memory alive of how the road to unity must be followed.

CHAPTER 4

ON CONSTITUTIONAL FOUNDATIONS AND HUMAN RIGHTS

An attempt to agree on the constitutional foundations for European unification has first been made in 1929 by the Foreign Ministers Briand and Stresemann of France and Germany in the framework of the League of Nations. In May 1930, Briand submitted a memorandum, outlining the foundation of a "moral European Union". The organization envisaged was confederal in character; its principal institutions would be composed of representatives of member governments. The plans never reached the drawing board.

It was not before the end of the Second World War and the beginning of the "Cold War" that plans for a European Union were taken up again.[1] In May 1948, the Congress of Europe, assembled in the Hague, called for the "Union or Federation of Europe". More specifically, the Congress called for a Charter for the protection of human rights, the institution of a Court of Justice to ensure observance of such Charter, and the formation of a European Assembly. The Council of Europe was formed in 1949, in response to the Congress. Within its framework, the European Convention for the Protection of Human Rights and Fundamental Freedoms was signed in November 1950.

---

1 For an excellent survey of the constitutional history of the EU, see: Bundesverfassungsgericht, *Entscheidung* 30 June 2009, Document E.4.1.

To ensure the observance of the engagements undertaken, the Convention provided for a European Commission of Human Rights and a European Court of Human Rights. The Statute of the Council, however, fell short of a "constitution" for the European Union or Federation, proposed by the Congress. It was an arrangement for intergovernmental cooperation; the Assembly it created, would have no more than consultative powers.

The idea of a European union or federation was carried a significant step further by the Schuman plan of 1950 and the institution of the European Community for Coal and Steel in 1951 by six West European states. The distinguishing feature of the plan was the proposal to form a federal Europe in stages. Rather than drafting a federal constitution, states should identify common interests and entrust the management of these interests to a common "supranational" authority. The ECSC Treaty provided for a High Authority responsible to a Parliamentary Assembly, for a Court of Justice and a Council of Ministers. Underlying the idea of unifying Europe in stages, was the assumption (strengthened by the formation of EEC and Euratom in 1957), that the dynamics of economic integration would ultimately produce the desired European union or federation. In substance the Community treaties included the kind of provisions to be written in a constitution, with the exception of those pertaining to the protection of fundamental human rights. The European Convention on Human Rights continues as an institution separate from the European unification efforts. As a consequence, the European protection of human rights is not embedded in a European structure with the power to enforce observance. Hence the efforts to include human rights in basic European Union Treaties, especially since the Southern and Eastern enlargements of the EU.

As the dynamics of the process of economic integration unfolded, the outcome did not confirm the original assumption. Agreement on the federal destination of Europe was seriously undermined by the policies of the French Fifth Republic since the 1960s, the enlargement of the communities and the broadening of the scope of their activities.

By the time, the new dynamics of the collapse of the totalitarian system in 1989-1991 took over from the internal dynamics of West European economic integration, community Member States experienced great difficulty in agreeing on the conclusion and ratification of a definite new Treaty on European Union. The transformation from Communities to Union went through different stages with the treaties of Maastricht, Amsterdam and Nice, the abortive effort to adopt a Constitution for Europe and in 2007 the Treaty of Lisbon. In this chapter we shall review the efforts to give European unification a solid constitutional foundation, including those towards the formulation of fundamental human rights.

THE RULE OF LAW AND THE DEMOCRATIC STATE

The solution to the problem of protecting the dignity and fundamental freedom of the human person, "has always been sought in obeying laws and not masters... And the problem of political freedom has always been interwoven with the question of legality, for it goes back to the problem of curbing power by making it impersonal", wrote Giovanni Sartori.

According to Böckenförde: The *Rechtsstaat* aims at the limitation and restriction of the power and the mastery of the state in the interest of the freedom of the individual, and at the substitution of the 'mastery of the law' (*Herrschaft der Gesetze*) for the mastery by men; the primacy of law over politics appears to be the ever recurring postulate of political theory concerning the *Rechtsstaat.*

Sartori then goes on: "Basically, the legal solution to the problem of freedom can be sought in two very different directions; either in rule by legislators or in the rule of law.

In the first approach, law consists of written rules that are enacted by legislative bodies; that is, law is legislated law. In the second, law is something to be discovered by judges: It is judicial law. For the former approach, law consists of statutory, systematic lawmaking; for the latter, it is the result of piecemeal law finding (*Rechtsfindung*) by means of judicial decisions. From the first viewpoint, law may be conceived as the product of sheer will; from the second it is the product of theoretical inquiry and debate".[2]

The distinction, Sartori makes, is derived from Dicey's well-known exposition on the Rule of Law. The distinction reflects the classical philosophical dispute between law as reason or will, and the close connection between natural law and the rule of law. It also reflects the cultural difference between the more liberal, universalist tradition in Anglo-American legal thinking, and the more nationalist approach in European and German thinking. If there is a universal law, it can be found; if laws belong to "us" as particular groups, they must be made. In modern constitutional states, attention must be drawn to an additional "political" difference, concerned with the question of legislative supremacy. Should such supremacy be granted to the legislative body or to an independent judiciary? Advocates of the first stress the representative character of the legislative body, and its ability to reflect the will of the people

---

2 Giovanni Sartori, *Liberty in Law*, In: Kenneth S. Templeton (ed), *The Politicization of Society*, Liberty Press 1979, p. 269; E.W. Böckenförde, *Recht, Staat, Freiheit*, Suhrkamp Taschenbuch 1991, p. 168.

as laid down in the Constitution. They consider the judiciary as insufficiently representative and more likely to resist change. Advocates of the second consider judges to be best able to uphold the constitutional order and the human liberties contained therein. The supremacy of the legislature normally prevails in parliamentary democracies with a unitary form of state. The supremacy of the judiciary in exposing the law of the Constitution, prevails in federal states and in international law, marked by the Anglo-American legal tradition.

The rule of law or the Rechtsstaat

In Dicey's exposition, the rule of law, "which forms a fundamental principle of the (English) constitution", has three meanings:

"It means, in the *first* place, the absolute supremacy or predominance of regular law as opposed to the influence of arbitrary power, and excludes the existence of arbitrariness, of prerogative, or even of wide discretionary authority on the part of the government." In this meaning, the rule of law is linked to the "liberal" fight against the absolute power of the state. In its English context, the idea of the supremacy of the law was also related to the struggle between common law judges and Parliament for legislative supremacy. In this struggle parliament prevailed. The sharp difference, Dicey and Sartori made between the common law and continental law, or between the rule of law and the *Rechtsstaat* no longer applies today.

The rule of law "means, *again*, equality before the law, or equal subjection of all classes to the ordinary law of the land administered by the ordinary Law Courts". Dicey, here, contrasted the English system to the French system of administrative law or administrative tribunals. Apart from his misunderstanding of French administrative law, the distinction has at present lost much of its relevance. The common law countries have accepted a system of administrative tribunals. The independence of the judiciary is an accepted principle in both systems of law.

The 'rule of law', "*lastly*, may be used as a formula for expressing the fact that with us the law of the constitution, the rules which in foreign countries naturally form part of a constitutional code, are not the source but the consequence of the rights of individuals, as defined and enforced by the Courts;"[3] Here again, the difference no longer is as sharp, as Dicey would like. The growing body of statutory law in England, requires judges to interpret legislation. The growing quantity and complexity of legislative acts in all countries, requires judges to interpret them by reference to principles or norms outside them. In this respect English judges and judges in continental parliamentary democracies, like Belgium or the Netherlands lack the competence of challenging an act of parliament by reference to a "higher" rule of constitutional law. The principal guarantee against a violation of the basic human rights (apart from the European Convention on Human Rights) lies in the observance of the principles of government by consent (which is more than legislation by a majority of votes), legislative control on executive power, and independence of the judiciary.

In essence, the rule of law or the *Rechtsstaat*, are efforts to achieve the self-limitation of the state in favor of the

---

3 A.V. Dicey, *Introduction to the Study of the Law of the Constitution*, Liberty Classics 1982, pp. 120,121.

fundamental rights of its citizens, by principles of a procedural or formal character. [4]

The Constitutional State

These efforts were carried several steps further, by the idea to draft a written Constitution as the basic law for the political order. The convention of delegates who assembled in Philadelphia in May 1787, was the first to produce such a document for the United States of America. Under its influence and the impact of the French revolution, the overwhelming majority of modern states have adopted such constitutions.

Constitutions - in general terms - serve three objectives: to limit the arbitrary action of governments; to guarantee the rights of the governed; and to define the operation of the sovereign power.

The principal characteristic of a written constitution is its status as the basic law of the country. The principles and rules contained therein are of higher order (than legislative acts). Among the rules and principles to be protected are human rights, the system of checks and balances between legislative, judiciary and executive powers, the holding of elections, and (in federal constitutions) the range of powers attributed to the federal government and those left or attributed to the governments of constituent states.

These rules and principles, as they appear in written constitutions, are primarily formal in nature. The German Constitution, as Böckenförde explained also tried to transform

---

[4] According to Jellinek as quoted in W. Friedmann, *Legal Theory,* Third Edition, Stevens & Sons, 1953, p. 423

basic values of the ordering of the political community, into rules of positive, constitutional law. The Constitution no longer guarantees freedom unconditionally, but only within the *Wertgrundlage* (basic values) of the Constitution. Persons or political parties, who abuse their constitutional rights for the purpose of fighting against the basic liberal democratic order, forfeit their rights, contained therein.[5]

Protection against the infringement of the higher law of the Constitution by the government, is sought primarily in another procedural rule: written constitutions require special procedures for their amendment. These rules may provide for strengthened majorities in the legislative, for a constitutional referendum, a special convention, or combinations of them.

In addition, federal states and a number of modern strongly decentralized states, know the rule of constitutional review by the judiciary. The U.S. Constitution, in its article VI, writes, that "this Constitution, and the laws of the United States which shall be made in pursuance thereof; and all treaties made, or which shall be made, under the authority of the United States, shall be the supreme law of the land;".

Ever since the leading case of *Marbury vs. Madison* (1803), the U.S. Supreme Court has established its supremacy "in the exposition of the law of the Constitution" and its power of judicial review to declare a law repugnant to the constitution as void . In the constitutions of countries like Germany, Italy, Spain, Portugal and Ireland, the principle of judicial review is written in the constitution itself .[6]

---

5 Cf. Articles 18 and 21 of the German Constitution; Böckenförde, *Op. cit.* p.164.

6 The task of the French *Conseil Constitutionnel* is different.

The constitutional state today can be seen as the most advanced solution in the efforts to uphold the rule of law or the *Rechtsstaat.* Still, as is indicated by Böckenförde's reference to the *Wertgrundlage* of a liberal democracy, the question remains, whether the positive law of the Constitution in itself gives the ultimate answer to the problem of upholding the rule of law or the *Rechtsstaat.* The question is of importance, because - on the one hand - government by consent requires consent on the conditions of a just social order. On the other hand, totalitarian and despotic regimes have always invoked higher ideological or religious principles as their justification for abolishing the procedural guarantees written in constitutions.

Procedures and principles

Reference to certain basic values in the German Constitution, clearly was intended to foreclose a totalitarian abuse of constitutional rules. By the same token, it may be said to reject the hierarchical model in which "the law of nature" and authority should ultimately answer the question which rule of positive law ought to be observed. Reference (in article 18 of the German Constitution) to the liberal democratic basic order (*die freiheitliche demokratische Grundordnung*), reflects German popular consent, or a shared sense or conscience of justice, at the time the Constitution was written.

For Americans, writes Weinreb, "constitutional doctrine provides both a source and a repository of principles that are accepted not simply as positive law, at however high a level, but as a standard for positive law generally." Similar conclusions could be drawn with respect to the written constitutions in other democracies. The basic values or accepted standard referred to can neither be equated with an objective norm, nor with the sum of individual norms. They belong to particular political and social orders, and even within each of them, basic values or accepted standards can and did change over time. "Beyond its limited application to a particular community, the political ideal of just social order not only is unattainable in practice but is not susceptible of coherent exposition. No elaboration of the abstract ideas of liberty and equality can satisfy such an ideal non-arbitrarily because the ideas are antinomic. Yet we cannot do without them".[7]

Still, the experience of constitutional democracies does indicate a less limited application than Weinreb seems to suggest. The first experience is related to democracies as open societies and cooperating states. The second one is related to the time and circumstance chosen for creating a (new) constitutional order.

The enduring strength of the U.S. Constitution has much to do with the circumstance of its formulation and the spirit in which this was done. In contrast to the American experience, France's turbulent constitutional history since the revolution reflects the vagaries of statesmen, who wanted a constitution to fit their own rule. The nature and substance of the German Constitution of 1949 have much to do with a strong anti-totalitarian consensus and American political and constitutional influence.

Open societies and close cooperation in Europe and the Western world since the Second World War no doubt contributed to sustain and strengthen a shared commitment to basic principles of a democratic, constitutional order. The linkage between return to democracy, adherence to the European Convention on Human Rights and membership of Western and European organizations is an important factor

---

[7] Lloyd L. Weinreb, *Natural Law and Justice,* Harvard Univerity Press 1987, pp. 231, 234.

also in extending such commitment to basic constitutional principles. The political ideal of just social order no longer is unattainable beyond a particular community, because open societies forcefully spread the conviction that democracy and human rights contribute to peace.

Principles and a just social order

I must now briefly return to the distinction, Sartori made between legislative law that could be conceived as the product of sheer will, and judicial law as the product of theoretical inquiry and debate. The sharp contrast, while initially useful, does not withstand further analysis. Legislative law - *die Herrschaft der Gesetze* - in the *Rechtsstaat* of the continental European or civil law type, is much more a product of reason and debate than Sartori seems to suggest. Judicial law in the United States, is much more a product of political will than he is prepared to acknowledge.

Comparing the American and the French experience, Mary Ann Glendon, writes: "The American founders, no less than the French, (thus) tended to look to law as a way in which life in society could be brought under the control of reason. But where the French turned to abstract reason and legislation, the Americans relied more heavily on practical reason, a constitutional framework, and - despite the fact that they had rejected English rule - the common law tradition. The creative energy that went into constitution making in America was devoted in France to legislation and codification, mainly on private subjects".[8] While the French and many lawyers and statesmen in other civil law countries gave their efforts to the codification of civil and criminal law, these matters in early America were largely left to be worked out by judges. Today,

8 Mary Ann Glendon, *Abortion and Divorce in Western Law,* Harvard University Press 1987, p. 127.

as she remarks, both the civil law codes and Anglo-American case law have been similarly displaced as primary sources of law by the mass of fragmentary statutory and administrative regulations. Still, the process of adapting the law to changing social values, is markedly different in the common law and civil law systems. In the civil law countries, amendment to the Civil Code still is a great event, taken more seriously than constitutional change. Adapting legislation on controversial subjects in family, social or criminal law, is done by political compromise. In the United States, the adaptation of the law to changing values, is left primarily to the judges. Judge-made law on such great issues as Roosevelt's new deal legislation, abortion, or the slow evolution from slavery, through civil rights to affirmative action, has been the subject of sharp, sometimes violent conflict. Whereas the President, with the advice and consent of the Senate, has the power to appoint the Justices to the Supreme Court, this power is being employed to change the law through a change in the political composition of the Court.

In modern democracies, the "sharp contrast" thus may well be elsewhere than Sartori thought. The civil codes enacted by legislative bodies, codified principles and rules that had gradually evolved over a long period of history. Like judge-made law, civil codes were the outcome of reason and debate. Codified law and judicial law are both the outcome of law-finding; the distinction to be made here is between systematic and piece-meal law-finding. The real contrast today, in civil law and common law countries alike, is between law discovered through reason and debate, and statutory and administrative regulations beyond the field of public law - the field in which legislative bodies were directly qualified to intervene. Statutory regulations, often hastily drafted, are displacing reasoned codifications and judicial law as primary sources of law, thus eroding both the certainty of and the respect for the law.

The new post-totalitarian democracies encounter even more serious problems in this respect. Decades of totalitarian lawlessness had interrupted the process of law-finding, whether by codification or judicial decision. Deprived of meaningful constitutions and subject to arbitrary party-rule, administrative action had ceased to be subject to review by independent courts. For them accepting the mass of European laws, known as the *acquis communautaire*, entails the risk of a lopsided legal development: a huge body of statutory and administrative regulations without a solid basis in constitutional, civil and judicial law.

EFFORTS TO WRITE A CONSTITUTION FOR EUROPE

Few politicians appear to have realized that already in the 1950s a first effort was made to give Europe - of the six at the time - its own constitution. I referred to it already in Chapter 1 above and shall come back to it in this paragraph. The new equally unsuccessful effort began with the Laken Declaration of the European Council.

Why the Laeken Declaration on the Future of the European Union was wrong

The Declaration, that Europe has a leading role to play in the world: 'as the continent of humane values, the Magna Carta, the Bill of Rights, the French Revolution and the fall of the Berlin Wall; the continent of liberty, solidarity and above all diversity, meaning respect for others' languages, cultures and traditions',[9] expressed an unfounded illusion. True, Europe

---

[9] Document EC.89.

as a civilization is shaped by the fundamental values of the Christian religion, but the extent to which Europe has failed to live up to and act by them, should make us very modest. Most of the values proclaimed to be European values in boastful political declarations have been discovered, only after two world wars had left Europe in ruins. Just as wrong as claiming a world role was the following claim in the Declaration:

> "At long last, Europe is on its way to becoming one big family, without bloodshed, a real transformation clearly calling for a different approach from fifty years ago, when six countries first took the lead."

The 'real transformation' had taken place exactly because of the new method of organizing common action agreed upon in 1950. It had also taken place because of the peaceful resistance of civil society against totalitarian repression in East and Central Europe. The latter resistance was a moral revolution, made possible also by the attraction of the peaceful organization of common action in the European Communities.

It may well be that the constitutional foundation of 1950 could be strengthened by a better division and definition of competences in the European Union. However, when the different approach called for, implies an interpretation of the principle of subsidiarity in such a way, 'that any powers not assigned by the Treaties to the Union fall within the exclusive sphere of competence of the Member States' the 'different approach' turned out to be little else than a return to a more intergovernmental approach to European unification, a step back from the constitutional provisions in the original ECSC Treaty of 1951.

The Convention created by the Declaration went astray the moment it buried the need for a strengthened constitutional foundation under a long list of wishes, where to go with the European Union. The formulation of tasks for the future could be the subject of a strategy or policy paper or for future legislation, but not for a constitutional document. A constitution should restrict itself to formulate the basic rules of operation for the European Union. A constitution should not proclaim that Europe must become a global player on the world stage, it should restrict itself to prescribing procedural rules for democratic policy making.

The Convention: a misnomer

The Declaration failed to give the Convention a clear task. Was it the task of the Convention to draft a Constitution? According to the Declaration: 'The question ultimately arises as to whether this simplification (of the Union's instruments) and reorganization (of the Treaties) might not lead in the long run to the adoption of a constitutional text in the Union.' The answer, apparently, is: not yet, but may be later. By its composition and the intended nature of its 'final document', the Convention was set up as a debating society rather than as a 'constitutional convention'.

As to composition, the Heads of State or Government of the Member States and the institutions of the European Community were represented in the Convention. Neither its members, nor the Convention itself were given a clear mandate: 'The Convention will consider the various issues. It will draw up a final document which may comprise either different options, indicating the degree of support which they received, or recommendations if consensus is achieved.' The eventual outcome of the Convention had no legal status whatsoever: 'Together with the outcome of national debates on the future of the Union, the final document will provide a starting point for discussions in the Intergovernmental Conference, which will take the ultimate decisions.'[10]

The name 'Convention' given to the exercise thus was a misnomer. Had the Heads of State or Government in the European Council done some homework, they might have come across the Resolution adopted by the Foreign Ministers of Member States of the ECSC on 10 September 1952 in which they invited an Assembly ad hoc to draft a Treaty constituting a European Political Authority.[11] This resolution contained a clear mandate and provided for a composition worth a constitutional task, namely elected representatives - exactly the kind of procedure required to reaffirm the constitutional foundation laid by the Schuman-plan and the ECSC Treaty, and prevent the 'Convention' from getting bogged down in the quicksand of intergovernmental bargaining.

As it turned out, the Convention Chairman pushed through a text, hardly examined but accepted by consensus. The text was submitted to and reworked by the Intergovernmental Conference and signed by Member States. The text and its annexes, together a book of 500 pages make interesting reading. Although a majority of the electorate in France and the Netherlands rejected the Constitution, most of it reappeared two years later in the Treaty of Lisbon.[12]

---

10 Document EC.89.

11 For the text of the Draft Treaty, see Document EUD. 1. Members of the Assembly ad hoc were members of the ECSC Assembly + additional members from among the representatives to the Consultative Assembly of the Council of Europe. Text of the Ministerial Resolution in Document E. 5.1.

12 For the sake of comparison, the text can be found in documents EUD.3 and 4. The consolidated text of the Treaty of Lisbon can be found in Document EU.15.

TREATY OF LISBON: TRADITIONAL TREATY OR NEW CONSTITUTION?

"It is interesting to note that, at the governmental level at least, the integration of the Community and non-Community paths towards integration nor the actual idea of a constitution seemed to pose any difficulties. The political breaking points were as ever the arrangements directly affecting the allocation of competences between Member States and the Union, the extent of qualified majority voting and the status and justiciability of the Charter of Fundamental Rights", wrote Koen Lenaerts and Piet van Nuffel.[13] None of these breaking points were satisfactorily solved in the Treaty of Lisbon.

According to the Treaty on European Union (the treaty of Lisbon, entered into force on 1 December 2009):

> "Article 1.
> This Treaty marks a new stage in the process of creating an ever closer union among the peoples of Europe, in which decisions are taken as openly as possible and as closely as possible to the citizen.
>
> Article 2.
> The Union is founded on the values of respect for human dignity, freedom, democracy, equality, the rule of law and respect for human rights, including the rights of persons belonging to minorities. These values are common to the Member States in a society in which pluralism, non-discrimination, tolerance, justice, solidarity and equality between women and men prevail.

---

13 *Constitutional Law of the European Union,* Sweet & Maxwell 2005, p.75, See also Part II, Chapter 1 *supra.*

> Article 6.
> 1. The Union recognises the rights, freedoms and principles set out in the Charter of Fundamental Rights of the European Union of 7 December 2000, as adapted at Strasbourg, on 12 December 2007, which shall have the same legal value as the Treaties.
> The provisions of the Charter shall not extend in any way the competences of the Union as defined in the Treaties. The rights, freedoms and principles in the Charter shall be interpreted in accordance with the general provisions in Title VII of the Charter governing its interpretation and application and with due regard to the explanations referred to in the Charter, that set out the sources of those provisions.
>
> 2. The Union shall accede to the European Convention for the Protection of Human Rights and Fundamental Freedoms. Such accession shall not affect the Union's competences as defined in the Treaties.
>
> 3. Fundamental rights, as guaranteed by the European Convention for the Protection of Human Rights and Fundamental Freedoms and as they result from the constitutional traditions common to the Member States, shall constitute general principles of the Union's law."

True to its character as the latest result in the process of European integration, the Union Treaty is built on the assumption of a continuation of the internal dynamics of integration. Respect for human rights laid down in the European Convention for Human Rights does not as yet imply adherence of the Union to the Convention. Among the treaties is the EU Charter of Human Rights as adopted in 2000. The rights included in the charter are merely to be treated as general principles of Community law, according to article 52. Otherwise the Treaty consists of The Treaty on European Union, the one coming closest to a constitution; the Treaty on the Functioning of the European Union, replacing the EEC Treaty; the Treaty of Lisbon proper, containing the final, formal provisions; and a long list of 46 Protocols and 65 Declarations (explaining, qualifying or derogating from the treaty texts).

The best one can conclude from studying the Treaty, is written in the first sentence of its article 1, quoted above. In the ongoing process of transformation from the original Communities to an undisclosed destination as yet, the most salient feature is the lasting paradox, growing into a troublesome tension, in its evolution from a legal-normative point of view and a political decision-making point of view. As Weiler wrote: "If we were to ask a lawyer during the foundational period to compare the evolution of the European Community with the American experience, the lawyer would say that the Community was 'becoming more and more like a federal (or at least pre-federal) state'. By contrast, if we were to ask a political scientist at the same point in time to compare the European system with, say, the American system, the political scientist would give a diametrically opposite answer: 'They are growing less and less alike. The paradox can be phrased in non-comparative terms: from a legal-normative point of view, the Community developed in that first phase with an inexorable dynamism of enhanced supranationalism. European legal integration moved powerfully ahead. From a political-decisional-procedural point of view, the very same period was characterized by a counter-development towards intergovernmentalism and away from European integration."[14] The chapter from which I took this extensive quote was written before the European Council meeting of Maastricht in December 1991. The ongoing process of rewriting the treaty law while enlarging the EU, has turned an interesting paradox into a dangerously growing tension.

European Law: What it Consists of

European law consists of so-called primary and secondary law. The original treaties instituting ECSC, EEC and Euratom, together with the treaties of accession and follow-up treaties like the Single Act (1986) and the European Union Treaty (1991), (now replaced by the Treaties of Lisbon) are primary sources of law. The acts adopted by the institutions in implementation of the treaties are secondary sources of law. Taken together, European law is binding upon Member States and their citizens.

In its origin, primary European law is inter-state law. It reflects the oligarchic rather than the democratic character of the international legal order. Unlike constitutions which are drafted by representative parliaments or special, representative conventions (and eventually submitted to popular vote), primary European law is international treaty law. It has been negotiated by plenipotentiaries, designated by national governments. Guided since the 1980s by the European Council, EU Treaty making has become a highly politicized process in which the major powers predominate and from which the outcomes are political compromise, resounding

---

[14] J.H.H. Weiler, *The Transformation of Europe* In: *The Constitution of Europe; "Do the New Clothes have an Emperor?"and other essays on European Integration,* Cambridge University Press 1999 (reprinted in 2004), p.16. His book of essays is highly recommended reading!

declarations and vague often contradictory provisions. None of the European Union Treaties since 1991 would qualify for a prize or even a passing grade in our law schools. Like international treaties, the European Treaties have been submitted to parliament for approval or rejection, but without a power to amend the treaties so submitted. Requirement of popular approval by referendum has been the exception rather than the rule (in Denmark and Ireland it is required by the national constitution; in France, the government has twice and ad-hoc decided to do so). The relationship between European treaty law and constitutional law of Member States is often unclear. It is left to the constitutional authorities in Member States to adapt constitutional law to European law. In the Netherlands, amendments to the constitution were made in 1953 (and several times thereafter). The German Constitution was amended together with the ratification of the European Union Treaty in 1992 and the Treaty of Lisbon in 2009.[15]

The institutional provisions of the European Treaties, differ significantly from those in other international treaties. The three founding treaties (instituting ECSC, EEC and Euratom) were intended to be "pre-federal" or "supranational" in nature. Important legislative, executive and judiciary powers were transferred to new European institutions. The transfer of power was limited, however, to the tasks and functions of the three communities within the scope of their economic objectives. The core of their supranational nature can still be found in the Treaty on the Functioning of the EU. As we saw already in Chapter 1 above, the integration of the 'supranational' and the 'intergovernmental' in the EU Treaties, together with the processes of enlargement and broadening scope, has resulted in blurring the demarcation lines.

---

15 Cf. Bundesverfassungsgericht. Document E.4.1.

European Law: The Interpretation of the Court

As we saw as well in Chapter 1, the European Court of Justice during the foundational period, moved in the opposite direction. In the interpretation of the law of the European Communities an evolution, comparable to that of the early United States, must now be briefly mentioned.

The European Court of Justice "shall ensure the observance of law in the interpretation and application of (this) Treaty". Within the context of European law, the Court has the power of judicial review. The legality of the Treaties cannot be challenged and they take priority over all other rules of Community law, as determined by the Court. In a series of leading judgments, the Court has developed the more far-reaching doctrine of European law as an autonomous legal order, taking precedence or being supreme over the legal order of Member States. In case of conflict European law (both primary and secondary) must prevail over the laws of Member States. In determining supremacy of European law, the provisions contained in the constitutions of Member States are no longer relevant. The supremacy of European law is to be established by the European Court.

As Weiler wrote, the Court developed a case law founded on four doctrines:
(1) the doctrine of direct effect;
(2) the doctrine of supremacy;
(3) the doctrine of implied powers; and
(4) the doctrine of human rights.

The first two were already referred to in Chapter 1 above. The fourth one will be discussed below in this Chapter. In *Les Verts v. European Parliament* (294/83) the Court in 1986 drew its conclusion from the four developed doctrines: "As a result of its complete system of legal remedies, the Community is a community based on the rule of law, whose foundation is the constitutional charter' constituted by the Treaties."[16]

The Court arrived at this conclusion by applying the teleological or systematic method of interpretation of the Treaties, based upon the intentions of the parties while concluding the treaties in 1951 and 1957. One should be allowed to wonder whether the Court's conclusions in the formative period are still valid for the European Union of 2009.

From the point of view of political theory concerning the *Rechtsstaat*, the Court's doctrine raises a number of pertinent questions.

The first question concerns the claim, that the European Treaties form the "Constitution" or the basic law of a new European legal order. They reflect the oligarchic nature of the international legal order, rather than the democratic nature of the constitutional order in Member States. Parliaments of Member States played a secondary role in treaty making. While asked to approve the treaties, they could accept or reject but not amend them. In treaty making, the supremacy of the governments rather than the supremacy of parliament, obtained. The same applies to implementing the treaties and law-making. The Council of Ministers holds the decisive powers in law-making. The supremacy of the Council has been strengthened by the provision, that the European Council:

> "shall provide the Union with the necessary impetus for its development and shall define the general political

16 In the words of Koen Lenaerts and Piet van Nuffel, *Op.cit. p. 17.* See however the Bundesverfassungsgericht in Document E.4.1.

directions and priorities thereof. It shall not exercise legislative functions" (article 15).

This provision places the European Council at the apex of the institutional hierarchy in the Union. Ministers in the Council of Ministers must abide by the political guidelines set by the European Council, according to the constitutional rules prevailing in each member state. The "guidelines" of the European Council themselves are not subject to judicial review by the European Court of Justice nor to political control by any parliament.

The substantive rules of the treaty on the functioning of the EU, mainly rules of economic administrative law, are detailed rather than general in character. They reflect - in their excessive length and their language - laboriously achieved intergovernmental compromises in a growing area of public law entered from the vantage point of their relevance for the functioning of the common market. They lack the clarity and brevity of a basic law. In attributing competences to the various European institutions, the emphasis is on protecting the powers of the intergovernmental Council against the supranational institutions, rather than on the "federal" problem of distinguishing the powers of the community and those of the constituent states.

The second question concerns the claim - implied in the first - that the Treaties are the source of a legal order conforming to the ideas of the rule of law or the *Rechtsstaat*. The treaties, unlike most constitutions, do not contain a "bill of rights".[17] The European Court, in its case law, considers the European Convention for Human Rights, as general principles of European law, but Member States so far resisted proposals

---

[17] For the EU Charter of Fundamental Rights, see the next section.

for the Community as such to adhere to the Convention. Two further rules, considered essential in this respect, namely a system of checks and balances and legislative control over the executive, are, at best, insufficiently included in the treaties. The Council clearly prevails in the power relationship between Commission, European Parliament and Council. Legislative control over the executive (the Commission) is severely limited by the legislative power of the Council. The independence of the judiciary is more assured by a common tradition in Member States than by the rules of the treaties. Judges are appointed in common agreement by Member States for a period of six years. National judges are called upon to apply European law (and ask the European Court for a preliminary ruling on its interpretation), but no European, federal-type, judicial organization has been created. The development of European law is determined primarily by the "sheer will" of the member governments to reach political compromises and by the European Court declaring the treaties to be a Constitution. If theoretical inquiry and reason are applied to the interpretation of European law, one would have to conclude that the constituent treaties - both in their procedural and substantive rules - fall short of the characteristics associated with the Constitution of a *Rechtsstaat.* As treaties under international law, they are a significant improvement over other or previous treaties constituting international organizations, but they are still far away from the federal-type constitution, the Court claims them to be.

Claim and Reality in the Treaty of Lisbon

The European Union Treaty, sharpened the contradiction between this "federal" claim and the real nature of the treaty. In terms of substance, constitutional law can be found in the European Union Treaty titles I-IV, articles 1-20 and in the Treaty on the Functioning of the EU, Parts I-II, articles 1-25. The constitutional status of the Charter of Fundamental Rights is, at best, unclear.

Article 5 reaffirms the principle of subsidiarity as a general principle for the law of the European Union:

> "Article 5.
>
> 3. Under the principle of subsidiarity, in areas which do not fall within its exclusive competence, the Union shall act only if and in so far as the objectives of the proposed action cannot be sufficiently achieved by the Member States, either at central level or at regional and local level, but can rather, by reason of the scale or effects of the proposed action, be better achieved at Union level."

As it is formulated, the principle of subsidiarity is the exact opposite of the federal principle that "federal law breaks state law", as applied by the U.S. Supreme Court and as laid down in the Constitution of the German Federal Republic. In its wording, the article amounts to a protection of the powers of Member States against those of the Community, whenever their competences are "concurring" or competing. In its original meaning, subsidiarity had been a principle to protect the "lower" competence of (non-governmental) social organizations against the "supreme" powers of the state. In the meaning given to it in the Union Treaty, it reaffirms the supremacy of the powers of Member States as against the functionally limited powers transferred to the European Community. With respect to the areas of concurring powers, the principle thus is at variance with the interpretation given by the European Court of Justice to the relation between European law and the national law of Member States. The principle thus amounts to a widening of the gap between the Court's "federal" doctrine and the reality of a less than "confederal" European Union. As one can read in the Verdict of the German Constitutional Court of 30 June 2009, the gap may give rise to serious challenges of the Court's doctrine:

> "The *ultra vires* review as well as the identity review may result in Community law or, in future, Union law being declared inapplicable in Germany. To preserve the viability of the legal order of the Community, taking into account the legal concept expressed in Article 100.1 of the Basic Law, an application of constitutional law that is open to European law requires that the *ultra vires* review as well as the finding of a violation of constitutional identity is incumbent on the Federal Constitutional Court alone."[18]

At the same time, the European Union Treaty, including the amendments to the original Treaties, is a lengthy and confusing product of intergovernmental compromises. It would thus certainly be beyond reason to consider the treaties as a "source and repository of principles that are accepted not simply as positive law, but as standards for positive law generally". The European Union has broadened the scope for economic and social integration; it has widened the scope for intergovernmental cooperation inside the Treaty on the Functioning of the EU, as for instance in Title V, The Space of Freedom, Security and Law; it has given a place to intergovernmental cooperation in foreign and security policies in the Treaty on European Union. The Treaty can be termed a promising, political compromise, but not the "basic law" of a new constitutional, European order.

The Member States of the European Union thus appear to have missed the unique opportunity to lay such a foundation:

---

[18] Cf. Document E.4.1. paragraph 241.

a European Constitutional Charter, not much longer than the United States Constitution; containing basic purposes and principles and the institutional provisions for a new European Union.

FROM THE UNIVERSAL DECLARATION TO THE EUROPEAN UNION CHARTER

"Human dignity is inviolable. It must be respected and protected." Reads the first article of the Charter of Fundamental Rights in the European Union, solemnly proclaimed in December 2000 and included in the basic treaties forming part of the Treaties of Lisbon entered into force on 1 December 2009. According to the explanations relating to the complete text of the Charter: "The dignity of the human person is not only a fundamental right but constitutes the real basis of fundamental rights. The 1948 Universal Declaration of human rights enshrined this principle in its preamble." [19]

The Convention thus claimed to confirm in 2000 what has been the real basis, the underlying principle or normative concept of fundamental human rights since the end of the Second World War. The explanations clearly stress the importance of the principle, where they add: "It results that none of the rights laid down in this Charter may be used to harm the dignity of another person, and that the dignity of the human person is part of the substance of the rights laid down in this Charter. It must therefore be respected, even where a right is restricted." Can this claim be upheld?

---

[19] Document E.4.2. Explanations of the Charter. Document E.4.3. How The Charter was drawn up - The sources of rights.

The 1948 Universal Declaration of Human Rights

When discussing the drafting of the Universal Declaration of Human Rights 1948, Jacques Maritain described how men opposed in their theoretical conceptions, could come to a merely practical agreement regarding a list of human rights. Agreement apparently could be reached on the draft of a list of rights, provided the drafters were not asked why.

> "On the level of rational interpretations and justifications, on the speculative or theoretical level, the question of the rights of man brings into play the whole system of moral and metaphysical (or anti-metaphysical) certainties to which each individual subscribes. As long as there is no unity of faith or unity of philosophy in the minds of men, the interpretations and justifications will be in mutual conflict.
>
> In the domain of practical assertion, on the contrary, an agreement on a common declaration is possible by means of an approach that is more pragmatic than theoretical, and by a collective effort of comparing, recasting, and perfecting the drafts in order to make them acceptable to all as points of practical convergence, regardless of the divergence in theoretical perspectives."[20]

In the years following the Second World War, such practical agreement was achievable for two reasons. *First,* the awareness of the extent to which such rights had been flouted by Nazi-Germany and continued to be flouted in Stalin's Soviet Union and the East European states under Soviet

---

20 Jacques Maritain, *Man and the State,* University of Chicago Press 1960, at p. 79.

domination; *second* the underlying consensus that violations of fundamental human rights by certain national governments required international supervision. States and especially non-democratic and totalitarian regimes were to be held primarily responsible for massive human rights violations; the best solution would be to make human rights, already accepted in democratic states, part of international law.

The reasons for such practical agreements were given in the Preamble to the 1948 Universal Declaration of Human Rights:

> "*Whereas* recognition of the inherent dignity and of the equal and inalienable rights of all members of the human family is the foundation of freedom, justice and peace in the world,
> *Whereas* disregard and contempt for human rights have resulted in barbarous acts which have outraged the conscience of mankind, and the advent of a world in which human beings shall enjoy freedom of speech and belief and freedom from fear and want has been proclaimed as the highest aspiration of the common people,
> *Whereas* it is essential, if man is not to be compelled to have recourse, as a last resort, to rebellion against tyranny and oppression, that human rights should be protected by the rule of law,
> (...)
> *The General Assembly*
> *Proclaims* this Universal Declaration of Human Rights as a common standard of achievement for all peoples and all nations,....".

The Evolution of the Human Rights Debate

The texts, quoted above, do express the two reasons why agreement on the Declaration was possible in 1948. They also contain a number of essential propositions going well beyond the two reasons given above.

First, human dignity is introduced as the normative concept or underlying value, accepted by all peoples, for the development of international human rights law.

Second, recognition of the inherent dignity and of the equal and inalienable rights is also considered to be the foundation of freedom, justice and peace in the world. Protection of human rights by the rule of law is considered to be the peaceful alternative to rebellion against tyranny.

Third, the human rights proclaimed in the Declaration - like the normative concept of human dignity - are considered to be universal ones. That is to say: every-one, irrespective of the state or culture he/she belongs to, is entitled to enjoy these rights; and recognition of these rights is an obligation *erga omnes* for all states and societies.

Fourth, the rights proclaimed in the Declaration are a common standard of achievement (still) to be elaborated in enforceable rules of international law.

In political terms, the human rights debate was an ideological debate between Western democracies and communist regimes. The latter abstained in the final vote on the Universal Declaration of Human Rights, while all Western democracies voted in favour. During the era of East-West detente in later years a much more confusing debate followed, opposing neo-Marxists, anti-colonialists and communist regimes to the so-called capitalists of the Western world wrongly labelled as "progressives" versus "conservatives". The progressives emphasised economic and social human rights - *to be promoted by the state.* The conservatives stressed classical civil and political rights - *to be protected from the state.*

In legal terms, the human rights debate remained neatly within the confines of constitutional and positive law. The issue requiring most of the attention was the strengthening of the international human rights regime, or progress toward compliance with international rules through judicial process and enforcement of court rulings. The principal rules requiring definition and supervision were rules protecting the individual against state power and its abuse. The debate on economic and social rights resulted in non-binding declarations in the framework of the UN, the non-enforceable provisions in the European Social Charter and some new "programmatic" provisions in state-constitutions.

The issues connected with the protection of one individual against another were considered to be issues for civil and criminal law rather than for human rights law. In civil law countries, rules on them had been codified in the civil and criminal codes. In common law countries they had been built up in a long history of judge-made law. In both cases, codified rules or judge-made law were considered to be law of higher order than the newly defined human rights law. Such "separation" could be upheld until national courts and law-makers came to be faced with the need to make international human rights rules part of national law on the one hand; and on the other hand with demands to revise or re-interpret traditional codified or judge-made rules. New international human rights law, required amendments in the civil and criminal codes e.g. on racial discrimination or the rights of women and children. The two demands referred to, in the highly secularised Western democracies, also required amendments in the civil and criminal codes e.g. with respect to marriage and family law in the civil codes and with respect to abortion and euthanasia in the criminal codes. The new demands undermined the traditional consensus - or laid bare the absence of such consensus, also within democracies.

The double change - the end of ideological division in the world, and the new emphasis on the protection of individual rights - thus created some interesting reversals of alliances.

Liberals or secularists and Marxists, who used to be at cross purposes in the past on such questions as civil and political rights, and economic and social rights, now appear to agree, as post-ideological secularists and reconstructed democratic socialists on a strictly positivist approach to the promotion of civil and political rights. Legislation on such issues as abortion, euthanasia, birth control, and family law, is to be guided by the majorities one can muster in society and in parliament. With state-power receding from its position as the principal danger to human rights at least in the European democracies, these majorities are deemed to demand rights protecting and enhancing the self-assertion and self-development of the individual - including the right of women to abort an unwanted child, the right of individuals to extend family-rights to whatever relationship they prefer, and the right to decide on when and how to end life. State authorities are supposed to translate the democratic majority views into enforceable law and more: recently legalized acts and practices ought to be elevated to constitutional and European human rights.

Developing countries are assisted in birth and population control policies through programmes sponsored by United Nations agencies and paid for primarily by the United States and the European Union.

Human Dignity as a Normative Concept: What did and does it mean?

In trying to answer this question, we are faced immediately with a set of contradictions.

The recognition of the inherent dignity of all members of the human family appeared as the response of an outraged conscience of mankind against contempt for human rights and the barbarous acts perpetrated by totalitarian regimes. As Isaiah Berlin wrote: "Because these rules were flouted, we have been forced to become conscious of them. This is a kind of return to the ancient notion of natural law, but for some of us, in empiricist dress - no longer necessarily based on theological or metaphysical foundations."[21] Hersch Lauterpacht considered the American and French constitutional pronouncements as practical expressions of the accomplishments of the law of nature and added: "When in the twentieth century that achievement was put in jeopardy, the law of nature resumed, as we shall see, its historic function as the champions of the rights of man." For him, the theories of natural law are generalisations from actual experience. Therefore: "The rights of men cannot, in the long run, be effectively secured except by the twin operation of the latent forces of the law of nature and of the compelling force of the law of nations - both conceived as a power superior to the supreme power of the State."[22]

The normative concept of human dignity can be said to be such latent force of the law of nature. It assumes the character of a challenge or a protest when the dignity of the person is

---

[21] Isaiah Berlin, *The Crooked Timber of Humanity,* New York 1991, *European Unity and its Vicissitudes,* p. 204.

[22] H. Lauterpacht, *International Law and Human Rights,* London 1950, pp. 97, 98 and 93.

violated - as it did in 1948. It assumes the character of a driving force thereafter towards greater conformity of the positive law with the demands for freedom and justice. In the civil resistance against communist repression in East and Central Europe since 1968, "the idea of human dignity has become an idea of "concrete democracy", wrote Jozef Tischner. "Everyone feels this idea in one's own way, but the idea is basically held in common." [23] As a normative concept, human dignity apparently is self-evident. It is a "latent force" but a very powerful one, as the outcome of civil resistance showed in 1989. It is a force of the law of nature and can be recognized by everyone, because it is "written" in the conscience of everyone and of mankind. Still, mankind's conscience of the concept is a latent force, activated mainly when human dignity is being violated.

Reference to the normative concept of human dignity in international law points to a recognition of a higher source of law than the will of the state or consent between states. The same can be said of the acceptance of *ius cogens* - those principles in international law that are binding irrespective of the consent of states. Certain fundamental human rights are considered to be part of such *ius cogens,* among them for instance, the prohibition of torture and inhuman treatment. Torture is the violation *par excellence* of human dignity and is so universally recognized, also by those governments which hide their dismal human rights record behind arguments of cultural diversity. "It is significant that torture is the one form of violence today that a state will always deny and never justify."[24] The "law of nature" thus appears to have resumed its "historic function

---

23 Jozef Tischner, *The Spirit of Solidarity,* San Francisco 1984, p. 43.

24 Amnesty International, *Report on Torture,* Duckworth 1973, p. 17. The report with which Amnesty launched its (still ongoing) campaign against torture.

as the champion of the rights of man" (as Lauterpacht wrote) in international law. The legal-positivist approach to human rights, civil law and criminal law in Europe - I noted above - contradicts these developments in international law.

This latter contradiction is both surprising and disturbing. The normative concept of human dignity originated in Western-Christian civilization as did the human rights movement. It found its inspiration in the Christian concept of the person, whose rights and duties are determined by his transcendental destiny. The Western-Christian contribution to human dignity as a universal normative concept resulted from the distinction between faith and reason, between revelation and natural law and between spiritual and temporal power. Respect for human dignity was not simply the execution of a command by God, it was the outcome of interpretation by human reason how to treat each other as human beings. Despite its deep roots in the Bible and in Christian thinking, the concept only matured when challenged by the totalitarian ideologies of the twentieth century. In the Roman Catholic Church, the Second Vatican Council took human dignity as its core normative concept to come out in favour of the fundamental human right to freedom of conscience and religion. In the teaching of Pope John-Paul II, human dignity has grown into the key normative concept with respect to human rights, democracy, the rule of law and catholic social doctrine.[25] While the Catholic Church, since 1965, has contributed so much to mature and elaborate the concept as the principal foundation for promoting human rights, the European politicians and representatives appear to more and more disown the very source of their human rights approach... a surprising and disturbing contradiction, indeed!

---

[25] Compare the masterful biography of Pope John-Paul II written by George Weigel, *Witness to Hope, The Biography of Pope John Paul II.*, New York 1999.

If Michael Ignatieff is correct in expecting: "to see the moral consensus which sustained the Universal Declaration in 1948 splintering still further" in the next fifty years,[26] not cultural diversity in the world, but the spiritual crisis in Europe is to be blamed.

The European Charter of Fundamental Rights

As noted above, the legal-positivist approach to human rights, civil law and criminal law in Europe contradicts developments in international law. External policies and international law-making contradict domestic policies and legislation in several respects.

In part, this contradiction goes back to the origins of the international human rights movement. Since the Enlightenment, substantial progress had been made towards human rights, democracy and the rule of law in the domestic, constitutional order of America and Western Europe. International human rights after the Second World War were meant to promote the same progress elsewhere. They were to be written for others, not for ourselves. It is no coincidence that the European Communities/Union began to pay attention to human rights in connection with its enlargements to South, Central and Eastern Europe. Nor should one any longer be surprised by boastful political declarations of intention of the kind produced in article 21 of the European Union Treaty.

Another reason for the contradiction is to be found in the nature of European law, as it developed since the formative years - the growing tension between the "federal"claim as expressed in the ECJ's case law and - in human rights - the

---

[26] Michael Ignatieff, *Whose Universal Values? The Crisis in Human Rights,* Praemium Erasmianum Essay 1999, Amsterdam 1999, p. 54.

political unwillingness to accept "federal" supervision of a constitutional bill of rights. The Charter of Fundamental Rights is far from being "a compelling force" or a power superior to the power of the states, despite the consistent elaboration of such rights in the case law of the ECJ.[27] The Charter was conceived in 2000 to teach candidate countries. It was not meant to become a constitutional bill of rights, enforceable by the ECJ. It was issued as a political declaration by the European Council and just happened to end up as the EU Charter in the Treaties of Lisbon. According to its article 52.5 (added in 2007):

> "The provisions of this Charter which contain principles may be implemented by legislative and executive acts taken by institutions, bodies, offices and agencies of the Union, and by acts of Member States when they are implementing Union law, in the exercise of their respective powers. They shall be judicially cognisable only in the interpretation of such acts and in the ruling on their legality."

A look at the sources of the rights in the Charter makes clear that the purpose of the Charter has not been a bill of enforceable rights, but a compilation of political principles to be implemented as our European Mandarins see fit. The compilation is a curious mix of traditional human right provisions, social and economic rights and policy principles. The principles derive from the European Convention, European Social Charters (not enforceable) and primary and secondary sources of European law. Contrary to a clearly formulated bill of rights, some rights formulated as principles are wide open to manipulation and controversy. To conclude this chapter, I take a few examples from the approach to human rights in the Netherlands.

---

27 See Koen Lenaerts and Piet van Nuffel, *Op.cit.* par. 17-089, p. 735

Examples

The right to life in Article 2 for instance, has its source in article 2 of the ECHR and its sixth protocol (abolition of the death penalty). It reads:

> "1. Everyone has the right to life.
> 2. No one shall be condemned to the death penalty, or executed."

Article 2 ECHR, however, reads in its first paragraph:

> "Everyone's right to life shall be protected by law. No one shall be deprived of his life intentionally (save in the execution of a sentence of a court following his conviction of a crime for which this penalty is provided by law).

At the time the European Convention was signed (1950), abortion (*abortus provocatus*) and euthanasia were considered to be criminal offences directed against life, including when performed on request of the mother (abortion) or on the explicit and serious desire of the person (euthanasia), in the parties signatories to the Convention. In the substantive provisions of the Criminal Codes, abortion and euthanasia were specifically prohibited. With respect to abortion, "fundamental change has occurred in this area all over the Western world in a relatively short period of time. Within less than two decades all but three of these twenty nations abandoned strict abortion laws - introduced for the most part in the nineteenth century - in favour of a more permissive stance."[28] As Mary Ann Glendon

---

28 Writes Mary Ann Glendon, *Abortion and Divorce in Western Law, American Failures, European Challenges,* Harvard University Press 1987, p.11.

explains, the approaches of the European legislators and judicial authorities (among them the European Commission of Human Rights) differed from the approach of the U.S. Supreme Court since *Roe v. Wade* (1973). Alone among the Western democracies, the U.S. Supreme Court refers to a constitutional right of abortion for the woman; nowhere else is "the legal approach to abortion as indifferent to unborn life as it is in the United States."[29]

The Dutch Law of 1981 motivated the new rules and the amendments to the Criminal Code with the consideration that developments in the views with respect to the termination of pregnancy made new provisions desirable for both the legal protection of unborn human life and the right of the woman to assistance in case of undesired pregnancy.[30] As in other West European states faced with increasing circumvention of existing criminal law provisions, the solution was sought in a political compromise. While the right of the woman to terminate an unwanted pregnancy should be recognized, it was not to be seen as an absolute (or constitutional) right. In each case it should be weighed against the right to protection of the unborn life as a moral obligation to the community. As a serious moral issue, a demand for abortion should be handled seriously.

The approach taken by both the 1981 Law on Abortion and

---

29 In her book on p. 24.

30 Law of 1 May 1981 containing provisions with respect to the interruption of pregnancy. Note the difference between the abstract term "legal protection of unborn human life" and the concrete "right of the woman to assistance". The Law is based on the seventh draft submitted to Parliament in February 1979, after all previous drafts since 1970 had failed to obtain a majority. The Law was adopted with a majority of one vote, the decisive one from a catholic member of the Christian Democratic Party, who changed her mind two hours before the final vote.

the 2001 Law on Euthanasia, has been fundamentally the same in at least two respects:

First, the Criminal Code was so amended that abortion on the mother's request and euthanasia or assistance in suicide on request by the person concerned, were exempted from the list of punishable criminal offences.

Second, such limitative "legalized" abortion and euthanasia were subjected to detailed procedural rules on the submission of the requests, on the validity of the causes for such requests, and on the ways physicians were allowed to grant them.

The arguments advanced for replacing substantive by procedural rules were - given the changed views and practices in society - that legalized practice could better restrain abuse than continued illegal practice. The question, whether the state by so legalizing abortion and euthanasia on request, would further flout moral standards or, on the contrary, restrict immoral behavior by subjecting actual practice to new procedural rules and serious discussion, has been hotly and inconclusively debated ever since. Evidence so far is equally inconclusive. As Mary Ann Glendon remarked:"in general, strict and lenient abortion laws do not appear to be related in any simple way to abortion rates." In final analysis, she writes:

> "The mores, not the law, are the best protection of the weak and dependent. A law which communicates that abortion is a serious moral issue and that the fetus is entitled to protection will have a more beneficial influence on behavior and opinions, even though it permits abortion under some - even many - circumstances, than a law

> which holds fetal life to be of little or no value and abortion to be a fundamental right." [31]

According to article 9, Right to marry and right to found a family:

> "The right to marry and the right to found a family shall be guaranteed in accordance with the national laws governing the exercise of these rights."

The official explanation of the article writes: "This Article is based on Article 12 of the ECHR, which reads as follows: '*Men and women of marriageable age have the right to marry and to found a family according to the national laws governing the exercising of this right.*' The wording of the Article has been modernized to cover cases in which national legislation recognizes arrangements other than marriage for founding a family. This Article neither prohibits nor imposes the granting of the status of marriage to unions between people of the same sex. This right is thus similar to that afforded by the ECHR, but its scope may be wider when national legislation so provides."

The "modernization" of the wording of article 12 ECHR is - unknown to the drafters - ironic, first of all. The whole purpose of the human rights movement after the Second World War was to afford the human person European protection against the State. The modernized version in article 9 withdraws this protection! In its modernized wording there is nothing left to protect. The purpose of article 12 (as of article 16 in the

---

[31] In her book referred to at pp. 59 and 61. Meant is the contrast between West European legislation on abortion, and the U.S. Supreme Court's approach to abortion.

Universal Declaration)[32] was quite specific and clear. The marriage vow between a man and a woman is given special protection because of the special purpose of founding a family. Such protection is bound to be undermined by recent developments giving unions between two persons of the same sex the same rights and status. Done in the name of the principle of equal treatment, it shows the extent of philosophical and moral confusion underlying the drafting of the European Charter.

A related philosophical and moral confusion appears in *article 21: Non-discrimination*

> "1. Any discrimination based on any ground such as sex, race, colour, ethnic or social origin, *genetic features*, language, religion or belief, political or any other opinion, membership of a national minority, property, birth, (*disability, age*) *or sexual orientation* shall be prohibited.
>
> 2. Within the scope of application of the Treaties and without prejudice to any of their specific provisions, any discrimination on grounds of nationality shall be prohibited."

According to the explanation, this article is primarily based on article 14 ECHR. However, the italicized grounds in the article

---

32 Article 16 reads:
(1) Men and women of full age, without any limitation due to race, nationality or religion, have the right to marry and to found a family. They are entitled to equal rights as to marriage, during marriage and at its dissolution.
(2) Marriage shall be entered into only with the free and full consent of the intending spouses.
(3) The family is the natural and fundamental group unit of society and is entitled to protection by society and the State.

above are not included in article 14 ECHR. The differences are substantial. When the principle of non-discrimination is extended from the *person he or she is* to how he or she decides to behave, it can be applied at random.

Internal and external human rights policies

One should, therefore, not be surprised when a democratic country like the Netherlands appears not to be aware of any problem, when its internal legislation on such sensitive issues like family law or euthanasia, contradicts its external human rights policies. The Netherlands are on record as strong advocates for promoting human rights and the rule of law in other countries. At the same time, the Dutch legislator did not want to have anything to do with Recommendation 1418 (1999) of the Parliamentary Assembly of the Council of Europe on "Protection of the Human Rights and Dignity of the terminally ill and the dying." Despite the Assembly's urgent request to uphold the prohibition against intentionally taking the life of terminally ill or dying persons, the Dutch went ahead with legalizing euthanasia.

Worse than the apparent contradiction, is the underlying confusion in the minds of the Dutch legislator: the majority in government and parliament is not even aware of any contradiction. In their view, the principal concern in external human rights policies is to help protect human rights against state-violence in other states. They see no reason for such concern in the issue of legalizing euthanasia in The Netherlands. What is at stake here, is entirely different, we are told. All they do is providing legislative consent by the state to acts, persons in the exercise of their individual autonomy are willing to decide to. The state of the Netherlands is seen no longer as the power against which the Dutch citizen should be protected; the state has become the "caring state" prepared to recognize and protect everyone's individual autonomy.

The confusion has an even deeper source. The crucial article 2 of the European Convention for the Protection of Human Rights and Fundamental Freedoms (1950) states in its opening paragraph:

> "Everyone's right to life shall be protected by law. No one shall be deprived of his life intentionally save in the execution of a sentence of a court following his conviction of a crime for which this penalty is provided by law."[33]

According to the rapporteur on matters of euthanasia in the Parliamentary Assembly of the Council of Europe, the new Dutch Law of 10 April 2001 is contrary to the Convention's Article 2. The Dutch Minister of Justice disagreed. In his view, the Convention provides for the protection of this right against a third party and not against the person, who *himself/herself* asks to die. Apparently, the fundamental Article 2 in the Convention is no longer read as the legal translation of the higher principle of the inviolability of human life. It is being reduced to no more than a prudent device for protecting the citizens against the abuse of power by the state. Respect for the inherent dignity of the human person as the expression of "the conscience of mankind", is being replaced by respect for the self-assertion and self-development of the individual in a permissive society.

The case of the Netherlands is revealing but not unique. The Dutch have a tendency to proclaim and legalize openly what is being practiced and concealed elsewhere in the democracies of Europe. Contrary to what Ignatieff wrote,

---

33 The death penalty has been abolished by the sixth Protocol to the Convention except for acts committed in time of war or imminent threat of war as provided in article 2 of the Protocol.

there is no:" deliberate silence at the heart of the human rights culture"[34]; there is a failing conscience in the very societies from which the normative concept of human dignity emerged.

Unfortunately, the EU Charter of Fundamental Rights, despite its first article on Human dignity, is an example of Europe's fragile conscience rather than a confirmation of the initial purposes of the Universal Declaration and the European Convention.

---

34 On p. 44 in his essay referred to in footnote 26.

CHAPTER 5

THE ECHTERNACH PROCESSION: FROM POLITICAL COOPERATION TO EXTERNAL ACTION

"Article 21

1. The Union's action on the international scene shall be guided by the principles which have inspired its own creation, development and enlargement, and which it seeks to advance in the wider world: democracy, the rule of law, the universality and indivisibility of human rights and fundamental freedoms, respect for human dignity, the principles of equality and solidarity, and respect for the principles of the United Nations Charter and international law. The Union shall seek to develop relations and build partnerships with third countries, and international, regional or global organisations which share the principles referred to in the first subparagraph. It shall promote multilateral solutions to common problems, in particular in the framework of the United Nations.

2. The Union shall define and pursue common policies and actions, and shall work for a high degree of cooperation in all fields of international relations, in order to:

(a) safeguard its values, fundamental interests, security, independence and integrity;
(b) consolidate and support democracy, the rule of law, human rights and the principles of international law;

(c) preserve peace, prevent conflicts and strengthen international security, in accordance with the purposes and principles of the United Nations Charter, with the principles of the Helsinki Final Act and with the aims of the Charter of Paris, including those relating to external borders;
(d) foster the sustainable economic, social and environmental development of developing countries, with the primary aim of eradicating poverty;
(e) encourage the integration of all countries into the world economy, including through the progressive abolition of restrictions on international trade;
(f) help develop international measures to preserve and improve the quality of the environment and the sustainable management of global natural resources, in order to ensure sustainable development;
(g) assist populations, countries and regions confronting natural or man-made disasters; and
(h) promote an international system based on stronger multilateral cooperation and good global governance.

3. The Union shall respect the principles and pursue the objectives set out in paragraphs 1 and 2 in the development and implementation of the different areas of the Union's external action covered by this Title and by Part Five of the Treaty on the Functioning of the European Union, and of the external aspects of its other policies.

The Union shall ensure consistency between the different areas of its external action and between these and its other policies. The Council and the Commission, assisted by the High Representative of the Union for Foreign Affairs and Security Policy, shall ensure that consistency and shall cooperate to that effect."

Article 21 is the opening article of Title V in the Lisbon Treaty on European Union. Against the background of efforts made since 1950 to achieve political unity, the article reflects a long history of pretence and impotence, of confusion and failure. The pretence, going back to another era, is that European unification as such contributes to world peace and the European Union therefore should play a global role. Based upon this pretence is a long list of illusions, expressed in documents since 1960, that Europe has a role of its own to play in international relations. The impotence, going back to the Gaullist era of the 1960s, results from the illusion that political unity and world relevance can be achieved through intergovernmental cooperation. The persisting confusion is the one between political unification as a process leading towards the final goal of federal unity, and political cooperation as another area - foreign policy and defense - for concertation of national policies. Concertation without a full score and one conductor, as we all know, ends in cacophony or silence. Originally the conduct of a common commercial policy by the European Communities was to foreshadow and shape a future common European foreign policy.

Article 21 also governs, according to article 205 of the Treaty on the Functioning of the European Union, the conduct of external relations. It indicates a dynamic opposite to the one envisaged by the founders of the European Communities. Instead of extending the new method of common action from external economic relations to foreign policy in general, article 21 envisages the opposite; the external economic relations of the Union are to be subjected to intergovernmental foreign policy coordination.

The history of political unification efforts can be divided into three periods:

(1) The first one from 1952-1969 covers the transitional period

of the European Communities in which political unity was seen as the completion of the European economic integration process.

(2) The second one runs from 1969-1986, the period governed by the Hague compromise on European Political Cooperation as a separate activity between governments of member states of the European Communities and the substantial increase of bilateral and multilateral treaty relations with third countries.

(3) The third period following the SEA is marked by efforts to find a place for a Common Foreign and Defence or Security Policy alongside the widening scope of community external relations, in the European Union Treaties of Maastricht (1992), Amsterdam (1997), Nice (2000) and Lisbon (2007) and to write the over all European Council leadership in the conduct of external relations into law.

The efforts to achieve political unity are intertwined with the desire to gradually unify the conduct of foreign and defense policies of member states. From the federal and Schuman's perspective, a common European foreign and defense policy would be the keystone of the edifice called a united Europe. From the perspective of Europe's major member states, it would be the last symbol of sovereignty to give up... if ever. For former French President Charles de Gaulle, it was *never* to be given up.... on the contrary. For that reason, political union talks ended in failure in the 1960s. Thereafter three issues could never be settled satisfactorily. The first one concerns the method of foreign policy making, whether the community or the traditional intergovernmental one. The second one concerns the borderlines between foreign and security policy on the one side and EC external relations and NATO security policies on the other. The third one concerns the competence to represent member states and the Community/Union in international relations, the so called *ius communicandi*. In the meantime, the external relations of the European Community/ Union continued to grow in scope and extent. Foreign and security policies continued to be conducted primarily from the national capitals.

EUROPEAN POLITICAL UNITY: A RECORD OF CONFUSION AND FAILURE

The draft-treaty embodying the Statute of the European Political Community adopted by the Assemblée ad hoc on 10 March 1953 made it quite clear in its first article that it was to establish a community of a supranational character, within the North Atlantic Alliance.

Article 2 formulated as the first and second mission of the Community:

> "- to co-operate with the other free nations in ensuring the security of Member States against all aggression;
>
> - to ensure the co-ordination of the foreign policy of Member States in questions likely to involve the existence, the security or the prosperity of the Community;".

In line with the spirit and the provisions of the ECSC Treaty, it was the responsibility of the supranational community to cooperate with the other free nations and to ensure such coordination in so far as necessary for the existence, security and prosperity of the Community. The Community was to have juridical personality. The mission referred to was further elaborated in Part III, Chapter 3, articles 67-74.[1]
The formulation was in line with the pre-federal nature of

---

1 For the full text see Document EUD. 1. See also Chapter II. 1 above.

the supranational communities and with the federal aim of European unification. It was the Community's mission to cooperate with NATO and develop external relations in diplomacy and trade. The draft-treaty conformed to the original inspiration of the Schuman Plan. It was drawn up, on the invitation of the six governments by a constituent assembly and clearly intended to create the political institutions for a supranational community.[2] The Assembly ad hoc met under the presidency of Paul-Henri Spaak and considered its work of historical importance. Following the defeat of the EDC Treaty in the French National Assembly, the same Paul Henri-Spaak presided over the committee that would prepare the Treaties of Rome instituting the EEC and Euratom - acting much from the same, original inspiration as the Schuman Plan.

When the French National Assembly rejected the EDC Treaty in August 1954[3], the Statute disappeared in the archives and West German participation in defense and security was arranged through the (intergovernmental) WEU and NATO.

We shall never know whether there was sufficient agreement for establishing the European Political Community as envisaged by the draft-statute, nor whether EPC would have been helpful on the intended road to political unity. What we do know is that in France the original inspiration of Schuman, vanished with the institution of the Fifth French Republic in 1958.

The new President, Charles de Gaulle, of the new Republic came to power with very different ideas about European unification and international relations from the leaders of the Fourth French Republic. He would soon make quite clear what

---

2 See Documents E. 5. 1- 1D and Chapter II. 1 above.

3 Cf. my *Western Cooperation,* Second Revised Edition, Chapter II. 6.

he thought in carefully staged press conferences. Guessing his intentions became a new game. Journalists and European politicians debated the question - what is he going to say? - before every press conference, and what did he mean to say? - thereafter. Despite de Gaulle's clarity of language and thought, he was never well understood. As a consequence the issue raised by him - whether time had not come for political union - became a source of confusion from the outset.[4] We can clearly document the confusion through two sets of documents: the press conferences of de Gaulle before and after the breakdown of political union negotiations; the outcome of the two Summits of 1961 and the three draft treaties on political union of 1961/1962.[5]

Charles de Gaulle held most traditional if not outmoded opinions on international diplomacy and the role of France in the world. Foreign policy is to express the raison d'Etat, which for France meant French prominence and lasting control over Germany.

The failure of the East-West Summit in May 1960 in Paris, reaffirmed his opinion that "Europe" under his French leadership should become more independent from the United States of America and more cooperative towards the Soviet Union. At the same time he made clear that the path to be followed must be that of organized cooperation between sovereign states. In other words: Community Europe had to be replaced by an intergovernmental Political Union directed by regular meetings between Heads of State and Government. As he said in his

---

4 Cf. my "*European Political Integration: A Record of Confusion and Failure.*" In *The European Yearbook XI.* 1965, pp.135-165.

5 Press Conferences, letter to German Chancellor Adenauer, instructions to Prime Minister Debré in Document E. 5. 4 ; Three draft treaties in Document E. 5. 2-3.

September 1960 press conference: "This means an organized and regular concert of responsible governments coupled with the work of specialized bodies in each field under the control of governments. This also means regular debates in an Assembly composed of delegates from national parliaments. And in my view this must mean the holding of a European referendum as quickly as possible so as to give the start of this new Europe the vital element of popular approval and participation." To which he added in his May 1962 press conference that he considered a political community (as envisaged by Schuman in 1950) an utopian and also objectionable structure: "Such an entity cannot be found without there being in Europe today a federator with sufficient power, authority and skill. Once again, it is quite natural for the European States to have a series of specialized bodies for them to use in solving the problems which are common to them, to prepare, and if necessary, to follow their decisions. But these decisions belong, and can only belong to the States, and they can only take them in concert." As he wrote to German Chancellor Adenauer in September 1960, political union must be based on French-German agreement. When the six could not agree, de Gaulle naturally resorted to a bilateral agreement with Germany, signed in January 1963.[6]

The basic confusion - never adequately solved - concerned the aim of starting negotiations on political union. De Gaulle deliberately used the term political union - instead of political community - to make clear that he proposed political cooperation between states as a method to recapture and maintain full governmental control over the process of unification. The other five favored political cooperation, that is in foreign policy in addition to economic integration, as a

---

6 The Treaty clearly is a French made political union *à deux*. Cf. Document E. 5. 5. Cf. also Chapter II. 1 above.

means to achieve political unity. They probably believed that the dynamics of economic integration would gradually lead foreign policy-making from intergovernmental concertation to full community decision-making.

The other confusion, much of French origin, relates to structure. Effective solidarity in Schuman's conception needed common institutions and common rules. In de Gaulle's conception, it needed French presidential leadership in an organized and regular concert of governments on the highest level. As in the Constitution of the Fifth French Republic, where foreign policy was the holy domain of the monarchical president, European foreign policy was to become the domain of the collective emperor called the European Council. Not only was de Gaulle's conception at cross purposes with the Schuman Plan; it would also be unworkable, as no other member state constitution provided for a monarchical presidency.

EUROPEAN POLITICAL COOPERATION: THE 1970 COMPROMISE

The Summit of The Hague in December 1969 came to a compromise. The French could pursue their Gaullist schemes for political union and the others had their way on the enlargement of the communities. Political cooperation would not come instead of community decision-making. It was allowed to move on alongside the communities with its own purposes and procedures. Political cooperation started with the adoption of the Davignon report on European Political Cooperation (EPC).[7] Officially the foreign ministers were to continue to study the best way to achieve political unification; in reality they were to meet regularly among themselves, outside the EC Council of Ministers, launching the odd practices of the

---

7 Text in Document E. 5. 6.

same ministers meeting with different hats and also in different locations. Their meetings were to be prepared by the heads of the political departments of their foreign offices (and not by the Commission of the EC).

The objectives were modest:

> "(a) To ensure greater mutual understanding with respect to the major issues of international politics, by exchanging information and .consulting regularly;
>
> (b) To increase their solidarity by working for a harmonization of views, concertation of attitudes and joint action when it appears feasible and desirable."

A second report was produced in 1973[8], following the enlargement of the European Communities. Pushed by the French, reluctantly accepted by the others, the new intergovernmental machinery alongside the EC began to take shape: more regular meetings of the foreign ministers, a political committee, a committee of correspondents, working groups and studies on the role of the embassies of the nine in foreign capitals. All of these "major" decisions were taken in regular summit meetings, growing - as proposed by French President Giscard d'Estaing - into the European Council. EPC was to be the special playground for the European Council, which of course met primarily to talk about foreign policy and Europe's important world role. Still, as the French had always worked for, the European Council would gradually become the highest authority also for community decision-making, as we saw already in Chapter 1 above. Through the European Council, "political cooperation" evolved from an alongside activity to the core of building the European Union.

---

8 Document E. 5. 7.

In the conclusions of the European Council meetings, ample attention would be given to declarations on world issues. Prime attention went to the Middle East.

The Middle East war of October 1973, followed by the energy crisis received priority attention. In November 1973 the nine came with their first Declaration,[9] announced and distributed as a policy declaration of great importance. The Declaration set the tone for a continuing stream of pro-Palestinian declarations without much policy follow up. There never was sufficient agreement among member states for a common Middle-Eastern policy, except for financial largesse towards the Palestinian authorities. It was not without irony that their political leaders published a Declaration on the European Identity, a month later in Copenhagen at the meeting where they received the unannounced visit from a number of Arab Foreign Ministers.[10] The French had wanted such a Declaration to underline Europe's identity as against the United States of America. The emphasis in European Political Cooperation would continue to be given to the Middle East and the Mediterranean area ever since - clearly and primarily to distinguish Europe from the United States as the prime mediator in the Israeli-Palestinian conflict.[11]

---

9 Document E. 5. 8. As a member, at the time of the Netherlands' delegation to the United Nations General Assembly in New York, we were instructed to bring it to the attention of other delegations and to avoid meetings with our Israeli fellow delegates - an instruction I refused to follow up.

10 Text in Document E. 5. 9.

11 Cf. S.I.P. van Campen, '*NATO Political Consultation and European Political Cooperation*' In; Frans A.M. Alting von Geusau, *Allies in a Turbulent World; Challenges to U.S. and Western European Cooperation,* Lexington Books, Heath and Company 1982.

The "conduct" of a Middle Eastern foreign policy, in a way, is paradigmatic for the nature of common foreign policy making and external action in the European Union as it evolved since 1969 and under the "leadership" of the European Council of Heads of State and Governments. It manifests at least four - disturbing - characteristics.

1. The policy is governed by the European Council and expressed primarily in the Conclusions of its meetings. The reader can follow the policy through the Conclusions and Declarations of the European Council from 1969-2011 as brought together on my website.[12] When we take the 1973 declaration as an example, the European Community/Union issues policy declarations without a clear follow up. Principal attempt is to distinguish Europe from US foreign policy, and thus to lean over backwards to support the Palestinian view on the solution of the Middle East conflict.

2. As a centre of soft rather than hard power, the Europeans try to compensate their lack of diplomatic power by huge financial and economic investments in - as far as the Middle East is concerned - the Palestinian Authority. Since 1973, several billion Euros have been invested in the Palestinian Authority without much transparency or identifiable results.

3. By far the largest number of documents produced by the European Council are foreign policy Declarations. What has been declared in common is not followed up in policy. Member states continue to go their own way, separate from and often in contradiction to the common declarations. The

---

12 European Council sessions numbered chronologically. Declarations, if published separately, are given the number of the related European Council session with an A added. The overwhelming majority of Declarations is on Foreign Policy.

absence of common policies is best reflected by the endless high level visits to the area. As one observer wryly remarked: when there is no agreement in the European Council, the High Representative is sent on a mission to the area.

4. The implementation of common policies - whenever done - is left to the Eurocrats. Their implementation lacks transparency and is hardly subject to parliamentary control, despite the very substantial amounts involved.

FROM POLITICAL COOPERATION TO EXTERNAL CFSP ACTION

The Single European Act, the European Union Treaty of Maastricht, the revision of Title V in the Treaty of Amsterdam, the amendments from the Treaty of Nice and the provisions in the Treaties of Lisbon - Title V in the European Union Treaty and Part V in the Treaty on the Functioning of the European Union - are all being presented as progress towards the integration of a common foreign policy into the law of the European Union. The reader can follow and evaluate that progress by comparing the Davignon Report of 1970 with the relevant chapters in the Treaties just mentioned. In case the reader would also like to consult the Constitution for Europe, he shall see that its third part on the Functioning of the European Union integrates CFSP into the title on external action.[13]

Despite the growth of provisions on procedures, the essential character of CFSP as an activity of an intergovernmental nature not subject to judicial control has been maintained and extended to the external relations of the EU. Much of what

---

[13] Basic European Treaty Texts can be found in a separate category on the website. Treaties, not entered into force are listed under subcategory EUD.

President de Gaulle wanted in the 1960s and was rejected at the time, found its way into Title V of the European Union Treaty of Lisbon. The European Council is in charge. There will be a political committee, the high representative for foreign affairs and security policy is appointed by the European Council and is given a central place inside the European Commission. The provisions on procedures and powers are of a baffling complexity and most likely unworkable.
According to article 24(1):

> "The common foreign and security policy is subject to specific rules and procedures. It shall be defined and implemented by the European Council and the Council acting unanimously, except where the Treaties provide otherwise. The adoption of legislative acts shall be excluded. The common foreign and security policy shall be put into effect by the High Representative of the Union for Foreign Affairs and Security Policy and by Member States, in accordance with the Treaties. The specific role of the European Parliament and of the Commission in this area is defined by the Treaties. The Court of Justice of the European Union shall not have jurisdiction with respect to these provisions, with the exception of its jurisdiction to monitor compliance with Article 40 of this Treaty and to review the legality of certain decisions as provided for by the second paragraph of Article 275 of the Treaty on the Functioning of the European Union."

To which article 27 adds:

> "1. The High Representative of the Union for Foreign Affairs and Security Policy, who shall chair the Foreign Affairs Council, shall contribute through his proposals towards the preparation of the common foreign and security policy and shall ensure implementation of the

> decisions adopted by the European Council and the Council."

The High Representative, thus is vice-president of the supranational Commission and chairperson of the intergovernmental Foreign Affairs Council acting unanimously, but without the power to adopt legislative acts. He is responsible to the European Council; not to the European Parliament like the other commissioners? Presumably he does not have voting rights in the Foreign Affairs Council? He is no more than the presiding official like the NATO Secretary-General. In the Commission there are at least six other commissioners dealing with external relations: the ones for development, trade, international cooperation-humanitarian aid and crisis response, enlargement and neighborhood-policy, energy, and climate action. Where does he stand in case of conflict between the Commission and the Council of Ministers, as he belongs to both? As Wessels writes:

> "Irrespective of the inconclusive written words of the EU primary law the body of the Heads of State or Government is the dominant master of the real world game in the EU system. The European Council is placed at the apex of the institutional architecture framing and constructing major dimensions of the EU polity, directing the EU politics and making decisions for major policies."

He concludes his most interesting paper:

> "With the creation of the office of the High Representative and the European External Action Service they have again opted for a complex and confusing path between a rationalized form of intergovernmentalism and a strengthened mode of supranationalism. In any

> case they have reinforced their own position at the apex and in the centre between the two areas."[14]

The provisions of CFSP and external action in the Lisbon Treaties appear to continue the record of confusion and failure from the 1960s.

There is no satisfactory answer to the simple question: who is responsible for conducting EU's foreign and external relations policy? Former US Secretary of State Henry Kissinger once asked for the phone number of the European Foreign Minister. Today's answer is: dial the number of the High Representative for Foreign Affairs and Security Policy. Once connected, there is a menu. Dial 1 for the President of the European Council; dial 2 for the Council of Ministers; dial 3 for the President of the European Commission; dial 4 for the High Representative and Chairperson of the Foreign Affairs Council; dial 5 for the German Foreign Office; dial 6 for the *Quai d'Orsay*; dial 7 for Whitehall; dial 8 for the Italian Foreign Ministry; dial 9 for the Spanish Foreign Ministry; dial 10 for the Polish Foreign Ministry; and the numbers 11-31 for the foreign offices of the other EU member states. The Lisbon Reform Treaties added up all the impossible political compromises without a clear delimitation of tasks and powers.

European foreign policy, apparently, is the preferred topic for politicians and scholars. There are more declarations and serious treatises on this subject than on any other one. One can consult the website of the European Council under foreign policy to find a continuous stream of declarations and statements, mostly on issues the EU can do nothing about but

---

[14] W. Wessels: "*The European Council Creating and Shaping the External Action of the EU*"; Text of the paper on my website: European Union/Documents/ER The Summitry Syndrome.

pretends to have an impact just by saying it.[15] Documents on important issues as strategy are vague and non-committal.[16] Among the tsunami of declarations, one can also find quite a few odd ones.[17]

On the more important international issues, the European Union mostly offers a continuing record of failure. The European Union pretended but failed to deal with the Yugoslav civil wars in the 1990's, including the Kosovo crisis. Despite a series of resounding documents on its Mediterranean policy and its dialogue with countries in the region, the EU had no clue how to deal with the Uprising in the Arab countries in 2011. The Union was deeply divided, when the UN Security Council adopted Resolution 1973 and authorized:

> "Member States that have notified the Secretary-General, acting nationally or through regional organizations or arrangements, and acting in cooperation with the Secretary-General, to take all necessary measures, notwithstanding paragraph 9 of resolution 1970 (2011), to protect civilians and civilian populated areas under threat of attack in the Libyan Arab Jamahiriya, including Benghazi, while excluding a foreign occupation force of any form on any part of Libyan territory, and requests the Member States

---

15 For a recent and excellent study on the topic, see: Stephan Keukeleire and Jennifer McNaughton, *The Foreign Policy of the European Union,* Palgrave MacMillan 2008. Foreign policy declarations can be found in the European Council documents on my website.

16 Cf. Document E. 5. 12A-B. The two documents are full of self-congratulatory statements, but have nothing of interest on the strategy of the Union for the next decade.

17 For the pleasure of the readers I collected a few odd ones in Document E. 5. 13

> concerned to inform the Secretary-General immediately of the measures they take pursuant to the authorization conferred by this paragraph which shall be immediately reported to the Security Council".

While France and Britain strongly sponsored such action, Germany was against and abstained from voting in the UN Security Council. As would turn out soon thereafter, the few EU members prepared to join in such measures, could not sustain military action without major US participation.

The conclusion to be drawn from this chapter of the history of European unification into the Twentieth Century is shocking and sad. There cannot be a common European foreign policy without full political unity; "soft power" is *Eurospeak* for impotence. De Gaulle's dreams of a Supreme Council ruling over Europe should be today's nightmare for the leaders of the EU member states after the glow of prominence and media coverage of their meetings is gone.

Summit Conferences have proven to be poor mechanisms for wise decisions. They are events of high publicity and personal vanity. Agreements are to be produced under great media pressure. Decision-making is undemocratic and lacks transparency. From (lack of) agreement at the Summit there is no appeal. European Council Conclusions and Declarations make poor reading. They are full of resounding, boastful and hypocritical statements. European Council conclusions lack legal force but have great political impact. The Lisbon Treaty implies more intergovernmental control over the community method of decision-making, especially in external relations. For the European Union the ever more frequent European Council sessions indicate the existence of a Summitry Syndrome to be diagnosed as a serious, possibly terminal disease. Since 1989 the disease has been spreading rapidly. Besides the ever more frequent European Council meetings, the EU political leaders had to attend 26 more Summit meetings in 2010 alone with third countries, according toWessels.[18]

EXTERNAL ACTION

Economic integration was conceived by the founding fathers of the communities as a means to reach the objective of political unity. The progressive establishment of the common market would require a common commercial policy towards third countries. The EEC Treaty provided for such a common policy at the end of the transitional period.[19] Member states would give up the power to conduct their own commercial policy. It was meant to foreshadow the shape of a future European foreign policy. Still, the treaty provisions with respect to external action reflected considerable reluctance to transfer external relations power to the Community. The three communities were declared to have legal personality, but were silent on the power of active and passive legation. When the European Commission decided to exercise these rights as the community's executive, it ran into serious conflict with Gaullist France (the so-called striped pants dispute). It was among the reasons for de Gaulle's empty chair policy in 1965.[20]

Article 228 prescribed the procedure for concluding community agreements with third states and international organizations. More restrictive procedures applied for commercial treaties

---

18 As recorded in his paper quoted above. Cf. note 14.

19 Cf. Document EU. 3: Part III, Title II, Chapter 3, articles 110-116; Part IV on the Association of Overseas Countries and Territories; Part VI, articles 210, 228-231, 238. Cf. my '*The External Relations of the European Communities*' In: *The Law of the European Communities and Greece,* Institute of Public International Law and International Relations of Thessaloniki, Greece 1980, pp. 15-45.

20 Cf. Chapter II. 1 above and the Luxembourg Compromise of 1966

and association agreements (articles 113 and 238). Due largely to disagreement among member states on replacing bilateral relations with state-trading countries[21] by community relations with them, the transitional period for matters of commercial policy was extended by five years.

The net result of these two conflicts is a complex system of representation and treaty making up to and including the latest version in the Treaties of Lisbon. The power of external representation is shared by the European Council, the Commission and member states. The more important agreements with third states are concluded in the form of mixed agreements; agreements signed and ratified by the Community/Union and all member states.[22]

The politicization of external economic relations - that is the effort to subject community policies to intergovernmental political agreement - started during the transitional period and received its clearest confirmation in the Paris Summit of 1972 following agreement on the first enlargement.[23] The statement of the Summit made it quite clear that it was henceforward up to the Heads of State and Government to set the agenda for external action. The actions outlined in paragraphs 10-13 are preceded by the following considerations:

> "4. The Community is well aware of the problem presented by continuing underdevelopment in the world. It affirms its determination within the framework of

---

[21] The communist countries belonging to COMECON. France in particular wanted to conduct her own policy of détente and industrial cooperation with the COMECON countries.

[22] Document E. 5. 14 shows the bilateral and multilateral agreements in force.

[23] Document ES. 4, par. 10-13..

a world-wide policy towards the developing countries, to increase its effort in aid and technical assistance to the least favored people. It will take particular account of the concerns of those countries towards which, through geography, history and the commitments entered into by the Community, it has specific responsibilities;

5. The Community reaffirms its determination to encourage the development of international trade. This determination applies to all countries without exception.

The Community is ready to participate as soon as possible, in the open-minded spirit that it has already shown, and according to the procedures laid down by the IMF and the GATT, in negotiations based on the principle of reciprocity. These should make it possible to establish, in the monetary and commercial fields, stable and balanced economic relations, in which the interests of the developing countries must be taken fully into account;

6. The Member States of the Community, in the interests of good neighborly relations which should exist among all European countries whatever their régime, affirm their determination to pursue their policy of détente and of peace with the countries of Eastern Europe, notably on the occasion of the Conference on Security and Co-operation in Europe, and the establishment of a sound basis for a wider economic and human co-operation;

7. The construction of Europe will allow it, in conformity with its ultimate political objectives, to affirm its personality while remaining faithful to its traditional friendships and to the alliances of the Member States, and to establish its position in world affairs as a distinct entity determined to

> promote a better international equilibrium, respecting the principles of the Charter of the United Nations. *The Member States of the Community, the driving force of the construction of Europe, affirm their intention to transform before the end of the present decade the whole complex of their relations into a European Union."*

The last (italicized) sentence, by the way, reads as the clearest expression of the Gaullist design for a European Union: to transform their supranational community into a European Union.

With the first enlargement, the external action of the European Communities would increasingly be characterized by Summit guidance, widening scope of external relations, a shift to multilateral relationships and a new emphasis on associations or special partnerships for political dialogue.

> "The development of relations between the European Communities, their member-states and the outside world has been a subject of perennial concern and controversy since the West European integration process began in the early fifties. In that decade primary attention was given to those states in Western Europe that were as yet unable or unwilling to join the economic communities. As a result of the successful launching of the EEC, the advent of Gaullism in France, decolonization in Africa and détente between East and West, attention shifted to worldwide relationships of the new economic 'world power'. The perceived erosion of the post-war bipolar system and the developing adversary relationship between the European Communities and the United States of America revived the old European desire to play a major role in world

politics. The latter desire was significantly nurtured by the enlargement of the Communities in 1972.

The issue of the Communities' external relations, which had never been a secondary issue in the fifties and the sixties, became the dominating theme in the changing international system of the seventies. Many Europeans considered enlargement as the starting position for launching Europe into a world role. All that appeared to be necessary was to stress a European identity distinct - this time - from United States policy and influence.

The fact, however, that a European identity could only emerge *from* unified European external relations policies was either overlooked or deliberately ignored. The enlarged European Community continued to be disunited in such vital policy issues as, for example, relations with Eastern Europe, relations with developing countries, monetary reform, and energy.

Notwithstanding the incapacity or unwillingness of member governments to move beyond the empty slogan of 'European identity', the sheer impact of a large common market on world trade relations induced several third countries to reckon with the prospect of a new formidable partner or competitor."[24]

This long quote from one of my earlier works, surprisingly, has not lost much of its relevance. The first enlargement of the European Communities/Union did the opposite of what federalists may

[24] From the preface I wrote to Frans A.M. Alting von Geusau, *The external relations of the European Community; Perspectives, policies and responses,* John F. Kennedy Institute 1974, Published by Saxon House and Lexington Books.

have expected from British membership. It strengthened the pursuit of the twofold Gaullist illusion, especially in the conduct of the Community's external action. Rather than building upon the internal dynamics of the need for a common trade policy once the common market is in place, external action came to be built on the illusion of Europe's independent world role as determined and guided by summit conferences. In terms of competences attributed to the European institutions, the increasing scope of external action has strengthened intergovernmental control over community policies.

Even the European Court of Justice appears to accept this reality in the evolution of its case law. In the so called ERTA case, the Court adopted the (federal) implied powers doctrine for the treaty-making powers of the EEC. In its Opinion 1/94, the Court accepted the need for close cooperation in negotiation, conclusion and fulfillment of an Agreement falling partly within the competence of the Community and partly within that of the Member States - that is so called mixed agreements.[25]

The widening *scope of external action* of the Communities/ Union was directly related to the objective - illusion - of the Paris 1972 Summit and all later European Council meetings of positioning the Union as a global power, preferably with its own sphere(s) of influence. Just as the United States claimed South America as its special sphere of influence, so Europe should claim the Mediterranean and Africa for her own sphere of influence. The two most important initiatives of the seventies were the adoption in 1972 of the idea of a Mediterranean policy, in addition to the Association Agreements concluded

---

[25] The issue raised by the Commission concerned the conclusion of the WTO Treaty. The text of the two cases can be found in document E. 5. 15A-B. Opinion 1/94 has been extensively debated in the E.J.I.L.

with Greece and Turkey; and the conclusion on 28 February 1975 of the Lomé Convention between forty six African, Caribbean and Pacific States, and the European Community and its member states.[26] In 2000 the Lomé Convention was replaced by the Cotonou Partnership agreement, concluded for 20 years. According to the official summary of the agreement:

> "The Agreement represents a new stage in the cooperation between the ACP States and the European Union (EU) which began in 1964 with the signing of the first Yaoundé Convention and continued with the four Lomé Conventions.
>
> The Agreement establishes a *new approach*, given the limited success of the main approach of nonreciprocal trade preferences in the previous conventions and the need to adapt to international developments such as globalization, technological progress and the far-reaching social changes in the ACP States. This new approach aims to strengthen the political dimension, provide more flexibility and entrust the ACP States with greater responsibilities.
>
> The new partnership is based on *five interdependent pillars*:
>
> - reinforcement of the political dimension of relations between the ACP States and the EU;

[26] Cf. Chapter 3 in my book referred to above; and Frans A.M. Alting von Geusau (ed), *The Lomé Convention and a new international economic order,* Publications of the John F. Kennedy Institute, Nr. 11, A.W. Sythoff, Leiden 1977.

- promotion of participatory approaches, involvement of civil society, the private sector and other non-State actors;

- development strategies and the objective of poverty reduction;

- the establishment of a new framework for economic and trade cooperation;

- the reform of financial cooperation."[27]

The scope of external action widened in the following ways: territorially the community/union extended its external relations from Western Europe to the whole world; in terms of subject matter external relations are no longer restricted to trade but extend to economic cooperation, political dialogue, cultural cooperation and human rights. In terms of structure, relations broadened from bilateral to multilateral and from reciprocal commitments to special partnerships. The widening scope is well reflected in the subsequent basic treaties. In the latest TFEU of 2007, external action includes the common trade policy extended to intellectual property and direct foreign investment, to development cooperation, economic, financial and technical cooperation, and humanitarian assistance and crisis response. Widening scope, however, did not imply further transfer of powers to the Commission in the category of exclusive Union powers. The governments are safely installed as the masters of external action, through the voting rules in the Council of Ministers, the overall leadership of the European Council and the position of the High Representative as vice-president the Commission.

---

[27] Text of the summary, the partnership agreement and the amendments in Documents E. 5. 16A-C.

Under the authority of the European Council, external action is the subject of many declarations, partnership agreements and summit conferences. Their impact and effect remain highly doubtful. Among the doubtful outcomes of EU's external action, the so called Mediterranean Union is a sad and shocking example, when reading the relevant documents in the light of the Arab uprisings in 2011. As early as 1972, the Paris Summit agreed to launch a Mediterranean policy. In 1995 the policy became a partnership in Barcelona.

> The Barcelona declaration, the official summary proclaims: "is intended to establish a comprehensive Euro-Mediterranean partnership in order to turn the Mediterranean into a common area of peace, stability and prosperity through the reinforcement of political dialogue and security, an economic and financial partnership and a social, cultural and human partnership."

It became a strategic partnership in 2004, certainly not because of the successful implementation of the Barcelona Declaration. As one can read in the Council Report:

> "While different countries face different challenges, it is possible to identify a number of challenges common to the majority of the countries involved. There is general agreement on the nature and scope of these challenges, which have been extensively documented in reports emanating from the countries concerned. These challenges will not be overcome by maintaining the status quo; political, social and economic reform is required. Such reforms can succeed only if they are generated from within the affected societies; they cannot and should not be imposed from outside.
> Many of the challenges derive from a single over-

> arching concern; the burgeoning challenge presented by a predominantly young population creating an ever-increasing demand for education and fulfilling employment. Reforms in the Mediterranean and the Middle East shall open to these young people the prospect of attaining a stake in their society and achieving their aspirations. Ensuring a stable and prosperous future for these young people is the major challenge facing their governments."

On the initiative of French President Sarkozy, the Partnership was upgraded again in 2008:

> The Paris Summit of the 'Barcelona Process: Union for the Mediterranean' (Paris, 13 July 2008) injected a renewed political momentum into Euro–Mediterranean relations. In Paris, the Heads of State and Government agreed to build on and reinforce the successful elements of the Barcelona Process by upgrading their relations, incorporating more co-ownership in their multilateral cooperation framework and delivering concrete benefits for the citizens of the region."

The continuous upgrading of the relationship only concealed the failure of the relationship. Despite all the objectives written in the documents - always with special emphasis on the plight of the Palestinians - none of them were realized. The Community/Union invested considerable amounts of financial support in the partnership, with little result and certainly without proper transparency towards the European electorate.[28] As if everything had been going according to plan, a new neighborhood-policy was proclaimed in May 2011, this time

---

[28] Selection of Documents in E. 5. 17A-E. See also Chapter II.2 above on the Good Neighbourhood policy and the Eastern Partnership.

including all problematic countries from the Maghreb to the Caucasus. As the document of 2011 declares:

> "With the entry into force of the Lisbon Treaty and the creation of a High Representative for Foreign and Security Policy and of the European External Action Service, *political and security co-operation* between the EU and its immediate neighbors can shift to a higher gear in a number of areas."[29]

Hope is a good breakfast but a bad supper. At the time of publication of this document, the Arab crisis was deepening and the EU itself was in a deep crisis. Even with an EEAS, there is nobody to shift the defunct partnership to a higher gear.

EUROPEAN EXTERNAL ACTION SERVICE (EEAS)

According to the original concept, the supranational community received legal personality, that included the power to communicate with third countries, the power to conclude international agreements and the power to take unilateral action under international law. The assumption of the federalists was that the political-community-to-be would gradually take over from member states. The striped pants dispute, to which I referred earlier, resulted from a conflict between Commission President Walter Hallstein and French President Charles de Gaulle over exactly that power to communicate with third countries. Hallstein correctly assumed that this power was vested in the executive - his Commission. He thus officially received representatives to be accredited to the Community by third countries, dressed in morning coat. His behavior was one of the reasons leading de Gaulle in 1965 to the policy of the empty chair discussed in Chapter II. 1 above.

---

[29] Document E. 5. 17E.

The outcome - referred to in the 1966 Luxembourg compromise - was a very complex arrangement. Foreign representatives had to offer their credentials to both the chairman in office of the Council of Ministers and the President of the Commission. The Commission was not allowed to send ambassadors - for a long time, the Commission had information offices abroad only. In international organizations and conferences, a variety of formula were applied. If the floor had to be taken on behalf of the EC, it was the Council Chairman in office first and the Commission thereafter.

With the formal establishment of an EEAS in 2010 on the basis of article 27.3 of the Lisbon TEU, the complexity in practice of the past is given legal expression:

> "3. In fulfilling his mandate, the High Representative shall be assisted by a European External Action Service. This service shall work in cooperation with the diplomatic services of the Member States and shall comprise officials from relevant departments of the General Secretariat of the Council and of the Commission as well as staff seconded from national diplomatic services of the Member States. The organisation and functioning of the European External Action Service shall be established by a decision of the Council. The Council shall act on a proposal from the High Representative after consulting the European Parliament and after obtaining the consent of the Commission."

A major improvement according to the 2009 Report of predecessor Solana in the foreign policy post: "The Lisbon Treaty provides new possibilities. The new institutional framework will allow us to align resources with priorities better. HR/VP Catherine Ashton, in her threefold capacity, will play a central role in delivering this, together with the Member States, the

Commission, and the European Parliament. With the European External Action Service, the EU will have a completely new and unique tool at its disposal: a foreign service which works on behalf of the EU as a whole, and which will allow us to act more coherently and effectively on the global stage. Establishing the EEAS is therefore both a key priority for the European Union, and a unique opportunity, which we must not allow to be wasted."[30]

The Council established the EEAS by Decision of 26 July 2010. The EEAS is to become a "functionally autonomous body" according to its article 1 par. 2:

> "2. The EEAS, which has its headquarters in Brussels, shall be a functionally autonomous body of the European Union, separate from the General Secretariat of the Council and from the Commission with the legal capacity necessary to perform its tasks and attain its objectives."

At first sight, this provision appears to present a proper way out of the striped pants dispute. The reality might well be different. As is stated in the motivations ("whereas"):

> "(3) The EEAS will support the High Representative, who is also a Vice-President of the Commission and the President of the Foreign Affairs Council, in fulfilling his/her mandate to conduct the Common Foreign and Security Policy ('CFSP') of the Union and to ensure the consistency of the Union's external action as outlined, notably, in Articles 18 and 27 TEU. The EEAS will support the High Representative in his/her capacity as President of the Foreign Affairs Council, without prejudice to the

---

30 His last report in Document E. 5. 18., p. 48.

normal tasks of the General Secretariat of the Council. The EEAS will also support the High Representative in his/her capacity as Vice-President of the Commission, in respect of his/her responsibilities within the Commission for responsibilities incumbent on it in external relations, and in coordinating other aspects of the Union's external action, without prejudice to the normal tasks of the Commission services.

(4) In its contribution to the Union's external cooperation programmes, the EEAS should seek to ensure that the programmes fulfil the objectives for external action as set out in Article 21 TEU, in particular in paragraph (2)(d) thereof, and that they respect the objectives of the Union's development policy in line with Article 208 of the Treaty on the Functioning of the European Union ('TFEU'). In this context, the EEAS should also promote the fulfilment of the objectives of the European Consensus on Development and the European Consensus on Humanitarian Aid."

How autonomous the EEAS is going to be and what functional autonomy might mean, must be read in connection with article 18 TEU:

"1. The European Council, acting by a qualified majority, with the agreement of the President of the Commission, shall appoint the High Representative of the Union for Foreign Affairs and Security Policy. The European Council may end his term of office by the same procedure.

2. The High Representative shall conduct the Union's common foreign and security policy. He shall contribute by his proposals to the development of that policy, which he shall carry out as mandated by the Council.

> The same shall apply to the common security and defence policy.
>
> 3. The High Representative shall preside over the Foreign Affairs Council.
>
> 4. The High Representative shall be one of the Vice-Presidents of the Commission. He shall ensure the consistency of the Union's external action. He shall be responsible within the Commission for responsibilities incumbent on it in external relations and for coordinating other aspects of the Union's external action. In exercising these responsibilities within the Commission, and only for these responsibilities, the High Representative shall be bound by Commission procedures to the extent that this is consistent with paragraphs 2 and 3."

The appointment procedure of the High Representative in article 18 differs substantially from the appointment procedures provided for the President and the other members of the Commission in article 17 TEU. The latter are to be elected by the European Parliament. After their election according to article17, par 7:

> "The President, the High Representative of the Union for Foreign Affairs and Security Policy and the other members of the Commission shall be subject as a body to a vote of consent by the European Parliament. On the basis of this consent the Commission shall be appointed by the European Council, acting by a qualified majority.
>
> 8. The Commission, as a body, shall be responsible to the European Parliament. In accordance with Article 234 of the Treaty on the Functioning of the European Union, the European Parliament may vote on a motion

> of censure of the Commission. If such a motion is carried, the members of the Commission shall resign as a body and the High Representative of the Union for Foreign Affairs and Security Policy *shall resign from the duties that he carries out in the Commission."*

According to the last italicized sentence, read in conjunction with article 18, the High Representative only resigns from one of his/her three tasks, but remains in office as CFSP high representative and as chairperson of the Foreign Affairs Council. How one person can be one third supranational commissioner and two thirds servant to the European Council is anybody's guess. Unless the European Parliament is prepared to fight it out, the High Representative is more likely to step out of the European Council's Trojan Horse into the Commission as guardian for the Council's intergovernmental supremacy over the external actions of the supranational Commission.
In any case, according to the Council decision of July 2010:

> "Article 9
> 1. The management of the Union's external cooperation programmes is under the responsibility of the Commission without prejudice to the respective roles of the Commission and of the EEAS in programming as set out in the following paragraphs.
>
> 2. *The High Representative shall ensure overall political coordination of the Union's external action,* ensuring the unity, consistency and effectiveness of the Union's external action, in particular through the following external assistance instruments:
> - the Development Cooperation Instrument,
> - the European Development Fund,
> - the European Instrument for Democracy and Human Rights ,

- the European Neighbourhood and Partnership Instrument,
- the Instrument for Cooperation with Industrialised Countries,
- the Instrument for Nuclear Safety Cooperation ,
- the Instrument for Stability, regarding the assistance provided for in Article 4 of Regulation (EC) No 1717/2006."

Within the institutional set up of the Lisbon Treaties and in the light of the history of the European Communities/Union, the High Representative has the authority of the European Council behind her to "ensure overall political coordination of the Union's external action".

The Council's authority is enshrined in articles 15 and 21 TEU, first paragraphs:

Article 15
"1. The European Council shall provide the Union with the necessary impetus for its development and shall define the general political directions and priorities thereof. *It shall not exercise legislative functions.*

Article 22.
1.On the basis of the principles and objectives set out in Article 21, the European Council shall identify the strategic interests and objectives of the Union.

2. Decisions of the European Council on the strategic interests and objectives of the Union shall relate to the common foreign and security policy *and to other areas of the external action of the Union.* Such decisions may concern the relations of the Union with a specific country or region or may be thematic in approach. They

shall define their duration, and the means to be made available by the Union and the Member States."[31]

The italicized sentences in article 9 of the Council decision and article 22 par.2 in the TEU make it clear that the European Council, much in the spirit of former French President Charles de Gaulle is not subject to the principle of conferral in article 5 par.1 TEU. Giving impetus and political direction is not subject to judicial or parliamentary control, unlike the exercise of legislative functions. Moreover EEAS is not supposed to replace the diplomatic services of member states. At best EEAS and the diplomatic services of the 27 member states are cooperating with each other in the external action of the European Union.

ONCE MORE: THE EUROPEAN UNION AND RUSSIA

Russia as we know it today was born officially on 1 January 1991, the date the Soviet Union came to an end. As the legally recognized successor state of the Soviet Union, Russia is not a new entity with a new approach to Europe, as we saw already in Chapter II. 2 above.

The attitude of the Soviet Union towards the European Communities evolved from outright hostility in 1957 to formal recognition in 1988.[32] Formal recognition only came after Gorbachev's *glasnost and perestroika* through a joint declaration of the EEC and COMECON of 25 June 1988. COMECON or CMEA was the Soviet dominated organization for economic cooperation between state trading or command

---

31 References to the Lisbon TEU are from the consolidated version in Document EC. 15A. References to the Council decision on the EEAS and other EEAS documents can be found in E.5. 19A-D.

32 For the earlier period see my: *Beyond the European Community. Op.cit.* p. 144 ff. and the sources referred to therein.

economy states in East and Central Europe.[33] As the European Commission wrote:

> "The Joint Declaration finally establishes official relations between the European Economic Community and COMECON. The two sides undertake to cooperate" In areas which fall within their respective spheres of competence and where there is a common interest".
> It is a milestone in relations between the EC and COMECON and more especially its European members. Even though it is limited to procedural matters, it opens the way to the establishment of diplomatic relations between the EC and the Individual East European countries and to bilateral agreements with each of them."[34]

It was a milestone indeed but a very different one than assumed by both sides. Diplomatic relations between the EC and individual East European countries were rapidly established, to begin with the Soviet Union itself, but COMECON disappeared in 1991. The declaration in fact opened the road to the Eastward enlargement of the European Union and a strategic partnership with Russia. The ambivalent relationship between the EU and Russia would remain, however. Russia would continue to look at Europe suspiciously and more so since ex KGB officer Vladimir Putin came to power.

---

[33] Created in 1949 as a reaction to the Marshall plan and disbanded in 1991. It linked the USSR with Bulgaria, Czechoslovakia, Hungary, Poland, Romania, East Germany (1950–90), Mongolia (from 1962), Cuba (from 1972), and Vietnam (from 1978), with Yugoslavia as an associated member. Albania also belonged between 1949 and 1961.

[34] Document E. 5. 20 The European Community's Relations with COMECON.

The European Union offered a strategic partnership in the illusion that it could help Russia to become a European style democracy. At the same time it made three things clear to Russia: strategic partnership was not to be a step to membership; it was not part of its Eastern good neighborhood policy; and it did not recognize the Russian near-abroad , the former Soviet republics, as its exclusive sphere of influence.[35]

In 1994 the "Agreement on partnership and cooperation establishing a partnership between the European Communities and their Member States, of one part, and the Russian Federation, of the other part" was concluded. It entered into force in 1997 for a period of 10 years (since 2007 silently renewed every year).

In 1999 the European Council adopted its common strategy on Russia. The agreement and the common strategy reflected both the pretence and the impotence of the European Union towards Russia, as one can read in the latter document:

> "*VISION OF THE EU FOR ITS PARTNERSHIP WITH RUSSIA*
>
> A stable, democratic and prosperous Russia, firmly anchored in a united Europe free of new dividing lines, is essential to lasting peace on the continent. The issues which the whole continent faces can be resolved only through ever closer cooperation between Russia and the European-Union. The European Union welcomes Russia's return to its rightful place in the European family in a spirit of friendship, cooperation, fair accommodation of interests and on the foundations of shared values enshrined in the common heritage of European civilization.

---

35 A selection of relevant documents can be found in E. 5. 21-29.

The European Union has clear strategic goals:

- a stable, open and pluralistic democracy in Russia, governed by the rule of law and underpinning a prosperous market economy benefiting alike all the people of Russia and of the European Union,

- maintaining European stability, promoting global security and responding to the common challenges of the continent through intensified cooperation with Russia."

They assumed that the Russian leaders would like Russia to become a democracy as the European Union and would need EU help to that end. They also assumed that this strategy could best be carried out through frequent bilateral summits - the well-known Gaullist assumption on heads of state meetings, now becoming a serious summitry syndrome after the end of Europe's division. At the end of 2011 some twenty-eight EU-Russian Summits have been held, but as one keen observer remarked, EU-Russian relations continue to be shallow and directionless.[36] Russia, as a self-declared sovereign democracy, is no longer moving towards democracy and human rights. EU criticism on the troubling trends in the opposite direction has become muted and impotent, as one can read in the selection of recent Summit communiqués. Putin's Russia prefers to play the power game of divide and rule and develops more and more bilateral relations with EU members separately. EU members are deeply divided on the two issues of primary interest to Russia: energy and security. A free trade agreement as envisaged by

---

[36] Katinka Barysch, *'The EU and Russia: From principle to pragmatism?'* and *'The EU and Russia: All smiles and no action?'* Policy Briefs, Center for European Reform, November 2006 and April 2011.

the 1994 agreement remains a distant prospect and Russian membership of WTO is still pending. Russia and the EU develop opposite policies in the "near-abroad" states like Belorussia, Ukraine, Moldova and Georgia, where Moscow continues to frustrate EU efforts to promote democracy and closer ties with them. The new plans offered by various summits are not signs of progress but efforts to hide lack of progress behind the appearance of newly formulated plans.

The strategic partnership agreement of 1994 was concluded in the chaotic Yeltsin era of post-Soviet Russia, in which there was some interest in imitating Western models and in seeking closer cooperation.[37] The concept of 'Sovereign Democracy' –used today by Putin and Medvedev - means primarily freedom from the West. It implies a profound distrust of the current European order, a preference for returning towards a state-centered European order. Russia under Putin is characterized by political centralism, state capitalism and an all-pervasive corruption instead of an overarching ideology. The current regime lacks a strategy for modernizing the country. Its European ambitions are mostly revisionist.

The problem of the European Union's vision on partnership with Russia is, like in so many other foreign policy and external

---

37 Interesting to read: Thomas Gomart, *EU-Russia Relations; Toward a Way out of Depression,* IFRI (Institut Français der Relations Internationales) and CSIS (Center for Strategic and International Studies), July 2008; Ivan Krastev, Mark Leonard and Andrew Wilson, *What Does Russia Think?* ECFR (European Council on Foreign Relations, September 2009; Irina Kobrinskaya, *Russia and the European Union; A Keystone Relationship,* Institute for World Economy and International Relations, Moscow; Published by Fondació CIDOB, Barcelona in November 2009. The Moscow Institute is the same one that published the 17 and 32 theses against the Common Market in 1957 and 1962.

action activities, twofold. The first one is lack of curiosity towards Russia as it is, and the resulting *pretence* that all there is to do is to remold Russia into a Western democracy. The second one is the illusion of a world role and the resulting *impotence* to turn summit declarations and political intentions into effective and unified foreign policies.

THE EUROPEAN UNION AND THE UNITED STATES OF AMERICA

No relationship has been more resilient, more reliable and more dependable than the one between Europe and the USA. since the Second World War.[38] This is true despite many (French inspired) efforts to assert a so called European identity - as against the US, or to use the EC/EU to muster the EEC troops for a trade or cultural war with the US.

Even more surprising is that little of importance has changed in this relationship since the end of the Cold War, despite the fact that the threat bringing the North Alliance into being in 1949 has disappeared in 1990.

The EU-US relationship followed the trend of the post-1989 era with respect to declarations, objectives and institutions.[39] The motivations are triumphant, the objectives broad and the institutions modest. Institutionally the relationship adopted the Gaullist model of regular (bi-annual) meetings on three levels: Presidents, Foreign Ministers, European Commission/US cabinet. The meetings are for consultation. The US President

---

[38] Cf my: *Beyond Containment and Division, Western Cooperation from a Post-Totalitarian Perspective,* Martinus Nijhoff 1992, 1994 (paperback), Chapters 3 and 4; and my: *Western Cooperation Op.cit.* 2009. In this chapter, I have not much to add to what can already be read in these two books.

[39] Cf. Document E. 5. 30, the transatlantic declaration of 1990; document E. 5. 31, a new transatlantic agenda.

must meet with the President of the European Council and the President of the Commission. They are not always sure what to discuss or what to conclude. As in other such meetings, the consultations are now called dialogues and apparently take place on a variety of levels on a variety of subjects.

The call for stronger institutions, more intensive cooperation and even a strategic partnership[40] from a number of research institutions in the US and Europe is not surprising. They, at least, have many forerunners since 1949. European-American relations owe their strength and durability to the American involvement in Europe since 1917, the 1947 Marshall Plan, the US policy of containment and the continuing American leadership in the Western alliance. In addition the relationship deeply involves every part of their democratic societies. As one can read in the annual economic reports on the transatlantic economy, the EU and the USA are each other's most important foreign, commercial markets.[41] Together they are the leading forces - for better and for worse - of the global economy.

Some European politicians may resent American leadership or denigrate American culture, the relationship is still going strong. The relationship does not need bi-annual summits, but having them does not harm it.

---

[40] Cf. Document E. 5. 31, *Shoulder to Shoulder: Forging a Strategic U.S.-EU Partnership.*

[41] Cf. Document E. 5. 32, *The Transatlantic Economy, 2011 report.*

EPILOGUE

FADING, FAILING, FRAGILE?

"If we are not willing to risk a partial dismantling of the EU, then the choice becomes as stark as can be in the lives of federations: deeper integration or collapse."

Speech of Radek Sikorski,
Polish Foreign Minister in Berlin, 28 November 2011

EUROPE'S FRAGILE CONSCIENCE

Those recognized as the 'Fathers of Europe', responded in conscience to the spectacle of ruins left by European politics in the first half of the twentieth century. They knew that: "to serve right and to fight against the dominion of wrong is and remains the fundamental task of the politician."[1] As Hannah Ahrendt wrote in 1945: "The problem of evil will be the fundamental problem of postwar intellectual life in Europe - as death became the fundamental problem after the last war."[2] The Fathers of Europe clearly understood that a radical break with the European past was necessary. After the Second World War and the onset of the Cold War, they saw it to be their task to reconcile France and Germany and to unify Europe. The Governments of the six states who concluded the ECSC Treaty in 1951, fundamentally agreed on:

(1) *The purposes* to be pursued: reconciliation, peace, solidarity and federal unity;

(2) *The road to follow*: concrete actions and the fusion of essential interests; and

(3) *The method of common action*: creating supranational institutions capable of giving direction to their future common destiny.

---

1 From the Address of Pope Benedict XVI to the German Bundestag. Berlin 22 September 2011. Full text on my website, European Union, Documents ER, Nr. 4.

2 As quoted by Tony Judt, *Post War A History of Europe Since 1945.* In his Epilogue, 'From the House of the Dead'.

> This agreement on the peaceful organization of common action has been solid enough to provide the constitutional foundation for more than sixty years of peace and cooperation and for managing the growth from a six-member ECSC to a twenty seven-member European Union.

Still, European conscience is fragile. Already in 1954, it was too weak in the French National Assembly to accept a European Defense Community. It was partly restored through the creation of EEC and Euratom, but soon faded, during the Gaullist era in France, again. Thereafter, the compromise reached at The Hague Summit (1969) and the first enlargement (1973) with Great Britain, Demark and Ireland weakened it further. In 1973 the British disagreed as much as in 1950 with the three fundamentals of the ESCS Treaty. This time Britain had post-Gaullist France on its side.

The Single European Act (SEA), after the years of crises in the 1970's, caused the integration process to deviate further from the spirit of the founding fathers. It moved the European Council from foreign policy forum to centre place. It enlarged the scope of action but blurred the distinction between community policies and intergovernmental coordination. It resumed the effort to transform the European Community into an Economic and Monetary Union (EMU). To that end the SEA created a new transitional period towards completing the internal market. With EMU in perspective, the completion of the internal market was no longer guided by the original three agreements. With the objective of removing all barriers to the freedom of movement for persons, goods, services and capital, the Eurocrats from the Commission and the Member States embarked on a program of detailed and intrusive regulation or harmonization of policies with an economic dimension.

In the absence of agreement on the purposes to be pursued. It was no longer possible to properly identify the interests deemed essential enough to be fused on the road to unity. The Treaty on European Union (TEU) in December 1991 marked the formal burial of the two original purposes of solidarity and political unity - a tragic irony as it coincided with the end of the Cold War. If ever, it was in the 1990's that these two original purposes would have made sense for Europe as a whole. The TEU of Maastricht thus marks a twofold deviation from the original spirit of the founding fathers. The transformation of Community into Union marked the end for political unity. EMU marked the end of real solidarity. Henceforward it was accepted that Britain and others could opt-out of EMU and other major programs. A so-called "two-speed" Europe, is not a Union in which states can reach the same goal at different points of time; it has become a Europe in which Member States can pursue different goals within the Union.

EMU also marked the new dictatorship of economic values in an era of globalization. The campaign slogan of presidential candidate Bill Clinton in America, "it's the economy stupid", was already written in the TEU of Maastricht! It would become the new guiding spirit for the EU and its enlargement in the decades thereafter. There is no more "sense of common purpose" beyond the market and the Euro, or in time of crisis even within the Euro zone. The history of European unification presented in this volume is a story of a fragile European conscience: in law and language, in virtues and values, in politics and economics, in rights and wrongs and in memory and forgetting.

ANY LESSONS LEARNED?

The first lesson, one could draw from the new method for organizing common action, is a positive one. The new institutional method introduced by Monnet, Schuman and the ECSC Treaty has significantly modified relations between nations and men, indeed. Europe, for the first time in its turbulent history, has become an expanding zone of peace and cooperation, characterized by the dependable expectation that conflicts and crises are being solved with peaceful methods. The underlying ideas formulated in the exceptional circumstances of a Europe ruined by war and translated into the law of the ECSC Treaty have proven to be a solid, constitutional foundation for the process of European unification. From this perspective, the drafting of "a constitution for Europe" in the early years of the 21st century was a sad example of organized forgetting.

A second lesson one could draw, is that crisis-resolution by peaceful methods has been producing more agreement than feared before the crisis, but less than hoped for. Despite recurrent crises, enlargement has proceeded apace. Modest institutional improvements have been possible, such as the merger of the institutions of the three original communities, direct elections for the European Parliament, the granting of limited budgetary and legislative powers to the European Parliament, and increased use of decision by majority in the Council of Ministers. Still, as the transformation from Communities to Union is showing more and more, the crisis-resolution capacity of the enlarged Union is in serious disrepair. The management of the sovereign debt crisis in 2010-2011 manifested very troublesome and expensive deficiencies. Summitry does not produce coherent foreign policies. It is an unsuitable instrument for conducting common economic and monetary policies. It leads to serious failures in the time of crisis.

A third lesson is that the most serious challenge to the new method for organizing common action is not enlargement with new members, but the opposition of member-states to the application of the new method within the extending scope of the European Union. That opposition, so to say, has been legitimized in the creation on French initiative of the European Council of Heads of State and of Government - a body standing above the European law, acting as the final instance in crisis-deliberation, but only capable of issuing guidelines to the institutions by laborious compromise and presidential conclusions. One should not overlook the irony in the history of European summits now formalized into regular meetings of the European Council. De Gaulle's proposal in 1962 was rejected exactly because of the purely intergovernmental nature of the summit meetings he wanted. The compromise agreed upon in 1969 had been that Summits could be used for promoting European Political Cooperation as an activity outside the scope of the European Communities. Today, the European Council stands at the apex of decision-making in all matters within the scope of the European Union.

A fourth lesson one could draw, is that agreement over the 'political finality' of the European Union is unlikely to be achieved. Despite the clear message of the sovereign debt crisis that one currency requires federal authority over economic, fiscal and budgetary policies, the political solutions offered for "economic government" are just a little bit more of the same. The European Union is to be given a fifth president in addition to the four already in the Treaties of Lisbon.[3] In other words and contrary to the original fundamental agreement, essential interest are no longer to be merged. They are to be dealt with in the European Council, which by its composition

3 The President of the Euro Summit in addition to the President of the European Council, the President of the Council of Ministers, the President of the Council of Ministers for Foreign Affairs and the President of the European Commission. See Summit Statement of 26 October 2011 in Document EC. 139

and task is incapable of giving direction to a future common destiny of the European states. At best the European Union will continue to be a common market for all, an Economic and Monetary Union for some and a political union for none; that is: an overload in *acquis communautaire*, two tiers for monetary and social matters, and twenty-seven speeds for foreign policy and defence.

A fifth lesson to be drawn, is that the transformation of Community into Union has adversely affected the legitimacy of the European unification process. The EU's diminished legitimacy has two aspects. The *one* is the growing gap between the endless stream of resounding declarations on principles, values and objectives and the increasing emphasis on national interests in actual negotiations. The *other*, related aspect is the growing gap between the Eurocrats (community and national officials) and the citizens of European Union, reflected for instance in the outcome of referenda, the low turn-out in European elections and the perception of the EU in the new Member States. Whereas the process of transformation and admission to the EU was a political success story, the transformation was a failure from the perspective of everyday life, as it caused pain, bitterness and disappointment for so many people through unemployment, corruption, growing inequality and immorality. Enlargement since the end of the twentieth century continues despite the fences erected in 1993; often by not applying the very principles of 1993. Deepening integration was repeatedly proclaimed as a priority task. Opaque negotiation processes produced just a little bit more of the same, from the 1991 Maastricht Treaty to the latest Lisbon Reform Treaties on European Union.

The most important lesson to be drawn, is that a Union directed by a collective Emperor in the garments of the European Council and standing above the law, is undermining rather than solidifying the process begun with the Schuman Declaration in 1950. The European Union is in serious trouble and not only due to globalization and the world economic crisis. In the glare of television cameras the appearance of compromise conceals lack of true progress and absence of common purpose - as has been made all too clear in the recent sovereign debt crisis.

EMU's Fragile Construction

The development and management of the Economic and Monetary Union (EMU) have become the core-business of the European Union. The financial, banking and sovereign debt crises of 2008-2011, have proven the EMU to be a fragile construction. The criteria for entering the Euro zone were loosely applied. Besides the European Central Bank (ECB), there is no institution capable of giving direction to the policies required to uphold monetary union. The criteria for sustaining the monetary union were laid down in the (non-binding) Stability and Growth Pact[4], adopted in 1997 on German initiative, but equally loosely applied. In 2003 the three leading states in the EMU - Italy, Germany and France - violated the criteria, but were not penalized. Thereafter the rules were relaxed for every state participating in the Euro zone.

It is not surprising, therefore, that the EU badly handled the crises since 2008. The only policy-instrument available for handling such crises was the European Council. Since the entry into force of the Treaties of Lisbon, the European Commission has been given a back seat. As a consequence the European Council stumbled, fully media-covered, from crisis to crisis with half-measures acceptable to the German Chancellor and her Bundestag. The French President could not but follow, the

---

4 Government annual deficit not to exceed 3% of GDP and national debt not to exceed 60% of GDP.

other fifteen had to accept, the outer ten were invited for drinks only.

The 'last chance' special session of the European Council/ Euro Summit took place on 26- 27 October 2011. On the three items mentioned, the concluding statement announced possible measures *to be taken by others*, but failed to deliver the required solutions.[5] The crucial and underlying question how to resolve the serious sovereign debt crisis in the European Union has not even been addressed. The same applied to the question, how to assure public accountability on the huge sums made available to the debt-ridden countries. Even more shocking is the neglect of the social consequences of the draconic austerity measures imposed on countries like Greece, Italy, Ireland, Portugal and Spain.

In its concluding statement the Euro Summit offered just more of the same on the governance structure of the Euro area. Policy-making continues to be handled by more meetings on the Summit level. As already mentioned, a fifth president is to be added to the list of presidents provided for in the Lisbon Treaties. The reality remains that Germany is in the lead with France coming along and the others bound to follow. Euro zone members with excessive debts and deficits are required to adopt draconic reforms to achieve debt and deficit reduction. Their implementation is to be checked and monitored by the European Commission. Necessary further integration is promised but not spelled out. The ten measures to improve the governance of the Euro area, listed in Annex 1, are just a variation on the well-known summitry practice. Still, it is for the first time that structures parallel to the EU structure for the twenty seven, are emerging for the Euro seventeen Member

[5] Cf. Document EC. 139. The October 2011 Summit was neither the first nor the last 'last chance' session.

States; a development that is bound to further undermine unity and solidarity in the European Union. In the light of the failure of the Stability and Growth Pact, paragraph 26 of the Statement, is the most deficient one. Instead of recognizing the need for supranational institutions capable of upholding the EMU, implementation is left to national measures. Nobody in the Summits appears to have learnt the lesson that a functioning EMU needs, in addition to the ECB, a European treasury, truly common European economic, budgetary and fiscal policies carried out by a capable and competent supranational European Commission. Robert Schuman would surely have understood.

The Conclusions of the 'last-chance' Summit tell us sadly that in times of crisis there is no real solidarity and there are no supranational institutions capable of giving direction to the EMU. In summitry Europe, leadership unavoidably returns to the strongest Member States, France and Germany. It is bound to be poor leadership. Consecutive French Presidents have made it quite clear that they are stuck to a summitry Europe. While preaching federalism, the German Government refuses any solution based on real solidarity within the European Union. In the absence of a shared common purpose, the French lack the political vision and the Germans lack the solidarity, required for unifying Europe.

EUROPE'S CONSCIENCE: FADING, FAILING AND FRAGILE?

In our early twenty-first century, Europe's conscience is fading, indeed

As Tony Judt wrote in 2008: "In the West we have made haste to dispense whenever possible with the economic, intellectual, and institutional baggage of the twentieth century and encouraged others to do likewise. In the wake of 1989, with boundless confidence and insufficient reflection, we put the twentieth century behind us and strode boldly into its successor swaddled in self-serving half-truths: the triumph of the West, the end of History, the unipolar American moment, the ineluctable march of globalization and the free market."[6] Elsewhere, Tony Judt wrote: "But we have become stridently insistent - in our economic calculations, our political practices, our international strategies, even our educational priorities - *that the past has nothing of interest to teach us.* Ours, we insist, is a new world; its risks and opportunities are without precedent."[7]

What Tony Judt refers to is what Milan Kundera called 'organized forgetting' in the totalitarian states of the twentieth century. Where ideology reigns, the past is even more uncertain than the future; history though must continuously be rewritten to suit the policies of the ruling leaders. It is the heritage affecting all of Europe, East as well as West. This 'organized forgetting' is a product also of the Western ideologies of progress, revived after 1989 in the ideology of economic growth through globalization and privatization.

> *The "European Union may be a response to history, but it can never be a substitute".*[8]

Herein lies the problem of Europe's *fading* conscience. The EU Summits, since 1991, with their conclusions on enlargement, monetary union and 'constitutional' reform have been trying exactly that: to present the EU as a substitute for history. The

---

6 Tony Judt, 'What Have We Learned, If Anything?' *The New York Review of Books,* May 1, 2008.

7 Tony Judt, *Reappraisals, Reflections on the forgotten twentieth century,* Penguin Press 2008. From his Introduction: The World We have Lost, p. 2

8 Tony Judt, *Post War, A History of Europe Since 1945,* Penguin Books 2005. Concluding sentence from the Epilogue to the book, p. 831

'collective emperor's' disowning of the past includes the Holocaust, specifically discussed in Judt's epilogue; it also extends to the spirit of the founding fathers of Europe, the spirit of *Solidarnosc* and the Christian heritage of Europe.

Europe's conscience is also failing

The EU has failed to recognize and resist the dictatorship of economic values installed by the new ideologies of globalization and privatization; in fact the EU supported both ideologies by the way in which the internal market was completed. Through instruments like the Public Procurement Directives, public services like railways and post were forcibly turned into private companies.[9] The interests of the citizen were replaced by the interests of the share-holders. Private profit replaced public service. Governments were expected to act in conformity with market rules, rather than pursue the common good.

The search for principles to provide a solid foundation for pursuing European unity degenerated into an open ended discussion on European values and the almost frivolous decision to write the European Human Rights Charter into the law of the European Union. Rather than recognizing the fundamental problem of evil (Hannah Ahrendt), the discussion moved beyond good and evil into a new language of value relativism. I would urge the reader to re-read part I (chapter 3 in particular) of this volume after having studied the history of European Unification proper in the second part.

---

9 See e.g. Dirk-Jan Eppink, *Life of a European Manadarin, Op.cit.*

The European Union since 1991 has seriously failed in its mission as intended by the founding fathers of the European Communities, and the founding fathers of Europe's re-unification since 1989.

EUROPE'S CONSCIENCE HAS BECOME VERY FRAGILE AS A CONSEQUENCE

"The conviction that there is a Creator God is what gave rise to the idea of human rights, the idea of the equality of all people before the law, the recognition of the inviolability of human dignity in every single person and the awareness of people's responsibility for their actions. Our cultural memory is shaped by these rational insights. To ignore it or dismiss it as a thing of the past would be to dismember our culture totally and to rob it of its completeness. The culture of Europe arose from the encounter between Jerusalem, Athens and Rome - from the encounter between Israel's monotheism, the philosophical reason of the Greeks and Roman law. This three-way encounter has shaped the inner identity of Europe. In the awareness of man's responsibility before God and in the acknowledgment of the inviolable dignity of every single human person, it has established criteria of law: it is these criteria that we are called to defend at this moment in our history."[10]

The tragedy of the European Union today is the denial of this European heritage in the name of economic growth and secular multiculturalism. Schuman was just as clear as Pope Benedict when on 19 March 1958 after his election, as the first President of the Common Assembly of the European Communities, he said: "Tous les pays de l'Europe sont impregnés de civilization chrétienne. Elle est l'âme de l'Europe,

---

[10] From the Address of Pope Benedict XVI to the German Bundestag. Full text on my website, loc.cit.

âme qu'il faut lui rendre."[11] Marcello Pera fully agreed. Europe is imbued with revolutionary Christian ethic principles. Without them democracy, human rights, the rule of law and European Unification would have been unthinkable.

Indeed, Schuman saw the Christian civilization to be the soul of Europe, a soul deeply wounded by the wild triumphs of the anti-European and anti-Christian ideologies of Nazism and Communism, and to be healed through European Unification. Such was the spirit of Schuman, now sadly missing in the European Union of the Treaties of Lisbon. Time has come for Europe to recover her soul and to return to the solid constitutional foundation of the original Schuman Plan. The European Union needs a true and short Constitution and a re-affirmation of the original threefold agreement on purposes, the road to follow and the method of common action. There is no alternative for emerging from the current deep moral crisis of European Unification.

The concluding words of the Papal Address to the German Bundestag are addressed to the European Union as well:

"As he assumed the mantle of office, the young King Solomon was invited to make a request. How would it be if we, the law-makers of today, were invited to make a request? What would we ask for? I think that, even today, there is ultimately nothing else we could wish for but a listening heart - the capacity to discern between good and evil, and thus to establish true law, to serve justice and peace."

---

11 As quoted in: Marcello Pera, *Pourquoi nous devons nous dire chrétiens, Le Libéralisme, l'Europe et l'éthique,* Editions Parole et Silence 2011; Traduit de l'italien avec une preface de Benoît XVI

SOURCES

Chapters I. 1-4 and II. 4-5 rely on previously written texts or presentations, most of them not yet published, with the exception of:

- "European Political Integration: A Record of Confusion and Failure" In The European Yearbook. XI. 1965 in chapters II.1 and II. 5.

- "Woher die Verwirrung?" In: *Europa der Grundrechte. Beiträge zur Grundrechtecharta der Europäischen Union.* Ed. Gudrun Lang. Wien 2003.

- "Die Liberale Gesellschaft und der Rechtsstaat." In: *Die Liberale Gesellschaft. Castelgandolfo-Gespräche 1992.* Ed. Krzysztof Micahlski. Stuttgart 1993.
In Chapter II. 4.

Unless otherwise indicated, documents on the website were retrieved from one of the following three documentary websites:

- Archive of European Integration, University of Pittsburgh
- European Navigator (ENA)
- Europa, the official website of the EU for recent documents

All of them were converted to PdF files.

ABOUT THE AUTHOR

Prof. Jhr. Dr. Frans A.M. Alting von Geusau (1933) studied Law at Leiden University, the Netherlands and European Studies at the College of Europe in Bruges, Belgium. He is Professor Emeritus of International Law and Western Cooperation, Tilburg University and Leiden University. Since 1994 Alting von Geusau is involved in the Phoenix Institute Summer Seminar for the Study of Western Institutions at the University of Notre Dame, Indiana U.S.A and since 2008 Professor of International Relations in the Advanced LLM program in International Law at Leiden University. More can be found on the website:

http://www.fransamaltingvongeusau.com

BOOKS BY THE AUTHOR

Published by Sythoff, Martinus Nijhoff, Kluwer Academic Publishers

- European Organizations and Foreign Relations of States, 1962, 1964 (reprinted)

- Beyond Containment and Division, Western Cooperation
  From a Post-Totalitarian perspective, Martinus Nijhoff Publishers, Dordrecht/Boston/ London. Hard-cover edition, 1992. Paperback, 1993.

In the series: Publications of the John F. Kennedy Institute. Center for Internationals Studies

1. Kernwapens voor Alle Landen? *(Het Wereldvenster, Baarn) 1967
2. Economic Relations After the Kennedy Round.*1969
3. Beyond the European Community 1969
4. The Future of the International Monetary System.** 1970
5. NATO and Security in the Seventies.* 1970
9. Energy in the European Communities.* 1975
10. European Perspectives on World Order. 1975

11. The Lomé Convention and a new international economic order.* 1977
12. Uncertain Détente.* 1979.
13. National Economic Security: Perceptions, Threats and Policies.** 1982

BY OTHER PUBLISHERS

- Denken Over Wereldvrede, Van Gorpen & Comp, 1972.
- The External Relations of the European Community.Perspectives, Policies and Responses*, Saxon House/Lexington Books, 1974.
- Allies in a Turbulent World. Challenges to U.S. and Western European Cooperation*, Lexington Books 1982.
- The Security of Western Europe, The Sherwood Press 1985.
- The Pacific Rim and the Western World. Strategic, Economic, and Cultural Perspectives**, Westview Press 1987.
- The Spirit of 1989. Europe on the Threshold of a New Era?, The Fourteenth Corbishley Memorial Lecture 1990, The Wyndham Place Trust, London 1990.
- De Som der Delen. Europa voor en na de omwenteling, Meulenhoff, Amsterdam 1991.
- Comment Faire la Transition Vers la Société de Droit? Réflexions pour Mes amis russes, Presses d'Europe, Nice 1998. Also published in Russian, State Library For Foreign Literature, Moscow, September 1997 (Kak Sowersjit Perechod k Pravovomoe Obzestroe ?).
- Europe : The New Christendom.* Special Issue of The European Legacy, Toward New Paradigms, M.I.T. Press. 1998, Volume 3, Number 2.
- Keren de Kansen? Op weg naar een nieuw milennium, Tilburg University Press 1998.
- European Unification in the Twentieth Century. A Treasury of Readings, Wolf Legal Publishers 1998.
- Sporen van de Twintigste Eeuw, Wolf Legal Publishers 2000 (reprint 2011)

- Western Cooperation. Origins and History, Wolf Legal Publishers 2002 (Analysis and Documents in two volumes).
- Highlights From Recent History. A Reader for "The New West and the New Europe", Wolf Legal Publishers 2003. (The Phoenix Institute Europe, Summer Seminar)

*) editor
**) co-editor

PUBLISHED BY WOLF LEGAL PUBLISHERS

In the Series: *Footprints of the Twentieth Century*

1. Cultural Diplomacy: Waging War With Other Means? 2009

2. The Illusions of Détente, 2009

3. Western Cooperation. Origins and History, (second edition) 2009

4. European Unification, 2012